AF443511

Life-Study
of
Ephesians

Messages 29-63

Witness Lee

Living Stream Ministry
Anaheim, California

First Edition, October 1991.

ISBN 978-0-7363-0962-2
(Complete set, softcover)
ISBN 978-0-87083-148-5
(Messages 29-63, softcover)

Published by

Living Stream Ministry
2431 W. La Palma Ave., Anaheim, CA 92801 U.S.A.
P. O. Box 2121, Anaheim, CA 92814 U.S.A.

Printed in the United States of America

10 11 12 13 14 15 / 12 11 10 9 8 7 6

CONTENTS

LIFE-STUDY OF EPHESIANS

MESSAGE TWENTY-NINE

THE REVELATION OF THE MYSTERY

In Ephesians 3, a parenthetical word, Paul begins to beseech the saints to walk worthily of God's calling. What Paul speaks regarding himself in this chapter is a pattern for one who would walk worthily of God's calling. In order to walk worthily of God's calling, we need to be a prisoner of the Lord, a steward, and a minister. As one imprisoned in Christ, Paul saw a heavenly vision. The more he saw of this vision, the more he experienced Christ and gained Christ. Paul was also a steward dispensing the riches of Christ to the members of the household of God. Furthermore, he was a faithful minister, one who ministered Christ to the members of the Body so that Christ might be expressed in the Body.

To walk worthily of God's calling is not simply to be kind, humble, and loving. It is to be imprisoned, confined, in Christ, where we see the vision. By seeing this vision, we experience Christ, and Christ is wrought into our being to make us stewards to dispense the riches of Christ into others. We also become ministers dispensing the riches of Christ to the members of the Body so that the Body may be built up. We all need to be imprisoned in Christ so that we may experience Him more and minister more of Him to others.

Having considered the stewardship of the grace in the previous message, we need now to see the revelation of the mystery. Ephesians 3:3 says, "That by revelation the mystery was made known to me, as I have written previously in brief." God's hidden purpose is the mystery, and the unveiling of this mystery is the revelation. To carry out this revelation is the apostle's ministry for the producing of the church. A revelation is an unveiling, the taking away of a veil. In the New Testament we have the revelation, the unveiling, of God's economy. In other ages and generations this economy was a hidden mystery. It was not made known to Adam, to Abraham, to Moses, to David, or to Isaiah and the other prophets. If they had been asked what God's economy is, they would have been unable to answer, for during their time the mystery was still veiled. God's economy, the dispensing of Himself into man to produce a Body for His Son, had not been revealed to them.

The Son of God is the embodiment of God. God's economy is to dispense Himself into a great number of human beings in order to produce a Body for this embodiment of Himself. This means that the Son of God as the embodiment of God requires a Body, an increase, an expansion. This expansion can be produced only by God's dispensing of Himself into His chosen people. This is the greatest mystery in the universe. Although many political leaders and dignitaries know nothing about this great mystery, by God's mercy we know what it is. Even the young sisters among us know what presidents and philosophers do not know. We know that God's economy is to dispense Himself into His chosen people in order to produce the Body as the expansion of the Son of God for the full expression of God in the universe. Nothing is greater or more important than this. Praise the Lord that not only do we know what God's economy is, but we are also in it! In fact, we even are it. We know it, we are in it, and we are it. By revelation this great mystery, which had been hidden until the coming of the Lord Jesus, has been unveiled to us.

I. THE REVELATION
TO THE APOSTLES AND PROPHETS

This mystery has been revealed to the apostles and prophets (3:5). Do you regard the apostles and prophets as outstanding people? The fact that the mystery has been revealed to them causes many to regard them as extraordinary. However, in 3:8 Paul, who was an apostle, referred to himself as "less than the least of all saints." According to

Paul's own word, the apostles and prophets were not extra-ordinary, for Paul said that he was less than we are. On the one hand, we may regard the apostles and prophets as extraordinary; but, on the other hand, we should consider them the same as we are.

Only in the book of Ephesians does Paul say that he was less than the least of all saints. Notice that he did not say here that he was less than the apostles, although in 1 Corinthians 15:9 he did say that he was "the least of the apostles." It is surely very significant that Paul inserted such a word into this section of Ephesians. If we did not have this verse, we would all be inclined to view the apostles as great men. Why did Paul mention this? It was because he was exhorting the believers to walk worthily of God's calling. As he made this exhortation, he presented himself as an example, saying that he was less than the least of all saints. If Paul had not uttered this word, we might be tempted to excuse ourselves by saying that Paul, who was a great apostle, could have such a walk, but that we are not able to have it. By inserting this word, Paul gave no place for such an excuse. In 3:8 Paul seemed to be saying, "Saints, don't think that I am greater than you. No, I am less. Since someone less than you can do this, then certainly you can do it also." We should not make excuses for ourselves. If Paul could have this kind of grace, we all can have it. If Paul could live such a life and walk worthily of God's calling, then we can also.

Many Christians think that only certain believers such as Peter are "saints." They even speak of Saint So-and-so. But according to the writings of the Apostle Paul, all believers are saints. As saints, we are not inferior to Paul. We all can walk in the same way he did.

The meaning of the Greek word rendered "apostle" is a sent one. If you send me to Los Angeles for a certain purpose, I am your apostle, your sent one. In the Bible an apostle is someone sent by God. Although John the Baptist was sent by God, he should not be considered the first sent one in the New Testament economy, because his ministry was during a transitional period. The first one sent by God in the New Testament economy was the Lord Jesus. Hence, He was the first Apostle (Heb. 3:1). The Lord sent out the twelve Apostles. These twelve, however, were not the only sent ones. In John 20:21 the Lord Jesus said to the disciples, "As the Father has sent Me, I also send you." This verse proves that all the disciples were sent ones. This means that every believer is a sent one. Even a young sister in junior high school is one sent to school by the Lord to minister Christ to her teachers and classmates. Likewise, if you are burdened for one of your relatives and the Lord sends you to him for the purpose of ministering Christ to him, are you not one sent by Christ? Yes, to your relatives you are Christ's apostle. You may even be an apostle to those in your own family. One day the Lord may send you to your mother to share Christ with her. At such a time you are an apostle to your mother. Therefore, in a sense, we all are the Lord's apostles, His sent ones.

In like manner, there is a sense in which all believers in Christ are prophets. Contrary to the concept of many Christians, a prophet is not primarily one who predicts the future; he is a spokesman for God. According to Hebrews 3, Moses, one called by God and sent to the children of Israel, was an apostle; he typified Christ as God's Apostle. When the Lord called him and sent him out as an apostle, Moses was timid and claimed that he could not speak well. Then the Lord told Moses that He would give him his brother Aaron as a prophet. Aaron was given by God to Moses not to predict the future on behalf of Moses, but to be his spokesman. By this we see that the ministry of a prophet goes along with that of an apostle. Moses was the apostle, and Aaron was the prophet.

On the one hand, we are apostles and, on the other hand, we are prophets. The young people are sent to school as apostles, but when they open their mouths to speak on behalf of the Lord, they are prophets. Likewise, if you go to your mother with the burden to minister Christ to her, you are an apostle. But as you speak for Christ, you are also a prophet. It is a shame to be a Christian for years without ever going to someone with the burden to minister Christ to him. It is also a shame to be a Christian without ever speaking to others on behalf of Christ. A normal believer is both an apostle and a prophet, a sent one and a spokesman.

Suppose, under the Lord's sovereignty, some of you are burdened to move to another city. You minister Christ to the people there, and after a period of time a number become believers. Then you all meet together as the church in that locality. Through whom was that church raised up? It was raised up by the apostles sent by the Lord to that locality. Because these sent ones also speak for God, they are prophets as well as apostles.

I emphasize this matter because we all have been strongly influenced by the concepts in Christianity. In Catholicism Peter has been elevated to be a pope, and others have been given high positions in the so-called holy service. But all believers are in the holy service, and all of us could be called "popes," because the word "pope" simply means "father." If you bring new ones to the Lord, begetting them with Christ, you become their spiritual father. In this sense, as a sent one and a prophet, you are a "pope," a father. My basis for saying that all can be such fathers is the fact that every believer is a sent one and a prophet. If you are not a sent one and a prophet, then you are not faithful to the Lord and not obedient to Him. Suppose the Lord sends you to a remote region with the burden to minister Christ to the unbelievers there. This means that you are the apostle sent to that area. Because you are the one to speak for God, you are also the prophet. As the apostle and prophet, you are the "pope." Even the least among the saints in the Lord's recovery may be sent forth to be such a "pope," a genuine father.

Regarding apostles and prophets, we all have been drugged by religious concepts. I hope that this message will be a strong antidote to this drug. I am serious in saying that we all must be apostles and prophets. Suppose a certain sister works as a nurse in a hospital. Do you think God wants her merely to be a nurse? No! God sends her to that hospital to be an apostle and a prophet. God's authority is always with such a person. If you practice your apostleship and prophethood, God will be with you as your authority. Many times we do not have authority because we fail to practice our apostleship. Wherever we are, at home, at school, or at work, we need to be there as those sent by the Lord to minister Christ to others by speaking for Christ.

The apostles and prophets, however, must bear a particular sign to prove that they are apostles and prophets. This sign is the revelation of the mystery. If you go to someone without this revelation, you are neither an apostle nor a prophet. When you contact people for Christ, you must let them know in a proper way that you have seen something they have not seen. It is by having this revelation that we have the boldness to say that we are God's sent ones and God's spokesmen. If a young brother has such a revelation, he can say to his unbelieving father, who may have a doctorate in physics, "Father, you know a great deal about science, but you don't know anything about Christ. I know Christ, for I have seen the revelation concerning Him. Christ is my life. He lives in me, He is one with me, and He is everything to me." If you have this revelation, then you are an apostle and a prophet. Do you not have the revelation concerning Christ and the church? Certainly you do. Therefore, go to your relatives and friends to tell them of what you have seen.

A. In Spirit

Verse 5 says that the mystery has been revealed to the apostles and prophets in spirit. The word "spirit" here refers to the human spirit of the apostles and prophets, a spirit regenerated and indwelt by the Holy Spirit of God. It can be considered the mingled spirit, the human spirit mingled with God's Spirit. Such a mingled spirit is the means by which the New Testament revelation concerning Christ and the church is unveiled to the apostles and prophets. We need the same spirit to see such a revelation.

When we speak to others about Christ and the church, we should not speak from our mind, emotion, or will. Rather, from our spirit we should tell others what we have experienced of Christ and the church. The principle here is that emotion touches emotion, mind touches mind, and will touches will. Likewise, only spirit can contact spirit. If you speak to others from your emotion, you will not be able to touch their spirit. But if you speak out from your spirit, their spirit will be touched.

B. Concerning Christ and the Church

The revelation received by the apostles and prophets is not a revelation of the many secondary matters in the Bible. It is the revelation concerning Christ and the church. In order to dispense Christ to others, we need to have this revelation.

II. THE MYSTERY OF CHRIST

In 3:4 Paul speaks of the mystery of Christ. The mystery of God in Colossians 2:2 (Gk.) is Christ, whereas the mystery of Christ here is the church. God is a mystery, and Christ, as the embodiment of God to express Him, is the mystery of God. Christ is also a mystery, and the church, as the Body of Christ to express Him, is the mystery of Christ.

A. Hidden in Other Generations but Revealed in the New Testament Age

This mystery was hidden in other generations, but has been revealed in the New Testament age. The mystery of Christ, the church, which is His Body, was hidden in the Old Testament ages. None of the Old Testament saints knew anything regarding this mystery. But it is revealed in the New Testament to all believers through the apostles and prophets. Today our ministry is simply to carry on this revelation.

B. The Church, the Body of Christ

1. With the Nations as Joint-heirs and Joint-partakers of the Promise

We have pointed out that the mystery of Christ is the church, which is the Body of Christ. Regarding the church as the mystery of Christ, verse 6 says that "the nations are to be joint-heirs and a joint Body and joint-partakers of the promise in Christ Jesus through the gospel." The term "joint-heirs" indicates that in God's New Testament economy, the nations, the chosen and redeemed Gentiles, are joined with the believing Jews to be the heirs of God, inheriting God. The term "joint Body" indicates that the saved Gentiles are joined with the saved Jews to be the one Body of Christ for His unique expression. The term "joint-partakers" indicates that the Gentile believers are joined with the Jewish believers to partake of God's promises given in the Old Testament concerning all the blessings of God's New Testament economy. Joint-heirs are related to the blessing of the household of God; a joint Body is related to the blessing of the Body of Christ; and the joint-partakers are related to the blessing of the promises of God, as found in Genesis 3:15; 12:3; 22:18; 28:14; and Isaiah 9:6. Both the blessing of God's household and the blessing of Christ's Body are particular, whereas the blessing of God's promise is general, all-inclusive.

2. Brought Forth out of
the Unsearchable Riches of Christ

The church as the Body of Christ is brought forth out of the unsearchable riches of Christ (3:8). The church is not brought forth out of doctrines or systems of organization. As the Body of Christ, the church can only be brought forth out of the riches of what Christ is.

3. For Expressing
the Multifarious Wisdom of God
to the Rulers and Authorities in the Heavenlies

According to God's intention, the church is to express His multifarious wisdom to the rulers and authorities in the heavenlies (3:10). This is to shame Satan and his followers. Satan's plots afford God the opportunity to express His wisdom in a multifarious way through the church.

4. According to the Eternal Purpose Which God Made in Christ

The producing of the church to be the Body of Christ is according to the eternal purpose which God made in Christ in eternity past (3:11). The formation of the church is not accidental, but eternally planned.

5. For the Dispensation of God

God's purpose in having the church is to dispense Himself into His chosen people (3:9). Hence, the church as the Body of Christ is the dispensation of God.

LIFE-STUDY OF EPHESIANS

MESSAGE THIRTY

THE RICHES OF CHRIST
PRODUCING THE CHURCH

Chapter three of Ephesians reveals that the Apostle Paul had a walk worthy of God's calling. As one with such a worthy walk, he was a prisoner, a steward, and a minister. In this chapter Paul told us that the revelation of the mystery concerning Christ for the church has been given to the apostles and prophets (v. 5). Paul's revelation of Christ was mainly a revelation of Christ's unsearchable riches. Because Paul's walk was governed by his revelation of Christ, he could not keep from speaking of the riches of Christ. The apostle's preaching was focused on the riches of Christ, not on the doctrines. The riches of Christ are what Christ is to us, such as light, life, righteousness, and holiness. These riches are unsearchable; it is beyond our ability to trace them out. Since we also can be apostles and prophets, there is the need for us to see the unsearchable riches of Christ.

Many Christians have the mistaken concept that the apostles in the universal church and the elders in the local churches are high officials, far above the so-called laymen or common believers. As we pointed out in the foregoing message, the Apostle Paul, realizing that such was a wrong concept, purposely indicated that the apostles and prophets were not extraordinary. On the contrary, they should be regarded simply as leading ones among the saints in the churches. They take the lead to receive the revelation concerning Christ for the church, to live Christ, to experience Christ, to enjoy Christ, and to minister the riches of Christ to others. If the enjoyment of the riches of Christ were available only for certain exceptional persons of high rank, then the rest of us would have no share in it. But in 3:8 Paul said that he was less than the least of all saints; yet he could preach the unsearchable riches of Christ as the gospel. The fact that Paul could do this indicates that we can do it also. Because he was less than we are, what was available to him is available also to us.

The apostles and prophets are not a special class of believers. Rather, they are ordinary believers like the rest of us. The difference between them and other believers is that they are leading ones. It is the same with the elders in the local churches. The elders are not extraordinary people of high rank, higher than other believers. No, they are simply those who take the lead in the church life. We all need to allow this concept to sink into our being.

In the Lord's recovery we must drop the thought of rank. There is no rank among us. At most, we just have some leading ones to take the lead to live Christ for the church life. There is no higher class, no special class, in the church. We have no leader. According to the Lord's word in Matthew 23:8-10, He is our unique Leader, and we all are brothers. We must drop the concept that the apostles and elders are special. We all are sheep, and the apostles, prophets, and elders take the lead to set an example, a pattern, of how to know Christ, to enjoy Him, to gain Him for the church life, and to dispense Him into others. This is a matter of setting an example, not a matter of rank or position.

I. THE RICHES OF CHRIST

In order to be apostles, prophets, stewards, ministers, and even prisoners in Christ, we need to know the unsearchable riches of Christ. These riches are for the producing of the church to be the fullness of Christ.

A. In Types

The riches of Christ are depicted in types. It is not easy to find all the types of Christ in the Old Testament. Some types are hidden. For example, the earth that emerges in Genesis 1:9 and 10 is a type of Christ. Many other types are found in chapter one of Genesis: light, the sun, the star, and the trees. Elsewhere in the Bible we see that the vine tree, the apple tree, the cedar, and the cypress are all types of Christ. Herbs also typify Christ. At the time of the Passover, the children of Israel ate not only the lamb, but also unleavened bread and bitter herbs. Wheat and barley are also types of Christ, and the henna flower spoken of in Song of Songs as well. Certain persons also typify Christ. Adam, Abel, Isaac, Jacob, Joseph, Moses, and Aaron are some of these who are types of Christ. The priests, the kings, and the prophets also typify Him.

The more I study the Bible, the more I realize how little I know it. A hundred messages could be given on Genesis 1, mainly on the types of Christ in this chapter. The Bible is deep and profound. Only when we get into its depths do we see the riches it contains. Beneath the surface of the Bible are the riches of Christ. Because these riches are so vast, it is difficult for anyone to say how many types of Christ there are in the Old Testament. Just this one matter of the types reveals many of the riches of Christ.

B. In Shadows

Along with the types, there are the shadows and figures of Christ. Although types and shadows are similar in certain respects, they are like human faces in that they not only share similarities, but also differ from each other. Types are mainly persons or things that signify Christ, whereas shadows mainly refer to rituals and practices in the Old Testament that portray Christ. According to Colossians 2:16 and 17, eating regulations, rituals, and holy days were shadows. By this we see that the laws, ordinances, and ceremonies in the Old Testament were shadows portraying Christ. But Adam, Aaron, and Moses were not shadows; they were types. The Sabbath day and the new moon, on the contrary, were shadows. Although the Sabbath was a rest, it was not the real rest, for the real rest is Christ. Likewise, the law as a testimony of God described what God was like. As a description and explanation of God, the law was a testimony of God. In this it was a shadow of Christ as the real explanation, definition, and testimony of God.

C. In Figures

A figure mainly refers to a situation that presents a certain picture. For example, the wandering of the children of Israel in the wilderness is a figure, a picture, of our experience in the Christian life today, which is often a life of wandering. The Passover is another figure. Although the Passover lamb is a type of Christ, the Passover itself is a figure depicting how Christ, our Passover, saves us from God's judgment and feeds us with what He is. Hence, the picture of the Passover is a figure of Christ.

Christ is so rich that He needs not only types, but also shadows and figures to portray Him. All the types, shadows, and figures of Christ in the Old Testament are descriptions, explanations, and definitions of what Christ is. We need to study all these matters in the Scriptures in order to know the riches of Christ.

D. In Prophecies

The riches of Christ are also seen in prophecies. In the Bible the first prophecy concerning Christ is Genesis 3:15, a verse which predicts that Christ as the seed of the woman will bruise the head of the serpent, Satan. This implies that Christ had to become a man born of a virgin, for He was to be the seed of woman. Christ is not the descendant of a man; He is the seed of a woman. This one verse reveals much of the riches of Christ.

Isaiah 9:6 is another prophecy regarding Christ. This verse gives us seven titles of Christ: Child, Son, Wonderful, Counselor, Mighty God, Eternal Father, Prince of Peace. In the Old Testament, there are a great many other prophecies of Christ. Even the short book of Zechariah contains many detailed prophecies concerning Him.

E. In Fulfillment

The riches of Christ are also seen in the fulfillment of the prophecies. Sometimes in the fulfillment of a prophecy in the New Testament something further is added. For example, the Old Testament reveals that Christ will be the lamb. But in the Old Testament, Christ is never called the Lamb of God. Nevertheless, in the fulfillment of the prophecy regarding Christ as the lamb, He is called the Lamb of God (John 1:29). What an addition this is!

When I was young, I was troubled by the fact that sometimes the New Testament writers added certain things when quoting the Old Testament prophecies concerning Christ. I thought that they should not have gone beyond what was written in the Old Testament. Later I came to see that Christ could not be limited by the prophecies concerning Him. When He came, He fulfilled more than what had been prophesied. Furthermore, our experience of Christ surpasses the fulfillment of the prophecies. Actually, this is not adding something; it is experiencing the unlimited Christ. In our experience Christ is not only the Lamb of God, but the Lamb of eternity. Thus, the prophecy is short, the fulfillment is longer, and the experience is eternal. When we experience Christ in the fulfillment of the prophecies concerning Him, we do not add anything. Rather, we enter into the eternal experience of the inexhaustible riches of Christ.

F. As Plants

Plants also portray the riches of Christ. Grass, flowers, grains, and trees all depict Christ's riches.

G. As Animals

Christ is typified not only by trees and plants, but also by animals. The lamb, the cow, the eagle, the lion, and the dove are all types of Christ.

H. As Minerals

In the Bible, a number of minerals also show forth the riches of Christ. Gold, silver, brass, and precious stones, for example, typify Him.

I. As Persons

We have pointed out that a number of persons in the Bible typify Christ. All these depict different aspects of Christ's riches. We see certain riches of Christ in Adam, others in Abel, and others in Joseph. Throughout the Bible, many other persons portray different aspects of the riches of Christ.

J. As All the Positive Things in the Universe

All the positive things in the universe point to Christ. For example, Christ is the real gravity. Without Him, we would drift away. If Christ did not hold us in place, we would not be able to stand. Christ is the One with the true holding power. According to Hebrews 1:3, He upholds the entire universe.

Because all the positive things in the universe signify Christ, Christ could use so many things as illustrations of Himself when He was on earth. For instance, He could use the door as a picture of Himself and say, "I am the door." Christ is the reality of every positive thing. He is not only the gravity, but also the air, the light, and every positive thing.

K. As Human Virtues and Divine Attributes

The riches of Christ also include both human virtues and divine attributes. Christ is the real love, patience, and forgiveness. Apart from Christ, we cannot love, be patient, or forgive, not even in relation to our wife or husband. But when we have Christ, we have all the human virtues and divine attributes.

II. THE RICHES OF CHRIST
FOR PRODUCING THE CHURCH

A. Through the Divine Dispensation
of Christ into the Believers

All the riches of Christ are for the producing of the church. This takes place through the divine dispensation of Christ into the believers. The church is produced not by teaching, nor by organizing, but by the dispensation of Christ. The more Christ is dispensed into us, the more life we have, the stronger life we have, the richer life we have, and the more uplifted the church life becomes. I love the ministry that dispenses the riches of Christ into the believers. By means of such a ministry, we have a proper, strong, uplifted church life.

B. By the Believers' Experience and Enjoyment of Christ

The riches of Christ produce the church through the believers' experience and enjoyment of Christ. On Christ's side, it is a matter of dispensation, but on our side, it is a matter of experience and enjoyment. When we experience and enjoy the very Christ who is dispensed into us, we become part of the proper church life.

III. TO EXPRESS GOD'S MULTIFARIOUS WISDOM

The riches of Christ also express God's multifarious wisdom (3:10). God's wisdom is manifold; it has many aspects in many directions. This wisdom is expressed before the rulers and authorities in the heavenlies, mainly before the evil powers of Satan. God desires to demonstrate to the powers of Satan how wise He is. Thus, the riches of Christ display His wisdom in a multifarious way. This is according to God's eternal purpose (3:11).

IV. RESULTING IN THE FULLNESS OF CHRIST

The experience of the riches of Christ results in the fullness of Christ, the Body as Christ's expression (1:23). The book of Ephesians speaks both of the riches of Christ and of the fullness of Christ. A tall, husky man is the fullness of America because he has enjoyed the riches of American foodstuffs. Throughout the years of his growth and development, he has consumed a great deal of meat, poultry, vegetables, and fruit. Therefore, as a full-grown man, he becomes the fullness of America. The riches of American foodstuffs did not make him this fullness until he ate them, digested them, and assimilated them. By absorbing the riches in this way, the riches became part of him. Likewise all the aspects of the riches of Christ do not become the fullness of Christ until they are eaten, enjoyed, digested, and assimilated by us. By absorbing these riches in such a way, we become the Body of Christ as His fullness to express Him. Thus, the Body of Christ is constituted of the riches of Christ that have been enjoyed and assimilated by us. Therefore, the Body is the result, the issue, of the experience and enjoyment of the riches of Christ.

LIFE-STUDY OF EPHESIANS

MESSAGE THIRTY-ONE

THE CHURCH FOR GOD'S WISDOM
ACCORDING TO HIS ETERNAL PURPOSE

In this message we shall consider 3:9-13. Verse 9 says, "And to bring to light what is the dispensation of the mystery, which from the ages has been hidden in God, Who created all things." God's mystery is His hidden purpose, which is to dispense Himself into His chosen people. Hence, there is the dispensation of the mystery of God. This mystery was hidden in God from the ages (that is, from eternity) and through all past ages, but now it has been brought to light to the New Testament believers.

I. GOD'S WISDOM

Verse 10 continues, "In order that now to the rulers and the authorities in the heavenlies might be made known through the church the multifarious wisdom of God." This verse speaks of God's wisdom. Chapter one speaks of the power of God (vv. 19-20), chapter two, of the grace of God (vv. 5-8), and chapter three, of the wisdom of God. God is very wise, and the universe reveals His wisdom.

We need to see the difference between wisdom and knowledge. In Colossians 2:3 the two are mentioned together. Wisdom is both higher and deeper than knowledge. Wisdom is seen in the initiation of something, for example, in the formulation of a new invention, and knowledge is seen in the practical application. If you have only knowledge and lack wisdom, you will not be able to initiate anything nor to invent anything. God is the unique Initiator. He has initiated many things, not by His knowledge, but by His wisdom. When He comes in to apply what He has initiated, He displays His knowledge.

In our case, wisdom is in our spirit, and knowledge is in our mind. If you do not know how to get into your spirit, you may have a great deal of knowledge, but you will not have any wisdom. But if you are a person in the spirit, you will be wise. Furthermore, in your mind you will have knowledge, prudence.

Verse 10 says that through the church the multifarious wisdom of God is made known to the rulers and authorities in the heavenlies. These rulers and authorities are the angelic rulers and authorities, both good and evil. The passage here especially refers to the evil ones—Satan and his angels. According to the New Testament, Satan has his kingdom, his angels, and his sphere of rule. Satan's sphere of rule is in the air and on the earth. The book of Daniel indicates that all nations on earth are under the rule of Satan in the air. Therefore, through the church God makes His wisdom known not mainly to human beings but to those rebellious angels who are the followers of God's enemy.

Verse 8 reveals that the church is produced from the unsearchable riches of Christ. When God's chosen people partake of and enjoy the riches of Christ, these riches constitute them the church, through which God's multifarious wisdom is made known to the angelic rulers and authorities in the heavenlies. Hence, the church is God's wise exhibition of all that Christ is.

Even the rebellion of Satan is within the realm of God's wisdom. If it were not for Satan's rebellion, God's wisdom could not be made known in a full way. If you are a person full of wisdom, the more troubles and difficulties you have, the more wisdom you will express. But if everything related to you is peaceful and without problems, you will have no opportunity to express your wisdom. Actually, when everything is going well, there is little need of wisdom. You need trouble in order to display your wisdom.

God also needs trouble. He even needs an adversary, Satan. Few Christians realize that God actually needs Satan. Although God needs us, He needs Satan even more. When I was young, I wondered why God did not cast Satan into the lake of fire immediately when he rebelled against Him. I questioned why God gave Satan so much freedom. I also asked why God put the tree of the knowledge of good and evil in the garden of Eden. If this tree had not been there, man would not have fallen. But without Satan and without the tree of knowledge, God's wisdom cannot be fully manifested. Satan and the tree of knowledge have created many opportunities for God's wisdom to be manifested in a multifarious way, that is, in various ways and aspects and from many angles. The Greek word translated "multifarious" indicates that God's wisdom has many sides, aspects, and directions. Only through problems can all the aspects of God's wisdom be manifested.

When some hear of such a word, they may be tempted to say, "Let us create more trouble for God. Let us do evil that good may come." Never say this. If you intend to create trouble or to do evil, you may find yourself unable to do so. For example, although it is easy to stand up, it is difficult to fall purposely. We need to realize our nothingness. On our own, we cannot succeed either in being defeated or in being victorious. If you try not to be defeated, you may be defeated. But if you want to be defeated, you may find that you cannot be defeated.

Consider the example of David. With respect to Bathsheba, David had a great failure. If God had not allowed him to fall in this matter, David could not have fallen. David's fall gave God an opportunity to express His wisdom. Through David's fall and repentance combined with God's forgiveness, David gained a son, Solomon, to be the builder of the temple. Later, David fell again, this time in numbering the army of Israel. But through this second fall David acquired the site on which the temple was built. For the building of the temple there was the need for both the builder and the site. If you read the Bible with understanding, you will see that David's falls were neither of David nor of God; they were of Satan. It was Satan who tempted David to commit immorality and to number the army of Israel. When David yielded to these temptations, Satan was pleased, convinced that he had damaged an excellent king whose heart was absolute for God. Satan, however, did not know that his temptations created opportunities for God's wisdom to be manifested.

Whatever the enemy of God does gives God the opportunity to show forth His wisdom. If we had never been poisoned and corrupted, we would not have needed God very much, and there would have been no need for God's salvation. The more sinful, corrupt, and damaged we are, the greater is our need for God and the more opportunity there is for God to do something for us.

In verse 10 Paul declares that God's multifarious wisdom is made known to the rulers and authorities in the heavenlies through the church. The church is the Body of Christ, the joint-heirs, and the joint-partakers. The church is composed of those who once were ruined, corrupted, and damaged. Before we were saved, we were vipers, poisonous serpents. Furthermore, we were dead in trespasses and sins. Moreover, we were scattered and divided, utterly unable to be one. Thus, all the members of the church were in a hopeless situation. Nevertheless, God in His wisdom is able to make us the church. Now we are not only redeemed, saved, cleansed, freed, liberated, and regenerated—we are also united. We are one with God and with one another. Therefore, we are the church.

The church is God's greatest boast. Although you may not care that much for the church, God cares very much for the church. Sometimes God may say, "Look, Satan, I have taken the very people whom you have ruined and I have made them into the church. Do you have the wisdom to do such a thing? You do not have this wisdom, but I have it."

After God had created man and had put him into the garden, Satan came in to intervene, convinced that the best way to ruin the man created by God for Himself was to inject his own evil nature into him. At the time of the fall, Satan as sin entered into man and, in many respects, caused man to be the same as he is. For this reason the Bible refers to fallen men as the offspring of vipers. Having come into man as sin, Satan has made himself one with man and has transmuted man's body into the flesh. But one day God became flesh (John 1:14). Eventually, Satan caused this One who had become flesh to be crucified. Firstly Satan instigated Judas to betray the Lord Jesus, and secondly he stirred up the Jews and the Gentiles to cooperate in crucifying Him. What Satan did not realize, however, was that in putting this One on the cross, he was actually crucifying himself. As Hebrews 2:14 says, "Since therefore the children have partaken of blood and flesh, He also Himself in like manner shared in the same, that through death He might destroy him who has the might of death, that is, the Devil." Through His own death on the cross, the Lord Jesus destroyed Satan. What a display of God's marvelous wisdom! This is one aspect of God's wisdom.

Another aspect of God's wisdom is revealed in 1 Corinthians 1. In this chapter Paul says that the Greeks, the philosophical people, seek wisdom. However, to us, the ones called by God and those who believe in the Lord Jesus, wisdom is Christ. Christ is God's wisdom. First Corinthians 1:30 says that it is of God that we are in Christ Jesus. For us to be in Christ is the wisdom of God. I cannot explain how God put us in Christ. Nevertheless, I have the deep conviction and assurance that we are in Christ. Praise the Lord that we are all in Him! In His wisdom God has put us in Christ.

According to 1 Corinthians 1:30, Christ is our wisdom with respect to righteousness, sanctification, and redemption. As our righteousness, Christ has dealt with our past, which was altogether unrighteous. For our present situation, Christ is our sanctification, and for the future, He is our redemption. One day our body will be redeemed, that is, transfigured. For Christ to be our righteousness, sanctification, and redemption requires much wisdom on God's part. Although Christ is our righteousness for the past, our sanctification for the present, and our redemption for the future, He is also our daily righteousness, sanctification, and redemption.

In order to understand this adequately, we need to see the full scope of God's economy. After the creation and the fall of man, God became flesh through incarnation. Then the Lord Jesus went to the cross and there crucified the flesh. After passing through death and resurrection, He ascended into the heavens, then descended, and entered into us as the life-giving Spirit in order to enliven our deadened spirit and to regenerate us. Having regenerated us, He now dwells in our spirit as life. In this life, the divine life, we have the law of life, the sense of life, and the fellowship of life. The Lord, however, is not only life to us; He is also the anointing within us. Furthermore, He is daily sealing us, saturating us, anointing us, and permeating us. As this takes place, we spontaneously live Him, and He becomes our righteousness. This is God's wisdom. Because of His wisdom God can boast to Satan of what He has done with corrupted and ruined man. Have you ever realized that what we are as believers today is of God's wisdom? Only God has the wisdom to initiate such a wonderful thing, to make sinful and corrupted people the members of Christ.

Through the work of the Spirit of life, a change is taking place in our very nature. It is a metabolic change, a change that sanctifies and transforms us. Thus, Christ is not only our righteousness, but also our sanctification. Furthermore, we are daily being redeemed, and eventually we shall be glorified. Christ is our righteousness, sanctification, and redemption, not only in an objective way, but in a very subjective way, in the way of mingling and changing us metabolically. All this is a testimony to God's multifarious wisdom. Many aspects of God's wisdom are manifested in His making Christ our righteousness, sanctification, and redemption. Our experience of Christ in these matters is according to God's manifold wisdom.

The church through which God's wisdom is so marvelously displayed is God's masterpiece. In the eyes of God the most wonderful thing in the universe is the church, for through the church God's multifarious wisdom is made known to Satan and his angels. The day is coming when

Satan and his angels will be put to shame. They will realize that everything they have done has given God the opportunity to manifest His wisdom. In the same principle, our failures, mistakes, defeats, and wrongdoings have also given God opportunities to display His wisdom. None of us likes to be mistaken; on the contrary, we all want to be right. Although I have always intended to do the right thing, I have nevertheless made many mistakes, even some big mistakes. I certainly hate these mistakes, but I can testify that they have afforded God the opportunity to show forth His wisdom. Therefore, I can thank the Lord for all my mistakes.

If we review our past, we shall realize that we have received more grace through our mistakes than through the things we have done without any mistake. Although I have made some major mistakes, through them I have received much mercy and grace. It seems as if the amount of mercy and grace received has been in proportion to the seriousness of the mistakes. Hallelujah, we are God's chosen people, and even through our failures He manifests His multifarious wisdom! However, we should not intentionally try to fail in order to receive God's mercy and grace.

II. GOD'S ETERNAL PURPOSE

Verse 11 says, "According to the purpose of the ages which He made in Christ Jesus our Lord." The purpose of the ages is the purpose of eternity, the eternal purpose, the eternal plan of God made in eternity past. It was made in Christ with a threefold intention for God's glory, for the blessing of God's chosen people, and for the shame of God's enemy. The main intention of God's purpose is to glorify God, to express Him through His chosen people. This is the greatest blessing to us. In this God's enemy is shamed to the uttermost.

III. OUR BOLDNESS, ACCESS, CONFIDENCE, AND GLORY

Verse 12 continues, "In Whom we have boldness and access in confidence through the faith of Him." In Christ we have access, entry, not only to approach God, but also to partake of His New Testament economy. Through the faith of Christ, we have such access with boldness in confidence to enjoy God and His eternal plan. We have boldness in Christ, we have access to God, we have confidence in God's purpose, and we also have the glory in the apostle's afflictions (v. 13).

LIFE-STUDY OF EPHESIANS

MESSAGE THIRTY-TWO

TO BE STRENGTHENED INTO THE INNER MAN THAT CHRIST MAY MAKE HIS HOME IN OUR HEARTS

In this message we come to 3:14-17, the first part of Paul's second prayer for the church, the prayer which is related to experience. The apostle's prayer in 1:15-23 is for the saints to receive revelation concerning the church. In 3:14-21 his prayer is for the saints to experience Christ for the church.

I. THE APOSTLE'S PRAYER FOR OUR EXPERIENCE OF CHRIST

A. "For This Cause"

The Apostle Paul begins his prayer in verse 14 with the words "for this cause." The cause for which Paul prayed is hidden in the depths of chapter three. We have seen that in this chapter Paul presents himself as a pattern of one who has seen God's economy. Paul received the revelation that God's economy is God's dispensing of Himself into His chosen ones to make them the expansion, the enlargement, of Christ, who is the embodiment of God, for God's full expression. Having received such a revelation, Paul became an apostle, a sent one. He was also a prophet, one who spoke for God. Paul not only spoke for God, but he even spoke forth God. As God's spokesman, Paul ministered the unsearchable riches of Christ to others so that they might see the same revelation and also become apostles and prophets. This means that Paul's desire was to produce more apostles and prophets. For this purpose he even suffered imprisonment. But the more he was confined in prison, the more revelation he received and the more of Christ he was able to minister to the believers to make them all apostles and prophets. All this is the cause for which Paul prayed in Ephesians 3.

When some hear that all the saints can be apostles and prophets, they may wonder about 1 Corinthians 12:29, a verse which says, "Are all apostles? are all prophets?" Not all are *the* apostles or *the* prophets, but, as 1 Corinthians 14:31 says, all can prophesy. *The* apostles and *the* prophets were those who took the lead in the New Testament. The difference between us and them is that they were the leaders and we are the followers. But this does not mean that we cannot do what the leading apostles and prophets did. In the same principle, the difference between the elders and all the other members in a local church is that the elders take the lead and the other members follow. This does not mean, however, that the other members cannot do what the elders do. On the contrary, all the members should do what the elders do, and they should do even more. How different this is from the concept in Christianity that the laymen cannot do what the ministers do! The elders are not a higher rank; rather, all are of the same rank. The only difference is that the elders take the lead, like sheep who walk at the front of the flock. Likewise, the leading apostles and prophets are not on a higher level than the rest of the saints. They take the lead, and we all follow them to do what they do.

When I came to this country, I came with a revelation concerning Christ for the church. Having received such a revelation, I was sent here to speak for God and even to speak forth God. I am simply a follower of *the* apostles and prophets in the New Testament. My burden is for all the saints to become such followers. I hope that one day thousands will be sent out to speak for God. Although we cannot be the leading apostles, we can be the followers. In like manner, we cannot be *the* prophets, but we all can prophesy. We all can be sent, and we all can speak for Christ. What a privilege, a mercy, and a grace to be the followers of the leading apostles and prophets!

B. Unto the Father

In verses 14 and 15 Paul says, "For this cause I bow my knees unto the Father, of whom every family in the heavens and on earth is named." Notice that here Paul does not refer to God, but to the Father. The "Father" here is used in a broad sense, signifying not only the Father of the household of faith (Gal. 6:10), but the Father of every family in the heavens and on earth (v. 15). The Father is the source, not only of the regenerated believers, but also of the God-created mankind (Luke 3:38), of the God-created Israel (Isa. 63:16; 64:8), and of the God-created angels (Job 1:6). The Jews' concept was that God was Father only to them. So the apostle prayed to the Father of all the families in the heavens and on earth, according to his revelation, not as the Jews, who prayed only to the Father of Israel, according to the Jewish concept.

Since God is the source of the angelic family in the heavens and all the human families on earth, so it is of God that every family is named, just as producers give names to their products and fathers give names to their children.

II. TO BE STRENGTHENED

In verse 16 we have the subject of Paul's prayer: "That He would grant you, according to the riches of His glory, to be strengthened with power through His Spirit into the inner man." In contrast to the prayer in chapter one, which is a prayer for revelation, this is a prayer for experience. The need in chapter one is for us to see the things related to the Body of Christ, to see how the Body comes into existence and how it is constituted. But it is inadequate simply to see the revelation; we also need the experience of what we see. Because we need to experience Christ in a subjective way, Paul prayed that we would be strengthened with power into the inner man.

A. By the Father
according to the Riches of His Glory

In verse 16 the word "strengthened" is modified by four phrases: "according to the riches of His glory," "with power," "through His Spirit," and "into the inner man." Firstly, we are strengthened according to the riches of the Father's glory. Glory is the expression of God. John 1:18 says, "No one has ever seen God; the only begotten Son, Who is in the bosom of the Father, He has declared Him." In this declaration of God there is glory, for the declaration of God is the manifestation of God, which is glory. When the Lord Jesus expressed God on earth, God's glory was manifested.

All the families in the heavens and on earth express God to some extent. With their expressions of God, there are the riches of His glory. The apostle prayed that the Gentile believers might experience God in a full way according to the riches of His glory, that He might be expressed through the Gentile believers by their experiencing Him in a full way.

What then are the riches of God's glory? The riches of glory in verse 16 are related to every family in verse 15. Every family is an expression of God to a certain degree. Because the Father is the source, the origin, of every family in the heavens and on earth, every family is His expression. The family that expresses the Father the most is the family of the believers. Therefore, Paul prayed to the Father that we might be strengthened for the purpose of expressing Him to the uttermost.

B. With Power

We are also strengthened with power. This power is the resurrection power referred to in 1:19-20; it is this power which operates in us (3:20). This power raised Christ up from among the dead, uplifted Him to the heavens, and put everything under His feet. With such a power God is strengthening us.

C. Through His Spirit

It is through the Spirit that the Father strengthens us. He strengthens us by the indwelling Spirit. This does not mean that the Spirit is not with us or that the Spirit will come down from the heavens to strengthen us. The strengthening Spirit has been with us since He regenerated us. He is still within us now. Through this indwelling Spirit, the Father strengthens us from within.

D. Into Our Inner Man

Verse 16 also says that we are strengthened into the inner man. The inner man is our regenerated spirit with God's life as its life. It is our spirit regenerated by the Spirit of God (John 3:6), indwelt by the Spirit of God (Rom. 8:11, 16), and mingled with the Spirit of God (1 Cor. 6:17). In order to experience Christ unto all the fullness of God, we need to be strengthened into the inner man. This implies that we need to get into our spirit, where we can be strengthened through the Holy Spirit.

Because human beings are souls, not spirits, our personality or our person is in our soul. This is the reason the Bible refers to men as souls (Exo. 1:5; Acts 2:41). Both the body and the spirit are vessels used by the soul. Therefore, as souls, we have an outward vessel, the body, and an inward vessel, the spirit. When we repented and believed in the Lord Jesus, the Lord came into us and regenerated us with Himself as our life. Before we were regenerated, there was no life in our spirit; we simply had our human life in our soul. But through regeneration we now have the divine life in our spirit. Therefore, our spirit is no longer merely a vessel; it has become our person with the life of God. But what about our human life and our old person in the soul? The old person, the soul with the human life, has been crucified on the cross, and now our new person is the spirit with the divine life. Our spirit regenerated with the divine life is now our inner man.

It is very difficult to remain in the spirit. We all are accustomed to going out from the spirit, not to going into the spirit and staying there. According to my experience, I can testify that I am not inclined to stay in the spirit. Because it is so easy for me to get out of the spirit, I am still learning to remain in the spirit. Whenever we stay in the spirit, we are strengthened; but whenever we go out from the spirit, we are weakened. Have you ever noticed how easy it is for your mind to wander when you are praying? When you are not praying, you may not think of certain things. But when you begin to pray, you may suddenly find your thoughts dwelling on one thing and then another. You may even make a fast trip to another part of the world. This is the reason we need to be strengthened into our inner man. The more we are strengthened, the more the parts of our inner being are brought back into the spirit, into our inner man.

We need to be strengthened in order to stay in our spirit and not to be distracted by thoughts regarding so many things. In order to pray without being distracted, we need to be strengthened into our inner man. Oh, how we need to be strengthened so that our whole being may come back to the inner man and stay there!

The revelation in chapter three of Ephesians can be seen only when we are in the spirit. As verse 5 says, the mystery is made known to the apostles and prophets *in spirit*. Being strengthened into the inner man is the secret of seeing the revelation of the mystery. We need to be strengthened so that our whole being might be brought back to our spirit.

In our spirit we are also filled with the riches of Christ unto all the fullness of God (v. 19). The Greek word rendered "unto" in verse 19 means "resulting in." Our being filled with the riches of Christ results in the full expression of God. This is the fullness of God.

III. CHRIST MAKING HIS HOME IN OUR HEART

The first part of verse 17 says, "That Christ may make His home in your hearts through faith." Our heart is composed of all the parts of our soul—the mind, the emotion, and the will—plus our conscience, the main part of our spirit. These are the inward parts of our being. Through regeneration, Christ came into our spirit (2 Tim. 4:22). Subsequently, we should allow Him to spread Himself into every part of our heart. Our heart is the totality of all our inward parts and the center of our inward being; therefore, when

Christ makes His home in our heart, He controls our entire inward being and supplies and strengthens every inward part with Himself.

In verse 17 Paul says that it is through faith that Christ makes His home in our hearts. Faith is the substantiating of things unseen (Heb. 11:1). Christ's indwelling is mysterious and abstract. We realize it not by our physical senses, but by the sense of faith.

The first three chapters of Ephesians are on the church, and the last three chapters are on the walk worthy of God's calling for the church. However, actually only the first two chapters are on the church, for chapter three marks the beginning of Paul's exhortation concerning a walk worthy of God's calling. In Ephesians 3 Paul presents himself as a pattern of one who could carry out God's eternal purpose concerning the church. If we had only chapters one and two without chapter three, we would have the teaching and even the vision regarding the church, but we would not have the way to fulfill the vision. In chapter three we see how the church is constituted and realized in a practical way. This chapter is concerned neither with the revelation of the church nor, strictly speaking, with the walk worthy of God's calling for the church; rather, it is concerned with the practical experience of the church being constituted.

The church life is constituted of those in the pattern of the Apostle Paul. We all need to follow Paul in receiving the revelation in our spirit and in being strengthened into our inner man. When Paul bowed his knees to the Father, he was so strong in his inner man that nothing could shake him or disturb him. Because his whole being was in his spirit, nothing outward could trouble him. We also need to be strengthened to such an extent that nothing will be able to carry us away from our inner man. Furthermore, we need Christ to make His home in our hearts so that we may be wholly occupied and possessed by Him.

When we are strengthened into our inner man and Christ makes His home in our hearts, we are able to see the revelation. We need to receive the same revelation given to the leading apostles and prophets. Paul could not receive this revelation for us; we must receive it ourselves personally and subjectively by being strengthened into our inner man. This revelation concerning Christ and the church is the economy of God, the hidden mystery. Whether or not we are today's apostles and prophets depends on whether or not we have seen the revelation. If we do not have the revelation, then we cannot be apostles and prophets. If I had come to this country without this revelation, all my speaking would have been in vain. But I did come with a revelation, and I have spoken according to this revelation. This made me a follower of the apostles and prophets in God's New Testament ministry. Today all the saints, including the young people, can be such followers.

When we were saved, Christ came into our spirit. Now we must give Him the opportunity to spread Himself throughout all the parts of our inner being. As we are strengthened into the inner man, the door is opened for Christ to spread in us, to spread from our spirit to every part of our mind, emotion, and will. The more Christ spreads within us, the more He settles down in us and makes His home in us. This means that He occupies every part of our inner being, possessing all these parts and saturating them with Himself. As a result, not only do we receive the revelation, but we also are filled with Christ. Then wherever we may go, we shall be the apostles, the sent ones, and the prophets, those who speak for Christ.

LIFE-STUDY OF EPHESIANS

MESSAGE THIRTY-THREE

TO APPREHEND THE DIMENSIONS OF CHRIST
AND TO KNOW THE LOVE OF CHRIST

In this message we shall consider the matters of apprehending the dimensions of Christ and of knowing the love of Christ (3:18-19). In verse 18 Paul speaks of the breadth, length, height, and depth, but he does not say to what these dimensions refer. Surely they refer to Christ. We need to be strong to apprehend with all the saints the breadth, length, height, and depth of Christ.

THE STEPS TO APPREHENDING
CHRIST'S DIMENSIONS
AND TO KNOWING HIS LOVE

In verses 16 through 19 the word "that" is used four times: "that He would grant you…to be strengthened…into the inner man," "that Christ may make His home in your hearts," "that you…may be strong to apprehend…and to know," and "that you may be filled unto all the fullness of God." In each case the Greek word rendered "that" may also be rendered "in order that."

The first "that" is the result of Paul's prayer. Paul bowed his knees unto the Father and prayed that He would grant us to be strengthened into our inner man (vv. 14-16). Thus, the result of Paul's prayer is that the Father would grant us such a strengthening.

The second "that," found in verse 17, is that Christ may make His home in our hearts through faith. This is the result of being strengthened into the inner man.

Some may say that the third "that" is parallel to the second, but I agree with those who claim that it is a further result. This means that the second "that" is the result of the first, that the third is the result of the second, and that the fourth is the result of the third.

In chapter three Paul prayed that we would be strengthened. If we have been strengthened into the inner man, Christ can then make His home in our hearts with the result that we are strong to apprehend with all saints what is the breadth, length, height, and depth of Christ and to know the knowledge-surpassing love of God. The result of all this is that we are filled unto all the fullness of God. Here we see several steps. From Paul's prayer we go on to being strengthened; from being strengthened we proceed to Christ's making His home in our hearts; and from this we progress to the apprehending and the knowing and finally to being filled unto all the fullness of God. It is by these steps that we can apprehend the dimensions of Christ and know His knowledge-surpassing love.

THE FULLNESS OF GOD

The fullness of God is the expression of God. We have pointed out that the Body is not the riches of Christ, but the fullness of Christ (1:23). As the riches of Christ are being digested and assimilated into us, they are metabolized. By this process of metabolism we become the fullness of Christ as His expression. Many Christians regard the riches and the fullness as synonymous. The riches of Christ are the various aspects of Christ for our enjoyment, whereas the fullness is the result, the issue, of the enjoyment of these riches. For example, when we eat and digest the riches of American foodstuffs, we become the fullness of America. As the fullness of America, we are the expression of America. Ephesians 3:19 does not say that we are filled with the riches of God, but that we are filled unto the fullness of God. This means that we are filled with the result that we become the expression of God. The expression of God today is the church, which is the Body, the fullness of Him who fills all in all. Hence, the fullness of God in 3:19 is the fullness of Christ, which is the Body, in 1:23. The Body is constituted through our enjoyment of the riches of Christ.

Chapters one and two cover the revelation of the church, and chapter three covers the constitution of the church. In chapter three we see that Paul, who was a leading one and a pattern, received the revelation and enjoyed the riches of Christ. These riches were metabolically constituted into his being to make him a part of the Body. All who would follow him to be today's apostles and prophets must be the same as Paul in these matters. Then the church will be constituted to become the fullness of Christ and the fullness of God. In order for this to take place, Paul prayed that we might be strengthened into our inner man with the result that Christ could make His home in our heart and thereby occupy, possess, permeate, and saturate our whole inner being with Himself. In this way we are filled with Christ, and we become strong to apprehend the dimensions of Christ and to know the knowledge-surpassing love of Christ. Eventually, we shall be filled with Christ to such an extent that we become the fullness of God.

As we pass through all these steps, we need to apprehend the dimensions of Christ. The Greek word translated "apprehend" means not only to know, but also to grasp, to lay hold of intensively. In order to grasp the dimensions of Christ, we need all the saints; for this we must lay hold of Christ corporately.

THE UNIVERSAL DIMENSIONS OF CHRIST

The dimensions of Christ are the breadth, the length, the height, and the depth. These dimensions are the dimensions of the universe. Only God Himself knows the measurements of the universe. We can measure the distance from one point in the universe to another, for example, from the earth to the moon, but we cannot measure the universe itself. Now the very dimensions of the universe are also the dimensions of Christ.

Christ is our real universe. Elsewhere we have pointed out that Christ is our earth, our good land, and also our sun and morning star. Now, according to verse 18, we have the boldness to say that Christ is our universe, for His dimensions are the dimensions of the universe. Ephesians 1:23 speaks of the fullness of Him who fills all in all, and 4:9 and 10 reveal that He who descended into the lower parts of the earth also ascended far above all the heavens that He might fill all things. When we enter into the new heaven and the new earth to dwell in the New Jerusalem, we all shall realize that Christ the Lord is our universe.

EXPERIENCING THE BREADTH AND LENGTH

In our experience of Christ, we firstly experience the breadth of what He is, and then we experience the length. This is horizontal. When we advance in Christ, we experience the height and depth of His riches. This is vertical. Firstly we experience Christ spreading as the breadth and the length. Later we experience Him rising up as the height and finally descending as the depth. As we shall see, our experience of Christ must eventually become three-dimensional, like a cube.

If we have only the length of Christ, without any breadth, our experience will be a "line," that is, an experience that is long and narrow to an extreme. Our experience of Christ, however, should not have only one dimension, like a line, but it should have two dimensions, like a square, and then three dimensions, like a cube. It is of great importance that we all have a two-dimensional, or a "square," experience of Christ. If we have only a "line" experience of Him, this "line" will eventually continue until it reaches an extreme. All extremists are "one-liners," those whose experience of Christ is on a single "line." If you experience Christ properly and normally as the breadth and the length, you will be kept from going to an extreme. Do not go too far out on the "line" of a narrow and long experience of Christ. Rather, experience Him in a "square" way as the breadth and as the length. By experiencing Christ continually as the breadth and length, our experience will be like a solidly woven "carpet," not a long, single "thread."

Some examples will help to make this matter clear. For a number of years, I listened to a certain great Bible teacher.

He was extremely knowledgeable in the Scriptures. Although he spent very little time in prayer, he was constantly reading the Word and writing notes in his Bible. After talking about the Bible for a period of time, he would excuse himself in order to smoke his pipe. Then he would resume his discussion of the Scriptures. With him there was a "line" of only one dimension—an extreme emphasis on studying the Bible—but there was not the normal spreading of Christ in two dimensions as a "square" in his experience.

A sister in my home town also had a "line" experience. She did not read the Bible, but devoted a great deal of time to prayer. Being extremely earnest in prayer, she decided to fast and pray for many days. On the seventh day some of the brothers and sisters came to me very concerned about her situation. When we visited her, she was in bed, weakened because of seven days of fasting. We encouraged her to take care of her health, but she was offended by our suggestion. On the very next day, she died. This is an example of how a "line" experience can lead people to an extreme, even lead them astray. Sooner or later every "line" experience leads astray. Therefore, we need to be balanced. These two examples show that we need to take time both to pray and to study the Word.

Another extreme experience relates to the church meetings. Not long ago some among us decided that they no longer needed the meetings of the church. They preferred simply to enjoy the Lord at home. There is nothing wrong with enjoying the Lord in our homes, but we should not stretch such an experience until it becomes an extreme. Others, on the contrary, care only for the meetings. In their Christian life they reserve no time for prayer, for Bible study, or for enjoying the Lord at home. All they care about is the meetings. This also is an extreme.

How easy it is to have "line" experiences of a single dimension! It seems that not many saints desire the two-dimensional experiences, like a carpet. In order to have an experience of Christ like a solidly woven carpet, we need to be balanced in many ways. To be balanced is to be enriched.

We need both the breadth and the length; we need the two-dimensional, "square," experiences of Christ.

In order to experience Christ in His universal dimensions, we need the church life. We need to experience Christ with all the members of the Body. In particular, we need the church meetings, for in the meetings we are balanced. Through messages and the testimonies of the saints, we are balanced. If we experience the dimensions of Christ in the church life, we shall gradually be woven into a "carpet." We shall not be thin lines of "thread." What is needed today is not lines of "thread," but a "carpet" woven through the balanced experience of Christ in the church.

When we experience Christ in this way, we find that His breadth and length are immeasurable. Christ is immeasurable in His spreading forth. As we experience Christ in His spreading, we come to see that the dimensions of the universe are the very dimensions of Christ.

EXPERIENCING THE HEIGHT AND THE DEPTH

After we experience the breadth and length of Christ, we begin to experience the height of Christ and then the depth. Do not think that we firstly experience the depth of Christ. No, firstly we ascend and then we descend. Before we can have the depth, we must have the height. The spiritual experiences of the depth of Christ come from the experiences of the height of Christ. This means that firstly we grow upward and then we are rooted. Therefore, the proper understanding of the experience of the height and depth of Christ is contrary to our natural concept, which places depth before height.

In our experience of Christ, we should go on from the two dimensions to three, from a "square" to a "cube." A cube is solid. Both in the tabernacle and in the temple the Holy of Holies was a cube. The dimensions of this cube in the tabernacle and temple respectively were ten cubits and twenty cubits. The New Jerusalem will be an eternal cube, twelve thousand stadia in three dimensions. The church life today must also be a "cube." Furthermore, our experience of Christ in the church must be "cubical," three-dimensional, with many lines going back and forth in all three directions. When we experience Christ in such a three-dimensional way, we are solid. In our experience of Christ we are firstly a "square" and then a "cube." When we become a cube, we cannot fall, and we cannot be broken. Christ is the universal cube, and the church life today is also a "cube," not a "line" nor even a "carpet." What about our experience of Christ? May the Lord open our eyes to see that our experience of Him must be a "cube." As we go back and forth and up and down in our experience of Christ, we eventually have a solid "cube."

ROOTED AND GROUNDED IN LOVE

In verse 17 Paul speaks of "having been rooted and grounded in love." We are God's farm and God's building (1 Cor. 3:9). As God's farm we need to be rooted for growth, and as God's building we need to be grounded for building up. Thus, in verse 17 Paul has in mind the matters of life and building. In speaking of our having been rooted and grounded, Paul indicates that the experience of Christ is for life and building. As those who have Christ making His home in our hearts and who are strong to apprehend the dimensions of Christ and to know His knowledge-surpassing love, we must have both the life and the building. All that we experience of Christ must be for this.

Paul says specifically that we are rooted and grounded in *love*. In order to experience Christ, we need faith and love (1 Tim. 1:14). Faith enables us to receive and realize Christ, and love enables us to enjoy Him. Both faith and love are not ours but His. His faith becomes our faith to believe in Him, and His love becomes our love to love Him. The love in which we are rooted and grounded is the divine love realized and experienced by us in a practical way. With such a love we love the Lord, and with that same love we love one another. In such a love we grow in life and are built up in life. Paul's thought here regarding the relationship between the experience of Christ and the matters of life and building is surely deep and profound.

The more we grow up, the more we are rooted. Although this is opposed to our natural concept, it nonetheless corresponds to our experience. If you consider your experience, you will realize that you have had the sense, not firstly of being rooted and then of growing up, but of growing up and then of being rooted. As we grow upward, we are rooted downward.

KNOWING THE LOVE OF CHRIST IN EXPERIENCE

In the first part of verse 19 Paul says, "And to know the knowledge-surpassing love of Christ." The love of Christ surpasses knowledge; yet, we can know it by experiencing it. According to our mentality, the love of Christ is knowledge-surpassing. Our mind is not able to know it. But n our spirit we can know the love of Christ through our experience.

The love of Christ is Christ Himself. Just as Christ is immeasurable, so His love is also immeasurable. Do not regard the love of Christ as something belonging to Christ. This love *is* Christ. Because Christ is immeasurable, His love is knowledge-surpassing; yet we can know it in our spirit, not by knowledge but by experience. If we compare what we have so far experienced of the immeasurable love of Christ to all there is to experience, it is like comparing a raindrop to the ocean. Christ in His universal dimensions and in His immeasurable love is like a vast, limitless ocean for us to experience.

LIFE-STUDY OF EPHESIANS

MESSAGE THIRTY-FOUR

TO BE FILLED UNTO ALL THE FULLNESS OF GOD

In 3:19 the Apostle Paul says, "That you may be filled unto all the fullness of God." When Christ makes His home in our hearts and when we are strong to apprehend with all the saints the dimensions of Christ and to know by experience His knowledge-surpassing love, we shall be filled unto all the fullness of God. All this fullness dwells in Christ (Col. 1:19; 2:9). Through His indwelling, Christ continually imparts the very element of God into our being. We can be filled with God to such a measure and can attain such a standard, even unto all the fullness of God. In this way we fulfill God's intention that the church should be the expression of God.

When the riches of God are in God Himself, they are His riches. But when the riches of God are expressed, they become His fullness (John 1:16). When we speak of the fullness of God, we imply that the riches of all that God is have become His expression.

THE CHURCH METABOLICALLY CONSTITUTED

When we get into the depths of 3:19, we see that the fullness of God is the church. Chapter three of Ephesians is not concerned with the organization of the church nor with the formation of the church, but with the constitution of the church. The church is neither organized nor formed; it is metabolically constituted in us through our experience and enjoyment of the riches of Christ. In order for the church to be constituted in a practical way, we need to be strengthened into our inner man. Then Christ must make His home in our hearts; He must occupy all the parts of our inner being and saturate them with His riches. Then we need to be rooted and grounded in love, rooted for growth and grounded for building. Following this, we must grasp the dimensions of Christ. This is to experience Christ in His universal dimensions both horizontally and vertically. Along with this, we come to know in our experience the knowledge-surpassing love of Christ. As a result of all these experiences, we are eventually filled unto all the fullness of God. Therefore, being filled unto the fullness of God is the outcome, the result, of all the deeper, higher, and richer experiences of Christ described in Ephesians 3.

THE HIGHEST DEFINITION OF THE CHURCH

The highest definition of the church is that the church is the fullness of God. Some may be troubled at such a statement and may wonder how this claim can be substantiated. In verse 21 Paul says, "To Him be the glory in the church and in Christ Jesus." According to the context, the church in verse 21 is the very fullness of God in verse 19. When in our experience we are filled unto all the fullness of God, the church comes into being in a practical way. It is at such a time that Paul says, "To Him be the glory in the church." This glory is the expression of God. Hence, in the fullness of God there is the expression of God. Therefore, the fullness of God is the church as God's expression.

Some translations of verse 19 say, "filled *with* all the fullness of God." According to this rendering, the fullness of God would have to be the element, the essence, with which we are filled. But this is a mistaken understanding of this verse. Here Paul is saying that we shall be filled *unto* all the fullness of God, that is, we shall be filled to be the expression of God.

THE RICHES AND THE FULLNESS

When I first began to speak on the difference between the riches of Christ and the fullness of Christ, some tried to argue with me by quoting John 1:16, "For of His fullness we all received, and grace upon grace." They said, "John 1:16 declares that of His fullness we have all received. Isn't this fullness the riches of Christ? How then can you make a distinction between the riches of Christ and the fullness of Christ?" When Christ was on earth with His disciples, would you say that the riches of God were there with Him or that the fullness of God was there with Him? If the riches had been with Him but the fullness had not, something would have been lacking; there would have been no completion. For example, suppose a glass jar contains just a few pieces of delicious candies. The jar contains some riches of the candies but not the fullness. However, after the jar is filled with the candies, it will have not only the riches but also the fullness. If the jar remains only partly filled, there will not be in the jar the expression of the candies. Because the fullness is the expression, without the fullness there can be no expression. Only when the candies fill the jar to the brim will there be the fullness as the expression of the riches.

When the Lord Jesus came, He no doubt brought all the riches of God with Him. However, with Him there were not only the riches of God, but there was also the fullness of God. This is the reason John 1:16 says that we all have received of His fullness; it does not say that we have received of His riches. If you take a piece of candy from a jar filled with candies, you will be receiving candy, not from the riches of the jar, but from its fullness.

The fullness is the completion of the riches. In Greek the word for "fullness" means completion. Hence, it is correct to render this Greek word as "completeness." The Greek word translated "of" in John 1:16 means "out from" or "out of." Thus, out of the fullness of Christ, the completeness of all the riches of God, we have all received.

Before retiring at night, I often enjoy a glass of protein drink, preferably a glass filled to the brim. As I drink from such a full glass, I partake of the fullness of the protein drink in the glass. When Christ came, He did not come only partially filled with the riches of God. On the contrary, He was filled to the brim. Hence, the fullness, the completeness of what God is, was present with Him. This fullness, this completeness, is the expression of God. The Lord Jesus was like the glass, and the riches of God with which He was filled unto all the fullness of God were like the protein drink. The disciples received not merely of the riches of God, but of His fullness.

METABOLICALLY ASSIMILATING
THE RICHES OF CHRIST

In the New Testament the fullness is the expression through the completeness of the riches. This is the reason that in 3:8 Paul speaks of the unsearchable riches of Christ and then in 1:23 and 4:13 speaks of the fullness of Christ. The riches of Christ are the various aspects of what Christ is, and the fullness of Christ is the result, the issue, of our enjoyment of these riches. As we enjoy the riches of Christ, these riches are assimilated into our being metabolically. Then they constitute us into the fullness of Christ, into the Body of Christ, the church, as His expression. Therefore, the fullness of Christ in 1:23 is the very fullness of God in 3:19. The fullness of God is the issue of the believers' being constituted metabolically through their experience of the riches of Christ.

In order to assimilate Christ metabolically, we need to be strengthened into our inner man. We also need Christ to make His home in our heart, that is, to occupy, possess, and metabolically saturate every part of our inward being with all that He is. Then we shall be rooted for the growth in life and grounded for the building. Furthermore, we shall become strong to grasp Christ experientially in all His universal dimensions. Along with this, we shall know through our experience the knowledge-surpassing love of Christ. When we have experienced Christ to such an extent, we shall be filled with the riches of Christ unto all the fullness of God. All this is for the constituting of the church in a practical way as the Body of Christ for His expression.

THE NEED FOR A VISION

We all need to see the vision of how the church is constituted. How we need to be strengthened into our inner man!

Every fiber of our being needs to be strengthened into our inner man. Not one part of our inward being should remain in a weak condition. We need to be strengthened so that the indwelling Christ can spread Himself throughout our being and make His home in our inward parts. As Christ spreads within us, He saturates every area of our inner being metabolically with all that He is. Then we are rooted and grounded in love, we lay hold of the dimensions of Christ, and we know His love that surpasses knowledge. Then, ultimately, we are filled unto the fullness of God which is the church. What a high revelation of the church this is!

In the light of such a vision we see that it is utterly wrong to regard the church as a material building where "services" are held. It is also not adequate to view the church merely as the *ekklesia,* the gathering together of God's called-out people. Although many Christians today use the term "the Body of Christ," few have any clear realization of what this term signifies. The Body of Christ is the expression of Christ. It is also the fullness of Christ, which is the fullness of God. This fullness of God comes into existence in a practical way by our being strengthened into the inner man, by Christ making his home in our hearts, by our being rooted and grounded in love, by our grasping the dimensions of the immeasurable Christ, and by our knowing Him as the knowledge-surpassing love. When we have been filled with all the riches of Christ and metabolically saturated with all that Christ is, we become the fullness of God. Surely this is the highest definition of the church.

Only by receiving such a vision do we truly know what the church is. Although chapters one and two of Ephesians give us a definition of the church, this definition is still not adequate. We need chapter three to show us how the church is constituted organically and metabolically with the riches of the living Christ. Not until chapter three does the church come into existence actually and in a practical way. As we have seen, in this chapter the church comes into being as the expression of God, that is, as the very fullness of God. It is at this point that Paul is able to sound a high praise, even a doxology: "To Him be the glory in the church." Now that the church has come into existence in a practical way, Christ can be glorified in the church. Such a church is not merely a gathering of God's called-out people; it is the actual fullness of God.

THE EFFECT OF THE VISION

We all need such a vision, such a revelation. If we see this vision, our being will be changed. If we are filled with this vision and then go forth to speak for God, we shall surely be God's sent ones and His spokesmen. We shall be today's apostles and prophets.

This vision unfolds the unique way for the Lord to build up His church. Only when we see this vision will the Lord have a way to accomplish on earth the building up of the church. After more than nineteen centuries of Christian history, what has been accomplished for the Lord? Consider today's situation. Hardly any have seen the vision in chapter three of Ephesians. May the Lord burden us to pray, "Lord, have mercy on me. I need to see this vision. I need to see the fullness of God and how it comes into existence. Lord, show me the constitution of the Body. Show me how the church can be constituted in a practical way." Once you have seen this vision, you will become a different person. You will be an apostle and a prophet. Wherever you go, you will be a sent one, and whenever you speak this vision, you will be God's spokesman speaking Christ for God's economy.

I can testify that I came to this country with this vision and with a unique burden. Those who have been with me over the years can testify that I have not changed my concept nor my speaking. In various aspects and from various angles, I have spoken just one thing—that God's economy is to dispense Himself into His chosen people to make them the expression of Christ. As we have seen in this message, this expression is the fullness of God.

FILLED UNTO THE EXPRESSION OF THE TRIUNE GOD

In these verses in chapter three of Ephesians concerning

the economy of God resulting in the fullness of God, we see the Triune God. The Father (v. 14) answers and fulfills the apostle's prayer through the Spirit (v. 16) so that Christ, the Son (v. 17), may make His home in our hearts. Thus, we are filled unto the fullness of the Triune God. This is the dispensing of the Triune God into our entire being that we may become His expression.

According to Ephesians 3, the Triune God is not to be the object of doctrinal debate; He is for the dispensing of Himself into the believers so that they may be filled unto the fullness, not only of the Father, nor only of the Son, nor only of the Spirit, but of *God*. Paul prayed that the Father would strengthen us through His Spirit so that Christ might make His home in our hearts and thereby fully occupy our inward being with the result that we might be filled unto the expression of the Triune God. How glorious and how marvelous! This is God's economy, God's dispensation. This is also God's New Testament revelation, our ministry, and the Lord's recovery.

THE CHURCH AS
THE CORPORATE FULLNESS OF GOD

We have seen that the fullness of God is the expression of God. According to John 1:16, the fullness of God came with Christ who is the embodiment of God's fullness (Col. 2:9; 1:19). With Christ, the expression was an individual matter. This expression, therefore, needed to be enlarged, to be expanded, from an individual matter to a corporate matter. The church today is to be the fullness of God in a corporate way. In the church God is not expressed through an individual; He is expressed corporately through the Body, through the believers who have together been filled to the brim with the riches of Christ. Therefore, the fullness of God is embodied in the church. The church as the embodiment of the fullness of God is the expression of the Triune God. This is the church in the Lord's recovery today.

LIFE-STUDY OF EPHESIANS

MESSAGE THIRTY-FIVE

GOD GLORIFIED IN THE CHURCH AND IN CHRIST

In this message we shall consider 3:20 and 21: "But to Him Who is able to do superabundantly above all that we ask or think, according to the power which operates in us, to Him be the glory in the church and in Christ Jesus unto all the generations of the age of the ages. Amen." These verses are a doxology, a high praise, even the highest to be found in the New Testament Epistles. Such a high praise could not have been uttered before the church had come into existence in a practical way.

As we pointed out in the foregoing message, in verse 19 we see the church as the fullness of God. The fullness of God here is the result, the issue, of our experience of the riches of Christ. After such a church has come into existence, the Apostle Paul sounds forth the doxology in verses 20 and 21, ascribing to God glory in the church and in Christ Jesus. Only after the church has come into being as the fullness of God can the glory of God be manifested.

THE FULFILLMENT OF GOD'S WORD
CONCERNING THE CHURCH

Although the church has been on earth for more than nineteen centuries, it has not yet reached the point of being the fullness of God. The highest definition of the church is that it is the fullness of God. We must admit that among us today we do not yet have the church as the fullness of God, as God's full expression. However, we believe that the church will come up to this level. The fact that the Lord has spoken such a word concerning the church is an indication that He will do what He has spoken. The Lord's word will not return void (Isa. 55:11). Whatever He speaks, He will perform. For example, when God spoke something in Genesis 1, it came to pass. Therefore, we believe that the Lord's word regarding the church as the fullness of God will be accomplished. Not only do we believe this word, but we also claim it and pray according to it. We need to pray, "Lord, You have spoken concerning the church as the fullness of God. Now You must fulfill what You have spoken." When the church on earth reaches the stage of being the fullness of God, we shall be able to say with Paul, "To Him be the glory in the church and in Christ Jesus."

THE WAY GOD IS GLORIFIED IN THE CHURCH

The words "but to Him" in verse 20 convey the thought that something has initially gone forth from God and is now returning to Him. In his prayer Paul asked that the Father would strengthen the saints according to the riches of His glory. This implies that the glory of God is wrought into the saints. In the doxology Paul said, "To Him be the glory" (v. 21). This implies that the glory of God returns to God after it has been wrought into the saints. Firstly, the glory of God is wrought into us; then it returns to God for His glorification. As an illustration, Isaac's wealth was firstly given to Rebekah for her beautification; then when Rebekah came to Isaac, all the wealth came back to Isaac with Rebekah for his glorification (Gen. 24:47, 53, 61-67). The apostle prayed that God would strengthen the saints according to His glory, but eventually God's glory, after being wrought into them, returns to Him along with the strengthened saints. This is the way God is glorified in the church.

We have seen that in verse 16 Paul prayed that the Father would grant us, according to the riches of His glory, to be strengthened with power into our inner man. To be strengthened according to glory is to have the glory of God worked into our being. This is the only way to be strengthened according to God's glory. Suppose a person who is physically very weak can be strengthened according to someone who is physically strong. This would mean that the strength of the strong one is wrought into the very fibers of the weak one. In the same principle, to be strengthened into the inner man according to the Father's glory means to have His glory wrought into our being. Firstly, the glory comes to us, and then it goes back to God. When the glory comes into our being, we are filled and strengthened. When it returns to God, He is glorified in the church.

The Greek word rendered "but" in verse 20 can also be translated "now." In such a case "now" would mean "in view of the fact that" or "based on the preceding." In verses 20 and 21 it seems that Paul was saying, "Now that the church has come into existence as the fullness of God, God can be glorified in the church. Before this time it was impossible for the glory to return to God. But because the church has become the fullness of God in a practical way, this is now possible."

It is correct to translate the Greek word here as either "but" or "now." In either case the word is not a meaningless insertion. The word "but" suggests that the glory which has come to us and which has been wrought into our being is now going back to God with us. The word "now" suggests that, in view of the fact that the church has come into existence as the fullness of God, God may at this time be glorified in the church. Both are true.

The church is the glory of God coming to us with God and going back to God with us. In such a church there is two-way traffic between God and us, and between us and God. By means of this two-way traffic, God's glory is wrought into us and God is glorified in us. This traffic is signified by the little word "but."

ABOVE ALL WE ASK OR THINK
CONCERNING THE CHURCH

In verse 20 Paul speaks of "Him Who is able to do super-abundantly above all that we ask or think." Strictly speaking, "ask or think" here refers to the spiritual things related to the church, not to material things. For these spiritual things, we need not only to ask, but also to think. We may think more than we ask. God fulfills not only what we ask for the church, but also what we think concerning the church, and God is able to do superabundantly above all that we ask or think for the church through the power which operates in us.

God's ability to do superabundantly above all that we ask or think, as revealed in verse 20, is different from His ability in creation. Verse 20 refers not to creation, but to the church. A number of times I have heard the saints quote verse 20 in testifying concerning their experience of God's material blessing. To quote this verse for such a purpose is to misapply it. Paul's concept here is related not to what God does outside of us, but to what He does inside of us. He specifically mentions "the power which operates in us." This is the inward power, the resurrection power, as mentioned in 1:19 and 20.

God's creating power is the origin of the material things in our environment (Rom. 8:28), whereas God's resurrection power accomplishes the spiritual things for the church within our inward being. In order for God to give us a good job, there is no need for resurrection power to operate in us. God's being able to do superabundantly above all that we ask or think is related not to His acts in our environment, but to His working organically and metabolically within us. As far as the environment is concerned, there may be times when God apparently does nothing for you. You may pray for a promotion, but He allows you to be laid off from your present job. During this time of unemployment, God may operate within you to enable Christ to make His home in you. When we are in a favorable environment, there may be very little opportunity for Christ to spread Himself in our hearts. But when we are placed in a difficult environment, the Lord may have more of an opportunity to spread within our inward being. From our side, it may seem beneficial for us to be in a good environment, but from the Lord's side, it may be better for us to be in a difficult environment, for then He may have greater opportunity to work within us.

The asking and thinking referred to in verse 20 should

be applied to the church. We need to ask and to think concerning the church, not concerning trivial things related to our environment. Our asking and our thinking should be focused on God's economy to dispense Himself into us to produce the church as the expression of Christ. When our asking and thinking concern the church, God will always do superabundantly above all that we ask or think. We need to ask and to think concerning Christ making His home in our hearts and concerning the church being filled unto all the fullness of God. If we ask and think in this way, we shall certainly be in the spirit. Then whatever we ask concerning the church will be answered, and it will be answered superabundantly. How we need to ask and to think concerning the church!

GOD GLORIFIED IN CHRIST

Verse 21 says, "To Him be the glory in the church and in Christ Jesus unto all the generations of the age of the ages. Amen." God's glory is wrought into the church, and He is expressed in the church. Hence, the glory in the church is to God; that is, God is glorified in the church.

God's glorification is not only in the church, but also in Christ. Hence, the word "and" is used here to emphasize this point. In the church the sphere of God's glorification is narrow, limited to the household of faith. But in Christ the sphere is much broader, because Christ is the Head of all the families in the heavens and on earth (1:22; 3:15). Hence, God's glorification in Christ is in the realm of all the families created by God, not only on earth but also in the heavens. Not only is the sphere in Christ much broader than that in the church, but the scope in Christ is eternal, as indicated by the phrase, "unto all the generations of the age of the ages." All the generations of the age of the ages constitute eternity. God's glorification in the church is mainly in this age, whereas God's glorification in Christ is for eternity.

The church is just one of the many families in the universe. The other families include the angelic family, the family of mankind, and the family of Israel. According to verse 15, God is the source of the angelic family in the heavens and of all the human families on earth. Of course, He is also the source of the church, which is the family, the household, of the believers. To say that God is glorified in the church means that He is glorified in just one of the many families. But to say that God is glorified in Christ means that He is glorified in Christ as the Head of all things. Christ is the Head over the angels, over mankind, over Israel, and also over the church. If God were glorified only in the church, He would not be glorified in an all-inclusive way. For Him to be glorified all-inclusively, He must also be glorified in Christ.

God will be glorified not only in this age, the age of the church, but also in the coming age, the age of the kingdom, and in the age of the ages, which is eternity. For God to be glorified in all the ages, from the present age throughout eternity, He must be glorified both in the church and in Christ.

THE CHURCH TAKING THE LEAD TO GLORIFY GOD

As the household of the believers, the church, we take the lead to give the glory to God the Father by having God's glory wrought into our being. In order for the glory of God to be wrought into us, we need to be strengthened into our inner man according to the riches of God's glory. Then this glory will come to us with God and, after being worked into us, will return to God with us. By means of this two-way traffic the church takes the lead to give the glory to God. In this universe, as the believers, we are the firstfruit. If we take the lead to give glory to God, all the other families both in heaven and on earth will follow us to glorify Him.

LIFE-STUDY OF EPHESIANS

MESSAGE THIRTY-SIX

KEEPING THE ONENESS OF THE SPIRIT

Ephesians 4:1 says, "I beseech you therefore, I, the prisoner in the Lord, to walk worthily of the calling with which you were called." This verse is somewhat a repetition of 3:1, which begins the apostle's exhortation in chapters four through six. This indicates that 3:2-21 is all parenthetical.

WALKING WORTHILY OF GOD'S CALLING

The book of Ephesians is divided into two main sections. The first, composed of chapters one through three, reveals the blessing and the position which the church has obtained in Christ in the heavenlies. Chapter three, in particular, reveals how the church comes into existence in a practical way through being constituted with the riches of the living Christ. The second section, comprising chapters four through six, charges us concerning the living and responsibility the church should have in the Spirit on the earth. The basic charge is that we should walk worthily of the calling, which is the totality of the blessings bestowed upon the church, as revealed in 1:3-14. In the church, under the Triune God's abundant blessing, the saints should walk worthily of the Father's selection and predestination, the Son's redemption, and the Spirit's sealing and pledging.

In walking worthily of God's calling, the church must have a certain kind of life and also bear responsibility to the full extent. Hence, in chapters four through six we see, on the one hand, the living the church should have, and, on the other hand, the responsibility the church should bear.

In exhorting the saints to walk worthily of God's calling, Paul spoke from his status as a prisoner in the Lord. His status as an apostle of Christ through the will of God authorized him to reveal the things concerning the church, to speak concerning the mystery of Christ. However, his status as a prisoner in the Lord qualified him to exhort us to walk worthily of God's high calling. Paul's living was surely worthy of God's calling. Furthermore, he bore the responsibility required by this calling.

In 3:1 Paul speaks of himself as "the prisoner of Christ Jesus," but in 4:1 he says that he is "the prisoner in the Lord." To be a prisoner *in* the Lord is deeper than to be a prisoner *of* the Lord. As such a prisoner, Paul was a pattern for those who would walk worthily of God's calling.

KEEPING THE ONENESS OF THE SPIRIT

To walk worthily of God's calling, to have the proper Body life, we need firstly to care for the matter of oneness. We must keep the oneness of the Spirit. This is crucial and vital to the Body of Christ.

Oneness, strictly speaking, differs from unity. Unity is formed by many people uniting together, whereas oneness is the one entity of the Spirit within the believers making them all one. Some Christians may have a certain kind of unity, but we in the Lord's recovery appreciate oneness much more than unity. In the Lord's recovery, we are not united—that is, we have not formed a certain kind of union—but we are one. Our oneness is a Person, even the Lord Jesus Himself realized as the life-giving Spirit. Today the Lord is the life-giving Spirit within us, and this Spirit is our oneness. Therefore, our oneness is not an objective Person far away in the heavens; it is a subjective Person indwelling us as our life.

This oneness is similar to the electricity in many lights that makes them all one in the shining. Although there may be dozens of lights in a large room, they are one in the electricity that flows within them. In themselves, the lights are not one; neither are they united to form one entity. The unique electricity in the lights is their oneness. This electricity does not unite the lights; it is the oneness within them. In themselves, the lights are individual and separate, but in the electricity they have oneness. It is the same in principle with the believers in Christ. The Spirit indwelling us is our oneness.

In 4:3 this oneness is called "the oneness of the Spirit." The oneness of the Spirit is actually the Spirit Himself. In the illustration of the electricity and the lights, the oneness of the electricity is the electricity itself. There is not another element, apart from the electricity, that is the oneness of the electricity. The oneness of the electricity is simply the electricity itself. In the same principle, the oneness of the Spirit is not something apart from the Spirit. On the contrary, it is the Spirit Himself. The oneness within us and among us is the very life-giving Spirit. Therefore, to keep the oneness is to keep the life-giving Spirit.

Many Christians talk about unity or oneness but neglect the Spirit. This indicates that they make oneness something separate from the Spirit. The more talk certain believers have had about unity, the more divided they have become. Some can even argue with one another in a fleshly way over the matter of unity. There is no need for us to talk so much about oneness. Oneness is like a dove. If we do not talk about it, the dove is present with us. But if we talk about it, it flies away. When we talk a great deal about oneness, we are in danger of losing it. We do not keep the oneness by talking about it; we keep it by staying in the life-giving Spirit. As long as we love the Lord and embrace Him, we keep the oneness; for, as we have strongly emphasized, oneness is the Person of Christ as the life-giving Spirit.

Keeping the oneness of the Spirit implies that we already have the Spirit. If we did not have Him, how could we keep Him? However, most Christians live apart from the Spirit most of the time. Any action taken apart from the life-giving Spirit is divisive. When we are one with the Spirit, living according to Him and doing all things in Him, we keep the oneness without making any conscious effort to do so. But whenever we act apart from the Spirit, we are divisive and lose the oneness. Therefore, instead of charging you to talk about oneness, I would encourage you to take care of the life-giving Spirit, who is the Lord Himself as life within you.

LOWLINESS, MEEKNESS, AND LONG-SUFFERING

Verse 2 says, "With all lowliness and meekness, with long-suffering, bearing one another in love." To have lowliness is to remain in a low estate, and to have meekness is to not fight for ourselves. We should have these two virtues in dealing with ourselves. Long-suffering is to endure mistreatment. We should have this virtue in dealing with others. By these virtues we bear one another; that is, we do not forsake the troublesome ones but bear them in love. This is the expression of life.

The word "all" governs both lowliness and meekness. It does not mean that there are many kinds of lowliness and meekness; it means that we should have lowliness and meekness in all things. Thus, we must keep the oneness of the Spirit with all lowliness and meekness.

The problem, however, is that in ourselves we cannot be either lowly or meek. If we are honest and sincere, we shall admit that we have no genuine lowliness or meekness. On the contrary, we tend to exalt ourselves and to fight in defense of ourselves. Just as we do not have lowliness or meekness, we are not long-suffering and we cannot bear others in love. Nevertheless, Paul charges us to have such a worthy walk.

If we would keep the oneness of the Spirit, we must have a proper humanity, a humanity with lowliness, meekness, and long-suffering and a humanity that bears others in love. If we do not have such a humanity as our "capital," then we cannot operate the "business" of keeping the oneness of the Spirit. The fact that the virtues in verse 2 are mentioned before the oneness of the Spirit in verse 3 indicates that we must have these virtues in order to keep the oneness of the Spirit.

A TRANSFORMED HUMANITY

In order to have the virtues spoken of in verse 2, we need a transformed humanity. In our natural humanity there is no lowliness, meekness, nor long-suffering. But these virtues are to be found in our transformed humanity, that is, in the humanity of Jesus. In Matthew 11:29 the Lord Jesus said that He was meek and lowly in heart. Meekness and lowliness are characteristics of the humanity of Jesus. Any meekness or lowliness that we may seem to have in ourselves is a pretense and cannot survive any real testing. Praise the Lord that the humanity of Jesus in His resurrection life can be ours today! The more we are transformed, the more of the humanity of Jesus we have. By having the humanity of the resurrected Christ, we spontaneously have the virtues required to keep the oneness of the Spirit.

A PICTURE OF GENUINE ONENESS

The genuine oneness in the Triune God is seen in the picture of the tabernacle with its forty-eight boards of acacia wood overlaid with gold. In themselves, the boards were separate from one another, but in the gold they were one. The bars that held the boards together were also made of acacia wood overlaid with gold. As we have pointed out elsewhere, the golden bars signify the uniting Spirit. The acacia wood signifies humanity, and the gold signifies the divine nature. In the uniting Spirit there is the element of humanity. This indicates that the uniting Spirit is not merely the Holy Spirit of God, but the Holy Spirit mingled with our spirit.

This mingled spirit is seen in Romans 8. Romans 8:4 says, "That the righteous requirement of the law might be fulfilled in us, who do not walk according to flesh, but according to spirit." The spirit here is our human spirit mingled with God's Holy Spirit. Furthermore, Romans 8:16 says, "The Spirit Himself witnesses with our spirit that we are the children of God." This verse clearly points to the mingled spirit, that is, the Spirit with our spirit. In the mingled spirit which constitutes the uniting bars, there is the transformed humanity with the virtues of lowliness, meekness, and long-suffering.

For years I tried to be meek and lowly, but I failed time after time. Eventually I learned that the lowliness, meekness, and long-suffering in 4:2 are not to be found in our natural humanity, but are characteristics of the transformed humanity, the humanity of Jesus Christ. This transformed humanity with all its virtues is typified by the acacia wood within the uniting bars. This indicates that in the uniting Spirit there is the transformed humanity, our humanity transformed by the resurrection life of Christ.

TRANSFORMATION AND ONENESS

Keeping the oneness of the Spirit requires transformation. For this reason, we should not expect a new believer to be able to keep the oneness of the Spirit. It is useless to charge the new ones to keep the oneness, because keeping the oneness of the Spirit requires transformation. If you have not been transformed, you will not have the lowliness nor the meekness necessary to keep the oneness. The more we have been transformed, the more we spontaneously inherit lowliness, meekness, and long-suffering. All these virtues are our heritage by transformation.

The oneness of the Spirit cannot be kept by babyish or childish Christians. It can be kept only by the transformed ones. Those who are natural and fleshly cannot be meek, lowly, or long-suffering. They cannot keep the oneness, because nothing in their natural being can ever enable them to keep it. Therefore, I wish to emphasize the fact once again that 4:2 implies the need of transformation. We have problems with oneness because we are so natural, so fleshly, and so much in ourselves. But if we have been transformed, we keep the oneness spontaneously because in our transformed humanity we have lowliness, meekness, and long-suffering.

THE UNITING BOND OF PEACE

Verse 3 speaks of keeping the oneness of the Spirit "in the uniting bond of peace." Christ has abolished on the cross all the differences due to ordinances. In so doing, He has made peace for His Body. This peace should bind all believers together and thus become the uniting bond.

Before Christ was crucified on the cross, there was no peace between the Jews and the Gentiles. According to 2:15, by Christ's abolishing in His flesh the separating ordinances and creating the Jewish and Gentile believers into one new man, peace was made between all believers. Furthermore, on the cross, Christ dealt with all the negative things between us and God. This means that He also made peace between man and God. Now there is no longer a separation between the Jewish believers and the Gentile believers nor between us and God. However, at the time Ephesians was written, some of the Jewish believers still held the concept that they should be separate from the Gentile believers. For this reason, Paul said that the middle wall of partition has been broken down and that the Jewish and Gentile believers must be one. Otherwise, there can be no oneness. And without the oneness there cannot be the one Body. Therefore, in 4:3 Paul says strongly that we must keep the oneness of the Spirit in the uniting bond of peace. If we would do this, we must realize that the differences between us have been abolished on the cross.

The uniting bond of peace is actually the working of the cross. By our experience we know that whenever we go to the cross, there are no differences between us and others. However, as soon as we come down from the cross, differences appear. This is true not only in the church life but also in our family life. Often the love between a husband and wife is buried beneath the differences that emerge when they come down from the cross. The only way to get rid of the differences is to go to the cross. When we go to the cross and remain there, the differences disappear, and we have peace. As we remain on the cross, this peace becomes the uniting bond in which we keep the oneness of the Spirit. Therefore, in order to keep the oneness of the Spirit we need both transformation and the cross.

Ephesians 4:2 indicates the need of transformation, and 4:3 indicates the need of the cross. We need to be transformed in order to have lowliness, meekness, and long-suffering; and we need to be crossed out in order to have the uniting bond of peace. Then we shall keep the oneness of the Spirit.

LIFE-STUDY OF EPHESIANS

MESSAGE THIRTY-SEVEN

THE BASE OF OUR ONENESS

In exhorting us to safeguard the oneness (4:3), the Apostle Paul points out seven things as the base, the very foundation, of our oneness: one Body, one Spirit, one hope, one Lord, one faith, one baptism, and one God and Father. These seven ones are of three groups. The first three can be grouped together, the Spirit with the Body as His expression and the Body related to the one hope. This Body, having been regenerated and being saturated with the Spirit as its essence, has the hope of being transfigured into the full likeness of Christ. The next three can also be grouped together, the Lord with faith and baptism, that we may be joined to Him. Then we have one God and Father, who is the Originator and source of all. The Spirit as the Executor of the Body, the Son as the Creator of the Body, and God the Father as the Originator of the Body—all three of the Triune God—are related to the Body. The third of the Trinity is mentioned first because the main concern here is the Body, and the Spirit is the essence of the Body. Then the course is traced back to the Son and then to the Father.

I. THE FIRST GROUP, RELATED TO THE SPIRIT

A. One Body

Verse 4 says, "One Body and one Spirit, as also you were called in one hope of your calling." The Body is mentioned before the Spirit because the oneness among us is related to the Body and is for the Body. The reason we need to keep the oneness is that we are all one Body.

B. One Spirit

There is a deep relationship between the one Spirit and the one hope. If we do not see this relationship, we shall not be able to know why Paul put the one Spirit and the one hope together with the one Body. The Spirit is the essence of the one Body. Without the Spirit, the Body is empty and has no life. The Body here is the Body of Christ, and the essence of the Body of Christ is the Spirit. Hence, the Body and the essence of the Body are one. It is impossible for the Body of Christ to have more than one essence. The unique essence of the Body is the Spirit.

The Spirit is in the Body. First Corinthians 12:13 says, "For in one Spirit were we all baptized into one body, whether we be Jews or Gentiles, whether we be bond or free; and were all made to drink of one Spirit" (Gk.). This verse reveals that the one Spirit is not only the essence of the Body, but also the life and the life supply of the Body. Without the one Spirit, the Body would be a corpse.

C. One Hope

The hope in verse 4 is the hope of glory (Col. 1:27). As saved ones, we have the hope that one day the Lord Jesus will come as our hope of glory and that through Him our vile body will be transfigured (Phil. 3:21). On one hand, we appreciate our bodies because they are useful and because without them we cannot exist in this world. On the other hand, our bodies are troublesome, for they are often weak and subject to illness. Therefore, we believers in Christ have the hope that one day our troublesome bodies will be metabolically transfigured by Christ to become glorified bodies.

If you find it difficult to believe that our vile bodies will be transfigured into glorious bodies, I ask you to consider the process a carnation seed undergoes to produce blossoms. In itself a carnation seed has no beauty. But by being sown into the soil and by growing normally, the seed is transfigured into a plant with beautiful blossoms. In speaking about the transfiguration of the body in 1 Corinthians 15, Paul compares our bodies to seeds (vv. 35-44). We have the solid hope that the day will come for the "seed" to blossom.

According to Romans 8, our hope also implies our manifestation as sons of God. We are sons of God today, but our sonship is hidden and even somewhat mysterious. For this reason, the worldly people treat us the same as everyone else, without any realization that we are sons of God. However, the time is coming when our sonship will be manifested. Then it will no longer be necessary to tell others that we are Christians. It will be apparent to all that we are sons of God in glory. The manifestation of the sons of God will also be the glorification of the sons of God. This is our hope.

Neither the transfiguration of our body nor our manifestation as the sons of God will merely be a sudden, unexpected occurrence. On the contrary, both our transfiguration and our manifestation are gradually taking place today. Yes, there is a sense in which transfiguration and manifestation will take place suddenly. But according to the truth of the New Testament and according to our experience, transfiguration and manifestation are also a gradual process in which we are involved today. This process is being carried out by the one Spirit, who is the essence, the life, and the life supply of the Body of Christ. The Spirit is presently working within us to transfigure us and to manifest our sonship. This is the reason Paul linked the one hope and the one Spirit to the one Body.

As believers, we are members of the Body of Christ. Although you are a member of the Body, are you satisfied with the way you are? If we are honest, we shall admit that the present situation of both ourselves and the church is less than satisfactory. We need to be transfigured. Within us as members of the Body and within the Body as a whole there is the one Spirit, who is the essence of the Body and the life and life supply of the Body. This Spirit is neither dormant nor idle; on the contrary, He is working energetically within us toward the goal of bringing us into the fulfillment of the hope of our calling. This is why we say that the transfiguration of the body will not be accidental. Today the indwelling Spirit is carrying out both the transfiguration of the body and the manifestation of the sons of God. Because we are in the process of transfiguration and manifestation, the rapture should not come as a surprise. Rather, it should be a normal experience.

Verse 4 implies that the indwelling Spirit today is carrying out the process of bringing the Body of Christ into glory as the fulfillment of our hope. Therefore, in this verse we have the one Body, the one Spirit, and the one hope. Because we all are in the one Body with the one Spirit and have the one hope, we are one. There is no reason for us not to be one, and there is no cause to be different. We are one Body, and we have the one Spirit working within us to bring us to the goal of our hope.

II. THE SECOND GROUP, RELATED TO THE LORD

A. One Lord

Verse 5 says, "One Lord, one faith, one baptism." This verse does not speak of one Son, but of one Lord. In the Gospel of John it is the Son in whom we believe (3:16), but in Acts, it is the Lord in whom we believe (Acts 16:31). In the writings of John, the Son is for life (1 John 5:12), whereas in Acts, the Lord, after His ascension, is for authority (Acts 2:36), a matter which concerns His headship. Here, as the Head of the Body (Eph. 1:22), He is the Lord. Our believing in Christ is related to both life and authority. Not many Christians, however, realize that they must believe in the Lord for authority as well as for life. As lost sinners, we were not only spiritually dead, but we were also without the Lord, without a head. But after believing in the Lord, we have both life and a head.

In Ephesians the oneness of the Body is related not only to life but also to headship. Christians are divided because they do not care for the Head. In verse 4 Paul covers life, which is closely related to the Spirit. But in verse 5 he deals with authority. Today few Christians care for life, and even fewer have any care for authority. By the Lord's mercy and grace, we in the Lord's recovery care both for life and for headship. We have not only the one Body with the one Spirit and the one hope, but also the one Lord with the one faith and the one baptism.

B. One Faith

In the New Testament faith denotes both the act of believing and the content of what we believe. Faith as our act of believing is personal and subjective. But faith as the content of what we believe is objective. The one faith in verse 5 is not our personal act of believing; it is the object of our faith.

As Christians we may differ concerning various doctrines, but we all have the one faith. We all believe in the Person of the Lord Jesus and His redemptive work. We believe that Christ is the Son of God incarnated to be a man, that He died on the cross for our redemption, that He was resurrected on the third day, and that He has ascended into the heavens. This unique faith is held by all genuine Christians.

It is through this faith that we are joined to Christ. As soon as a person comes to believe in the Person and work of Jesus Christ, the Son of God, he is made one with Christ. Before this he was outside of Christ, but now he is in Christ. This Christ is our Lord, our Head, and we are under His authority. We are members of His Body, and He is our Head.

If we would keep the oneness, we must take care of both life and authority. The life-giving Spirit is working within us so that we may be transformed in soul, transfigured in body, and fully manifested as sons of God. This is a matter of life. But we have not only the life-giving Spirit within us, but also the Lord as the Head of the Body. Hence, we must be submissive to the authority and headship of Christ.

C. One Baptism

In faith we believe into the Lord (John 3:36, Gk.), and in baptism we are baptized into Him (Gal. 3:27; Rom. 6:3) and terminated in Adam (Rom. 6:4). Through faith and baptism we have been transferred out of Adam into Christ and have thus been joined to the Lord (1 Cor. 6:17).

The reality of baptism consists in realizing and confessing that our natural being has been crucified and buried. Hence, baptism is the realization of death, burial, and resurrection. Through faith we are joined to Christ, and in Christ we are crucified, buried, and resurrected. Immediately after we believe in Christ, we should be baptized as a testimony of our realization of this fact. Baptism always follows faith. Through baptism, we have a complete and thorough transfer out of Adam and into Christ. Now we are in Christ who is our life and our Lord. No longer are we in Adam with Adam as our head. We are in Christ with Christ as our Head. Because the Lord, faith, and baptism are related in such a way, Paul spoke of them together in verse 5.

III. THE ONE GOD AND FATHER OF ALL

Verse 6 says, "One God and Father of all, Who is over all and through all and in all." God is the Originator of all things, and the Father is the source of life for the Body. In verse 4 we have life; in verse 5, headship; and in verse 6, origin or source. Because everything has a source, it is possible to trace things back to their origin. However, most Christians today, being superficial, do not care for the origin or source of things. We in the church life, on the contrary, must have sober discernment. This means that we must consider the matters of life, headship, and source, or origin. If we trace something back to its source, we shall not be cheated or deceived or led astray.

The Apostle Paul was a very discerning person, having received a keen discernment from the Lord. Beginning with the one Body, Paul traced the source all the way back to the one God and Father. This means that he went all the way back to the very source, to the origin.

In verse 6 Paul speaks of the one God and Father "Who is over all and through all and in all." The thought of the Trinity is implied here. "Over all" mainly refers to the Father; "through all," to the Son; and "in all," to the Spirit. The Triune God eventually enters into us by reaching us as the Spirit. Our oneness is constituted of the Trinity of the

Godhead: with the Spirit as the life-giving Spirit, with the Son as the Lord and Head, and with the Father as the source and origin. If we see this, nothing will be able to distract us or lead us astray. We shall have the proper discernment regarding the oneness and how to keep it.

The keeping of the oneness is a matter in the Triune God. This means that the Triune God Himself is the base of our oneness, its fundamental basis and very foundation. The Originator of our oneness is the Father, the Accomplisher of our oneness is the Lord, and the Executor of our oneness is the Spirit. In our experience, however, the Spirit is first because He is directly related to the oneness, to the carrying out of the oneness in the one Body. Following this, we have the Lord as the Accomplisher and the Father as the source. Therefore, our oneness is the Triune God realized and experienced by us in our Christian life.

Although many of us have been Christians for years, we have never heard that oneness is actually the Triune God becoming our experience. Our oneness is the Triune God— the Spirit, the Lord, and the Father—wrought into the Body. Along with the Triune God, we have the faith, the baptism, and the hope. One day we received faith and were brought into Christ. What a glorious visitation was this coming of faith! After we believed into Christ, we were baptized. We became members of the Body with the hope of glorification. This is our oneness. This oneness is the Triune God wrought into the Body, which comes into existence through faith and baptism and which has the hope of one day being glorified. May we all have the heart to care for this oneness.

LIFE-STUDY OF EPHESIANS

MESSAGE THIRTY-EIGHT

THE GIFTS PERFECTING THE SAINTS

Ephesians 4:7 says, "But to each one of us was given grace according to the measure of the gift of Christ." Concerning the Body, all the basic elements are one. This is covered in verses 4 through 6, where we have one Body, one Spirit, one hope, one Lord, one faith, one baptism, and one God and Father. Although the basic elements of the Body are one, the gifts, or the functions, are many and varied. The word "but" at the beginning of verse 7 brings out this contrast between the oneness of the Body and the variety of the gifts or functions.

GRACE ACCORDING TO THE GIFT

Verse 7 says that each one of us has been given grace according to the measure of the gift of Christ. Here grace is given according to the gift, but in Romans 12:6 gifts differ according to grace. Grace actually is the divine life that both produces and supplies the gifts. In Romans 12 it is the grace that produces the gift. Thus, the gift is according to grace. In Ephesians 4 it is grace that supplies the gift. Hence, here the grace is according to the gift, according to the measure of the gift. Grace according to the measure of the gift can be compared to our blood, which supplies the members of our body according to their size. The measure of the gift of Christ is the size of a member of His Body.

CHRIST GIVING GIFTS TO MEN

Verse 8 continues, "Wherefore He says, Having ascended to the height, He led captive those taken captive and gave gifts to men." "Height" in the quotation of Psalm 68:18 refers to Mount Zion (Psa. 68:15-16), symbolizing the third heaven where God dwells (1 Kings 8:30). Psalm 68 implies that it was in the ark that God ascended to Mount Zion after the ark had led the way to victory.

Verse 1 of Psalm 68 is a quotation of Numbers 10:35. This indicates that the background of Psalm 68 is God's move in the tabernacle with the ark as its center. The ark was a clear type of Christ. Wherever the ark went, the victory was won. Eventually this ark ascended triumphantly to the top of Mount Zion. This portrays how Christ has won the victory and ascended triumphantly to the heavens.

"Those" in verse 8 refers to the redeemed saints who had been taken captive by Satan before they were saved by Christ's death and resurrection. In His ascension Christ led them captive; that is, He rescued them from Satan's captivity and took them to Himself. This indicates that He has conquered and overcome Satan, who had captured them by sin and death.

The Amplified New Testament renders "He led a train of vanquished foes" for "He led captive those taken captive." "Vanquished foes" may refer to Satan, to his angels, and to us the sinners, also indicating Christ's victory over Satan, sin, and death. In His ascension there was a procession of these vanquished foes as captives from a war for a celebration of Christ's victory.

"Gifts" here does not refer to the abilities or enablements for varied services, but to the various gifted persons in verse 11—apostles, prophets, evangelists, and shepherds and teachers. After conquering and rescuing them from Satan and death through His own death and resurrection, Christ in His ascension made the rescued sinners themselves such gifts with His resurrection life and gave them to His Body for its building up.

Verses 9 and 10 are a parenthesis. This means that verse 11 is the continuation of verse 8. Verse 8 says that Christ gave gifts to men, and verse 11 says that He gave some apostles, some prophets, some evangelists, and some shepherds and teachers. "Each one" in verse 7 refers to every member of the Body of Christ, each of whom has received a general gift, whereas the four kinds of gifted persons mentioned in verse 11 are those who have been endued with a special gift. As we shall see, these are the leading apostles, prophets, evangelists, and shepherds and teachers. As followers, we all can be such gifts to the Body.

Verses 9 and 10 explain how Christ gave the gifts to the Body: "Now this, He ascended, what is it except that He also descended into the lower parts of the earth? He Who descended is the same Who also ascended far above all the heavens that He might fill all things." The "lower parts of the earth" refers to Hades, underneath the earth, where Christ went after His death (Acts 2:27). Christ firstly descended from heaven to earth in His incarnation. Then after He died on the cross, in His death He descended further, from earth to Hades. Eventually, in His resurrection He ascended from Hades to earth, and from earth to heaven in His ascension. By His descending in death and ascending in resurrection, He gave gifts to men.

CHRIST FILLING ALL THINGS

By descending and ascending, Christ also cut the way that He might fill all things. The thought here is profound. Firstly, Christ was in the heavens. In His incarnation He came down to earth as a man and lived on earth for thirty-three and a half years. Then He died on the cross and descended into Hades, ascended in resurrection from Hades to earth, and then ascended to the third heaven. By means of such a traffic of descending and ascending, He fills all things. Now Christ is everywhere, on the earth as well as in the heavens.

FOR THE PERFECTING OF THE SAINTS

In verse 12 we see the reason for Christ's giving of the gifts: "For the perfecting of the saints unto the work of ministry, unto the building up of the Body of Christ." The Greek word rendered "for" in this verse is weighty and significant. It indicates that Christ gave apostles, prophets, evangelists, and shepherds and teachers for the purpose of perfecting the saints. The saints are perfected "unto the work of ministry." The Greek word translated "unto" means "resulting in." Therefore, the perfecting of the saints results in the work of ministry. The many gifted persons in verse 11 have only one ministry, that of ministering Christ for the building up of the Body of Christ, the church. This is the unique ministry in the New Testament economy (2 Cor. 4:1; 1 Tim. 1:12). According to the grammatical construction, "the building up of the Body of Christ" is "the work of ministry." Whatever the gifted persons in verse 11 do as the work of ministry must be for the building up of the Body of Christ.

ARRIVING AT THREE THINGS

Verse 13 continues, "Until we all arrive at the oneness of the faith and of the full knowledge of the Son of God, at a full-grown man, at the measure of the stature of the fullness of Christ." According to this verse, the perfected saints will arrive at three things: at the oneness of the faith and of the full knowledge of the Son of God, at a full-grown man, and at the measure of the stature of the fullness of Christ. Christ has a fullness, the fullness has a stature, and the stature has a measure. We must arrive at the measure of the stature of the fullness of Christ. We shall cover this matter in a later message.

CHRIST'S UNIVERSAL TRAFFIC

Let us now consider in more detail how the gifts are given by Christ to the Body. We have seen that, concerning the Body, all the basic elements are one. However, the gifts and the functions are different. Christ has traveled from the heavens to the earth, from the earth to Hades, from Hades back to earth, and from the earth to the third heaven. It is by this universal traffic that the gifts have been given by Christ to the Body.

Consider the Apostle Paul as an example. How could a sinful, devilish persecutor of the church such as Saul of Tarsus become a gift to the Body of Christ? Only by the traveling of Christ throughout the universe. Christ traveled from the heavens to the earth. He was born in a manger in Bethlehem, and He lived for about thirty years in the little town of Nazareth. After He was crucified on the cross, He went down into Hades and took a tour of that region for three days. Then He came out of Hades on the day of His resurrection. Between His resurrection and ascension, He appeared to His disciples over a period of forty days. At the end of those forty days, He ascended into the heavens.

If we had Ephesians 4 without Psalm 68, we probably would not realize that when Christ ascended to the heavens He led a train of captives. He entered into the heavens as a conqueror with a train of captives. He presented these captives to His Father, who in turn gave them back to Him as gifts. Then Christ gave all these captives as gifts to men. One of these gifts was Saul of Tarsus. This is the way Christ gave gifts to men.

By His universal traveling Christ not only gathered up many sinners, but He also defeated Satan, the one who had captured them. At one time, we all were captives, those who had been captured by Satan, sin, and death. By traveling from heaven to earth, from earth to Hades, from Hades back to earth, and from earth back to heaven, on the one hand, Christ gained all of us and, on the other hand, He conquered Satan, who had usurped us and held us under his power of death. Having been released from Satan, sin, and death, we are now Christ's captives. All the angels know that when Christ ascended to the third heaven, He was leading a train of captives and that these captives were presented to the Father. What a victorious celebration this procession must have been! Although this glorious event was hidden from the eyes of men, it was seen by angels. They knew that an event of tremendous significance was taking place in the history of the universe. This is not a product of our imagination; it is a marvelous fact.

CAPTURED BY CHRIST

More than nineteen centuries ago we were captured by Christ and put into His train of captives. As those who have been captured by Him, we have no way to escape. Although we have never seen the Lord Jesus, we have no choice but to believe in Him because we have been captured by Him. Now that we are in His train, we cannot get away from Him. Not only have we been captured by Christ, but He has also presented us to the Father. After beholding us with great appreciation, the Father returned us to the Son as gifts. In this way we all were made gifts to the Body through Christ's universal traveling.

In His travels Christ died for our sins and accomplished all things for the fulfillment of God's purpose. He defeated Satan, and He released us from the enemy's usurping hand. Once we were Satan's captives, but now we are Christ's captives, those who have been led in His train to the height of the universe, presented to the Father, and given back to the Son as gifts to men.

According to the New Testament, we were saved before we were born. When people ask me when I was saved, I sometimes tell them that I was saved more than nineteen hundred years ago, at the time of Christ's crucifixion, resurrection, and ascension. We were redeemed in Christ's crucifixion, and we were regenerated in His resurrection. Even before Christ put us in His train of captives, we were already saved. By the time He presented us to the Father, we had already been saved and regenerated.

GIFTS TO THE BODY AND TO MEN

Now we can see the steps by which sinners have become gifts to the Body of Christ. These steps include Christ's incarnation, His human living, His death on the cross, His burial in the tomb, His descent into Hades, His resurrection from among the dead, and His ascension to the heavens to return to the Father. By means of these steps we, the sinners, have become apostles, prophets, evangelists, and shepherds and teachers. Now we are gifts to men. Wherever the Lord may send us in the days ahead, we shall be sent as gifts to the people there.

Not only the leading apostles and prophets are gifts, but every member of the Body is a gift. For example, my little finger is a gift to my body. It can do something for my body that no other member can do. None of us should regard ourselves as too small to be a gift. Sometimes it is the smallest members who are the most useful and who render the greatest comfort to the Body. Therefore, we all are gifts given by Christ to His Body. Because of Christ's universal traveling, we are no longer sinners, but sons of God, trophies to the Father, and gifts to the Body.

In Ephesians 4 we see the giving of the gifts, whereas in Psalm 68 we have the receiving of the gifts. According to Psalm 68, the Son received trophies from the Father as gifts. Then in Ephesians 4 the Son gave them all as gifts to the church. We, the saved ones, have been given not only to the church, but even to the whole world. Thus, wherever we may go, we shall be a great blessing to others.

In some of the foregoing messages I have pointed out that all the saints can be today's apostles and prophets. In this message I would like to point out that we also can be evangelists, those who preach the good news, those who proclaim the glad tidings. As we contact people in our daily living, we need to tell them the good news. If we are faithful to do this, we are evangelists. We are also shepherds and teachers, those who take care of others and instruct them in the way of the Lord and in the things concerning God's economy.

NO CLERGY OR LAITY

Ephesians 4:11 does speak of *some* apostles, prophets, evangelists, and shepherds and teachers. Perhaps you are wondering how I can say that *all* the saints can be such gifts to the Body. The gifts in 4:11 are the leading apostles, prophets, evangelists, and shepherds and teachers. We, of course, cannot be these leading ones; however, as their followers, we can be the same kind of persons. I certainly do not consider myself an apostle like Paul, who was a leading one. But as a follower of Paul, I do regard myself as one of today's apostles, today's sent ones. We all should have such a concept concerning ourselves. We all should be followers of the leading apostles, prophets, evangelists, and shepherds and teachers. If we are not such followers, we shall fall into a great heresy—the heresy of a clergy-laity system. We shall make the leading ones the clergy, and the followers will become the laymen. But in the church, the Body of Christ, there is no such thing as either clergy or laity. As gifts to the Body, we all are apostles, prophets, evangelists, and shepherds and teachers. As gifts given by Christ to the Body and to all mankind, we can be a great blessing to the whole world.

Ephesians 4 tells us that grace is given according to the measure, the size, of the gift. The grace produces the gifted persons and then supplies them according to the measure of the gift. All the gifted persons are for the perfecting of the saints unto the work of ministry, unto the building up of the Body of Christ, until we all arrive at the three items mentioned in verse 13. In a later message we shall consider these items in detail.

LIFE-STUDY OF EPHESIANS

MESSAGE THIRTY-NINE

THE BELIEVER'S STANDARD

In 1 Timothy 1:16 Paul says, "For this cause I obtained mercy, that in me first Jesus Christ might show forth all long-suffering, for a pattern to them which should hereafter believe on him to life everlasting." According to this verse, Paul was made a pattern of God's salvation. Paul, however, was a model not only of God's salvation, but also of one called by the Lord.

In the book of Ephesians the matter of God's calling is of great significance. In 1:17-18 Paul prayed that we would have a spirit of wisdom and revelation to "know what is the hope of His calling." In 4:1 Paul besought us, God's called people, to walk worthily of the calling with which we were called.

THE GOAL OF GOD'S CALLING

Not many Christians know the goal of God's calling. Many think that this goal is simply to receive grace and to be saved. Grace and salvation, however, are not the ultimate goal of God's calling. According to Ephesians, the unique goal of God's calling is the building up of the Body of Christ. In Matthew 16 the Lord Jesus said that He would build His church. The book of Acts and the Epistles reveal that the church is built up not by the Lord directly, but through the members of the Body. Christ builds the Body by the Body. God has called us for the fulfillment of this goal.

Ephesians 3:2 speaks of the stewardship of the grace of God, and 4:12, of the building up of the Body of Christ. Hence, the portion of Ephesians from 3:2 to 4:12 begins with the stewardship of the grace of God and ends with the building up of the Body of Christ.

The stewardship of the grace of God is not limited to Paul and the other apostles. Do not think that Paul was such a steward and that you are not. Paul's intention here is to impress the saints with the fact that they all have received the stewardship of the grace of God for the building up of the Body of Christ. According to 4:12, the building up of the Body is not the work of the apostles alone; it is the responsibility of all the saints. This verse reveals that the saints are perfected unto the work of ministry, unto the building up of the Body of Christ. The Greek word rendered "unto" in this verse also means "for the purpose of," "with a view to," or "resulting in." The perfecting of the saints results in the work of ministry, which in turn results in the building up of the Body of Christ. The Body is not built up directly by the apostles and the other leading ones; it is built up directly by the saints.

In 4:16 Paul says, "Out from Whom all the Body, fitted and knit together through every joint of the supply, according to the operation in measure of each one part, causes the growth of the Body unto the building up of itself in love." Verse 12 speaks of the saints, and verse 16 mentions "each one part." According to verse 16, the Body causes the growth of itself unto the building up of itself in love. In order for this to take place in a practical way, all the saints need to be perfected by the apostles and the other leading ones.

THE SAME AS PAUL

As we read this book of Ephesians, we need to get into Paul's burden and feeling. Paul's expectation was that every believer would be an apostle. This means that Paul expected every saint to be the same as he was.

Paul was not only an apostle; he was also a prophet, an evangelist, and a shepherd and teacher. Many of us, however, may classify the gifted ones mentioned in verse 11 into four distinct categories: the apostles, the prophets, the evangelists, and the shepherds and teachers. But Paul, the pattern of God's called one, was all of these. Paul certainly was a prophet. In his Epistles he uttered some great prophecies, such as those found in 1 Corinthians 15 and in 1 and 2 Thessalonians. Paul was also an evangelist. Who was a greater evangelist than he was? He preached the gospel wherever he went. Furthermore, Paul was a shepherd and a teacher. Day and night, he cared for all the churches and all the saints. Finally, who can deny that Paul was a teacher? If Paul was not a teacher, then no one in the New Testament was a teacher. Therefore, Paul was an apostle, a prophet, an evangelist, and a shepherd and teacher. His burden and intention in chapters three and four was to point out that every saint should be the same as he was in these respects.

Chapters three and four are part of Paul's charge concerning a walk worthy of God's calling. If we would have a walk worthy of God's calling, we need to be like the Apostle Paul. To have a worthy walk, we should devote our attention not only to such things as humility, kindness, and love, but to the important matter of being apostles, prophets, evangelists, and shepherds and teachers. If we are not such persons, then we do not have a walk worthy of God's calling. In these chapters Paul is an example, not of a victorious Christian nor even of a believer who is full of life, but of one who is an apostle, prophet, evangelist, and shepherd and teacher.

ALL DISCIPLES BEING APOSTLES, PROPHETS, EVANGELISTS, AND SHEPHERDS AND TEACHERS

Every Christian who is up to the standard is an apostle, prophet, evangelist, and shepherd and teacher. An apostle is not a king; he is a sent one. If I send you out to do a specific task, then you are my sent one, my apostle. In John 17:18 the Lord Jesus prayed to the Father, "As You have sent Me into the world, I also have sent them into the world." The "them" in this verse refers not only to the twelve Apostles, but to all the disciples. This indicates that all who believe in Christ should be sent ones. This is confirmed by the Lord's word to the disciples in John 20:21: "As the Father has sent Me, I also send you." All disciples of the Lord Jesus, both male and female, are to be sent ones. If you have been a

Christian for years without ever having been sent by Him, you are not up to the standard. If we consider our past experience, we shall realize that many of us have been sent—to our husband or wife, to our parents and relatives, and to our friends. Like Paul, we are sent ones, we are apostles.

We are also prophets. According to the Scriptures, a prophet does not primarily predict the future; he is one who speaks for God. For example, when Moses was called by God in Exodus 3 and 4, he told the Lord that he was not eloquent (4:10). The Lord said that He would give Aaron to Moses to be his prophet (4:14-16; 7:1). Aaron did not predict things for Moses; he spoke on his behalf. This indicates that to be a prophet is to be a spokesman. Just as we have functioned as apostles, so we have also been prophets, perhaps to our parents, relatives, and friends. As prophets, we speak on behalf of the Lord, telling others how the Lord loves them and desires to be life and everything to them. The more we speak in such a way, the more we function as prophets.

In speaking for God, we also preach the gospel. This means that we are evangelists. To be an evangelist is simply to preach the gospel.

In the same principle, we are also shepherds and teachers. In caring for the ones saved through our gospel preaching, we shepherd them and teach them. Hence, we are apostles, prophets, evangelists, and shepherds and teachers.

To have a walk worthy of God's calling is to be one who is sent by God, who speaks for God, who preaches the gospel, and who shepherds others and teaches them. If we are not such a person, we are not up to God's standard. Due to the influence of our religious background and environment, we are accustomed to thinking of apostles and prophets as extraordinary people. But an apostle is an ordinary Christian, a Christian who meets God's standard.

We should not have a false humility and say that we are too small, too insignificant, to be apostles and prophets. It is a fact that we can be sent out by the Lord, at least to our relatives and friends, and that we can speak for Him. It is a fact that we all can be and should be God's sent ones. We are of the same category as Paul, although, as apostles, we do not have, of course, as great a measure as he had.

THE STEWARDSHIP OF THE GRACE

Ephesians 3:2 says, "If indeed you have heard of the stewardship of the grace of God which was given to me for you." Do you realize that not only Paul was a steward, but that you are a steward also? Like Paul, you have received the stewardship of the grace of God. A steward is a serving one. For example, a steward or stewardess on an airplane serves the passengers and takes care of them. This indicates that a steward is not some kind of high official, but one who serves others. The service of a steward is called the stewardship. According to 3:2, our stewardship is the stewardship of the grace of God.

We all have received a certain amount of grace. In 4:7 Paul says, "But to each one of us was given grace according to the measure of the gift of Christ." By receiving grace, we spontaneously have the stewardship of the amount of grace we have received. By grace we have been constituted stewards.

Ephesians 3:2 says that grace has been given to Paul, and 4:7 says that grace has been given to each one of us. In the light of these verses, we should not consider that Paul was something that we are not. In fact, 3:8 reveals that Paul regarded himself as "less than the least of all saints." This indicates that all the saints can receive the same kind of grace as was given to the Apostle Paul. As to the person of Paul, he was the least among the apostles (1 Cor. 15:9); but as to his ministry, he was not behind the chiefest apostles (2 Cor. 11:5; 12:11). Yet, as one who received grace, he was less than the least of all saints. This implies that all the saints can receive the grace which he received. This can be compared to all the members of our physical body which receive the same lifeblood, however large or small they may be. But the ability, or the gift, that comes out of the lifeblood differs with the members. All the members of the Body of

Christ can have the same grace of life as Paul, but their gifts are not the same as Paul's gift was. If grace could be given to Paul, who thought of himself as less than the least of all saints, then it can certainly be given to all of us.

To Paul, it was not a matter of who had received more grace and who had received less. We need to forget all such comparisons. The important thing is that we see that we all can be the same as the Apostle Paul. Since one who was less than the least of all saints could be such a person as described in chapters three and four, then we have no excuse.

However, throughout the centuries, Christians have been under the influence of the natural concept. According to this concept, one of the early apostles was enthroned to be a pope. But we all can be "popes" in a proper sense, for a pope simply means a father. This indicates that we all can be spiritual fathers to those we bring to the Lord.

Our mind needs to be purged from the natural concept that uplifts the apostles above the ordinary believers in Christ. Apostles are simply those sent by God to carry out His purpose for the building of the church. Certainly we all can be such sent ones, and, having been sent, we all can speak for God as His prophets, His spokesmen. Do not be held back by traditional teachings. Instead, believe the fact that the stewardship of the grace of God has been given to every believer.

THE REVELATION OF THE MYSTERY

In 3:3 Paul says that by revelation the mystery was made known to him. Do you think that the mystery has been made known only to the Apostle Paul and not been made known to all the other New Testament believers? We all have received the revelation of the mystery, the very revelation given to Paul. The reason Paul wrote the book of Ephesians was so that all the saints might know the mystery of Christ. In the years the Lord's recovery has been in this country, the saints have seen more and more of the mystery of Christ. By receiving this revelation, we are constituted apostles and prophets, and we are qualified to speak concerning Christ and the church.

As prophets, we need to speak to those around us, regardless of whether we think that they understand what we are saying. Our responsibility is to speak wherever we are—at home or at our places of employment. Those who are parents need to speak to their children concerning God's economy. We also should contact our parents and relatives and tell them what we have seen regarding God's eternal purpose. Do not be concerned about what others may think of you. Speak so that the unbelievers may be brought to the Lord. If we do not speak, how can others be saved? If we speak, at least some of those who hear us will come to the Lord. What an impact there will be if all the saints in the Lord's recovery open their mouths and speak concerning Christ and the church! Many of us have been cheated by the enemy into thinking that we are not qualified to speak for the Lord. Do not expect brothers with certain outstanding gifts to do all the speaking. This concept is wrong. As those who have received grace and who have seen the revelation of the mystery of Christ, we are today's apostles and prophets, and we can speak for the Lord.

ALL SERVING ONES

In 3:7 Paul said, "Of which I became a minister according to the gift of the grace of God, which was given to me according to the operation of His power." The Greek word translated "minister" in this verse is the same word that is elsewhere in the New Testament rendered "deacon." In fact "deacon" is the anglicized form of the Greek word used here. A minister or deacon is a serving one, not a high official. In this verse Paul was saying that he became a servant. According to the natural concept, the ministers are above the elders, and the elders are above the deacons. But if we have the proper understanding of this verse, we shall see that the ministers actually are deacons, those who serve. The word "minister" is a good word, but its meaning has been spoiled by traditional usage. According to the New

Testament, to say that one is a minister is to say that he is simply a serving one. All believers in Christ are serving ones.

THE OPERATION OF GOD'S POWER

In 3:7 Paul speaks of the operation of God's power. This is the power of the resurrection life (Phil. 3:10), which operates within the apostle and all the believers (Eph. 1:19; 3:20). By such an inward operating power of life, the gift of grace was given to the apostle; that is, it was manifested in him.

The Greek word rendered "operation" in verse 7 is the word from which the English word "energy" is derived. Within us and among us there is a divine energizing. This operation, this energizing, was not exclusively for the Apostle Paul; it is for all the saints. This is proved by 4:16, which, using the same Greek word, speaks of the "operation in measure of each one part." The very same energizing that was in Paul is in every part of the Body. Such an energy is working within us today.

THE DISPENSATION OF THE MYSTERY

In 3:9 Paul speaks of bringing to light what is the dispensation of the mystery. The word "dispensation" here refers to the process of dispensing Christ as life, as the life supply, and as everything to the believers. We all have a part in such a marvelous dispensation. As believers we need to be brought up to God's standard, the standard set by the Apostle Paul.

LIFE-STUDY OF EPHESIANS

MESSAGE FORTY

THE WAY TO REACH THE STANDARD

In the last message we saw the believer's standard. In this message we shall consider the way to reach this standard.

Ephesians 3:1 says, "For this cause I Paul, the prisoner of Christ Jesus on behalf of you, the nations." This verse is not a complete sentence; it contains a subject but not a predicate. All the verses from 3:2 through 3:21 are a parenthesis, and Darby places them within parentheses in his translation. This means that 4:1 continues Paul's thought in 3:1. As Paul was writing this Epistle, a burden rose up in him in 3:2 to utter a parenthetical word. Then he continued in 4:1, "I beseech you therefore, I, the prisoner in the Lord, to walk worthily of the calling with which you were called." Here Paul completed the thought he began to express in 3:1. Thus, by putting 3:1 and 4:1 together we have a complete thought.

The lengthy parenthesis between 3:1 and 4:1 is an extremely crucial section of Ephesians. In this portion Paul indicated that he longed for all the believers to be the same as he was. As those who would walk worthily of God's calling, we must take Paul as our standard. In order that we might do this, Paul presented himself as an example. In chapter three Paul did not speak on the basis of being an apostle called by God, but he spoke on the basis of being a prisoner of the Lord. As such a prisoner, he was the standard model of one who walked worthily of God's calling. In chapter three of Ephesians Paul presented not only the standard, but also the way to reach this standard. Let us consider the various aspects of this way in some detail.

THE UNIVERSAL STEWARDSHIP

Firstly, we must all be stewards, just as Paul was (3:2). The stewardship is not limited to the leading apostles. Rather, it is universal; that is, it is for all the Lord's disciples. For example, the parable of the steward in Luke 16 was spoken to the disciples. This indicates that every believer, including all of us, must be a steward. I believe that, when Paul spoke of the stewardship in 3:2, he realized within him that the stewardship is for all believers.

In Ephesians 3 Paul develops a concept presented by the Lord Jesus in the four Gospels. The Gospels reveal that all the believers are both stewards and slaves (Matt. 25:14-30). According to the Gospels, a slave is not different from a servant, a steward. The concept in Ephesians 3 is that not only the apostles are stewards and servants, but that all the believers are stewards and servants.

Because of the influence of their religious background and environment, not many Christians regard themselves as stewards. Do you realize that you are not simply a believer, one who trusts in the Lord for salvation? Moreover, have you seen that you are not just a disciple, one who is disciplined and trained? Have you seen that you are a steward, one who serves others with the riches of Christ? We all need to regard ourselves as stewards. If we have this concept, our whole Christian life will be changed. We are all stewards; even we could be called waiters, those imparting Christ's riches to others as nourishing food. The "kitchen" in which all this food is prepared is the church. If you do not have anything with which to serve others, you may come to this "kitchen" and receive the supply.

RECEIVING GRACE

Because our stewardship is the stewardship of the grace of God, we need to receive grace, even the abundance of grace. Yes, we all can be God's sent ones and God's spokesmen, but in order to fulfill such a function, we must have grace. John 1:16 says, "For of His fullness we all received, and grace upon grace."

We have pointed out that all the believers are stewards. Furthermore, we as the stewards have the supply that comes from an excellent "kitchen." But when we contact the "customers," what shall we serve them? We need to serve them the very grace we have received.

Perhaps you are wondering how you can receive grace in a practical way. For this, we must get into the Word and pray with the Word. To get into the Word is to receive grace, and to pray with the Word is to touch reality. After getting into the Word and praying with the Word, we need to walk in spirit according to the Word. If we do these three things daily, we shall receive a continual supply of grace. With this grace, we shall be enlightened and shall experience the reality of God as grace. This grace spontaneously connects us to the church, giving us a vital link to the "kitchen." In this way we become proper stewards.

If we say that we are apostles, prophets, evangelists, and shepherds and teachers, but we do not get into the Word, pray, and walk in the spirit according to the Word, then what we have is just an empty title. We have no reality, and we have no way to reach the standard set by Paul.

In our prayer we should not be concerned about trivial matters. For example, do not pray about a minor problem with your health or about your temper. The more you pray about your temper, the more you will be troubled by it. Pray with the Word, especially with chapters like Ephesians 3. We should pray with the Word until it gets into us and fills us. When the Word gets into us and the Spirit fills our spirit, spontaneously our daily walk becomes worthy of God's calling. We shall then walk in spirit according to the Word, and we shall receive grace and experience grace. By receiving grace in this way, we are brought on to the standard established by Paul.

RECEIVING REVELATION

In order to reach the standard, we also need to receive revelation (3:3, 5). A prophet is one who is full of light, one who sees what others do not see. Those who are in darkness have nothing to say, but those who are in the light have a great deal to speak forth. Whenever we see something by revelation, we automatically have something to talk about. If we would be today's sent ones and prophets, we must receive both grace and revelation.

By receiving grace and revelation, we shall spontaneously become burdened to contact others. One who gets into the Word daily and who prays consistently will have a burden to speak to others about what he has seen and experienced. At the very least, he will have the desire to call someone on the telephone. Do not think that the grace and revelation you receive will allow you to remain passive or inactive. No, the grace and revelation will burden you to go to others and to minister to them. This is to be an apostle and a prophet in a practical way. It is useless for me or anyone else to charge you to be such a sent one and spokesman. The only thing that avails is for you to get into the Word, pray, and receive grace and revelation. Whenever you are enlightened by the Lord, you will be eager to tell others what you have seen.

The way to receive revelation is to get into the Word. I believe that Paul received revelation through his study of the Old Testament. Because he spent so much time in the Word, revelation could come to him by means of the Word. The Pharisees, however, could not receive revelation from the Word because they were closed and disobedient. Paul, however, was open. All the veils that covered him were taken away by the Lord. As we come to the Word, we should ask the Lord to remove the veils from our eyes. Although we do not know what veils are still upon us, the Lord knows, and He is willing to remove them. We need to pray, "Lord, I am coming to Your Word. Take away anything that veils my sight, and make Your Word open to me." If we pray in this manner, light will come in, and we shall receive revelation. Then we shall speak to others according to the light we have received from the Lord. Such a speaking, a speaking full of divine light, will greatly surprise the religious ones. Oh, the church people must be full of light, full of revelation!

ASKING PROPER QUESTIONS

In receiving revelation, we should not be concerned with minor things such as foot-washing, the method of baptism, or the size of the cup used at the Lord's table. I am troubled when saints question me regarding secondary matters, but neglect the matters of God's eternal purpose and God's economy. Once I visited a certain place where the people were supposed to be quite spiritual. During a fellowship meeting held for the purpose of answering questions, I was disappointed by the kind of questions that were asked. I was asked questions about minor things, but no one asked me about significant things such as the difference between the mystery of Christ and the mystery of God.

The questions we ask indicate where we are and what we are. For example, many of the questions addressed to me by my little grandchildren are nonsensical. I do not expect them to ask questions about profound subjects. In order to ask a high question, we need to have considerable knowledge and experience. As we read chapter three of Ephesians, we need to ask question after question. Here are some questions we should ask: What is the stewardship of the grace? What is the mystery of Christ? What is a joint-heir? What are the unsearchable riches of Christ? What is the dispensation of the mystery? What is the difference between ages and generations? What is the purpose of the ages? What does it mean to be strengthened into the inner man? How can Christ make His home in our hearts? If we seek out the answers to questions like these, we shall receive revelation.

After we receive light and revelation in answer to questions such as these, we shall have a great deal to share with others. We in the Lord's recovery must be speaking people, those who speak day by day because we have received revelation. The more we see, the more we shall desire to speak. This is the reason that I always have something to speak in the ministry. Actually, the more I speak, the more there is to speak. If we would be such speaking ones, we need to receive revelation. All the saints, not just the leading apostles, should receive revelation.

MINISTERS OF THE GOSPEL

In 3:7 Paul says that he "became a minister according to the gift of the grace of God." As we pointed out in the previous message, a minister is one who serves. Therefore, we should not just be stewards, but also ministers, serving ones.

The words "of which" in verse 7 refer to the gospel in verse 6. This indicates that Paul became a minister of the gospel, that is, one who served others with the gospel. We also are ministers of the gospel. This gospel is not concerned with heaven, but with the nations becoming "joint-heirs and a joint Body and joint-partakers of the promise in Christ Jesus" (v. 6). The gospel spoken of in verse 6 has to do with joint-heirs, a joint Body, and joint-partakers of the promise. All the saints can be ministers of such a high and rich gospel.

We need to preach the high gospel to our parents, neighbors, and friends. Tell them about becoming joint-heirs and joint-partakers of the promise in Christ. If they argue with you in a negative way, simply continue to speak positively to them about what you have seen in the book of Ephesians. Do not be worried that they may not be able to understand you. If you regularly speak to them in a proper way, they will eventually understand what you are saying. Let us all speak to others from the book of Ephesians.

STRENGTHENED INTO THE INNER MAN

If we would reach the standard established by the Apostle Paul, our whole being needs to be strengthened into the inner man. By being strengthened into the inner man, we shall be rooted and grounded in love and shall become strong to apprehend the dimensions of Christ, to know the knowledge-surpassing love of Christ, and to be filled unto all the fullness of God (3:16-19). Paul was a person with his entire being strengthened into the inner man. Therefore, he was rooted and grounded in love and knew the dimensions of Christ and the knowledge-surpassing love of Christ. What about us? Paul prayed that we would be strengthened into the inner man so that, ultimately, we might be filled unto all the fullness of God.

Do not think that Paul could be such a person, but that you cannot. The crucial point in chapter three is that Paul expected all the saints to be the same as he was. We all can and should be strengthened into the inner man. Likewise, we all should be rooted and grounded in love, and we all should be strong to know the dimensions of Christ, to know the knowledge-surpassing love of Christ, and to be filled unto all the fullness of God.

In chapter three of Ephesians we see that Paul's desire was for all the saints to be the same as he was. In verses 2 through 9 he expressed this from one angle, and in verses 16 through 19 he related it from another. From one angle, we are stewards, we have received grace, we have seen the revelation of the mystery, and we are ministers of the high gospel. We minister the riches of Christ so that the church may be produced in a practical way. From another angle, we need to be strengthened into the inner man so that we may be rooted and grounded in love and may become strong to know the dimensions of Christ, to know the knowledge-surpassing love of Christ, and to be filled unto all the fullness of God. From both angles, we need to be the same as Paul was. If we are the same as he was, we shall be walking worthily of God's calling, for we shall be up to the standard for a believer.

As he was about to beseech the saints to have a walk worthy of God's calling, Paul became burdened to insert the parenthetical word found in 3:2-21. In this parenthetical section, Paul presented himself as the standard of a normal, proper believer in Christ. He was one who had received grace, who was a steward, who had seen the revelation, and who had become a minister of the high gospel. He was one who preached the riches of Christ as the gospel for the producing of the church. As such a one, he was strengthened into the inner man, he was rooted and grounded in love, he knew the dimensions of Christ and the love of Christ, and he was filled unto the fullness of God, which is the church as the expression of the Triune God. Today we all can be such a person. Praise the Lord that in Ephesians 3 we have not only the standard, but also the way to reach the standard!

LIFE-STUDY OF EPHESIANS

MESSAGE FORTY-ONE

THE WAY TO BE PERFECTED

In 4:12 Paul speaks of the "perfecting of the saints unto the work of ministry, unto the building up of the Body of Christ." In this message we shall consider the way to be perfected.

GRACE ACCORDING TO THE MEASURE OF THE GIFT OF CHRIST

Ephesians 4:7 says, "But to each one of us was given grace according to the measure of the gift of Christ." Notice that in this verse Paul does not say, "to each one of you"; he says, "to each one of us." This indicates that Paul was including himself. He did not put himself in a special category, in a category separate from that of the other saints.

Grace has been given to each of us according to the measure of the gift of Christ. Each member of our physical body has a certain measure. For example, the measure of the ear is of one size, and the measure of the shoulder is of another. The words "the measure of the gift of Christ" refer to the size of a member of Christ's Body. With every member there is a certain size, a certain measure. Just as our blood supplies the members of our body according to their size, grace also is given to each member according to its size. Although there is more blood in the shoulder than in the ear, the quality of the blood is the same. Just as blood is the life supply to our physical body, so grace is the life supply to the members in the Body of Christ. Praise the Lord that all the saints are gifts of Christ to whom grace has been given!

THE WORK OF MINISTRY

Since verses 9 and 10 are parenthetical, verse 11 is the continuation of verse 8. Verse 11 says, "And He gave some apostles, and some prophets, and some evangelists, and some shepherds and teachers." As verse 12 makes clear, these have been given for the "perfecting of the saints unto the work of ministry, unto the building up of the Body of Christ." According to grammar, the phrase "unto the building up of the Body of Christ" is in apposition to the phrase "unto the work of ministry." This indicates that both phrases refer to the same thing. Hence, the work of ministry is the building up of the Body.

The apostles, prophets, evangelists, and shepherds and teachers perfect the saints unto the work of ministry. Whose work is this—the work of the gifted ones mentioned in verse 11, or the work of the saints? Is it the work of the perfecting ones, or the work of the perfected ones? The answer is that it is the work both of the perfecting ones and the perfected ones. The building up of the Body is not only the work of the apostles and the other gifted ones, but also the work of all the saints. I believe that the work of ministry in verse 12 refers more to the work of the saints than it does to the work of the apostles, prophets, evangelists, and shepherds and teachers.

The work of building the meeting hall in Anaheim is an illustration of this. Many brothers worked on the construction of the hall. But very few of these brothers were professional builders. Most of them had little experience in the building trades. The few experienced tradesmen took the lead, and gradually the inexperienced ones were perfected. Eventually, both the journeymen and the learners worked together on the building of the meeting hall. However, most of the work was done, not by the professionals, but by the learners. In the same principle, the work of ministry refers to the unique work of building up the Body of Christ. This work is the responsibility not mainly of the apostles, but of all the saints. Both the leading apostles and prophets and all the believers, including even the smallest member, work together to build up the Body.

THE CONCEPT OF HIERARCHY

At this point I need to say a frank and honest word about the degraded condition of today's Christianity. Christianity has become degraded largely because of the influence of the natural concept. According to the natural concept, in any group or society there should be ranks among the people, with some of a higher rank and others of a lower rank. Ignatius, one of the great church fathers, a good teacher and a pious man, made the mistake of saying that bishops are higher than elders. He said that the authority of the elders is local, but that the authority of the bishops is regional. Through such a concept the seed of hierarchy was sown. As the hierarchy developed, there were not only bishops, but also archbishops, cardinals, and, at the top, the pope. After the Reformation, this hierarchy was not abolished. Rather, it continued in various forms in the Protestant denominations, and it still exists today.

The concept of a hierarchy or a pyramid arrangement among the believers, fits into the natural concept. But if we have the light from the clear revelation in the New Testament, we shall see that the church is not a pyramid; it is a living organism, the Body, with Christ as the unique Head. In Matthew 23:8-10 the Lord Jesus said, "But you, do not be called Rabbi; for One is your Teacher, and you are all brothers. And do not call anyone your father on the earth; for One is your Father, He Who is in the heavens. Neither be called leaders, because One is your Leader, the Christ." Nevertheless, according to the natural concept, the twelve apostles are regarded as being above all the other saints. However, if you study the New Testament carefully, you will not find very much difference between the twelve apostles and all the other disciples. The grace in the New Testament is not given uniquely to the twelve apostles, but generally to all the disciples. In John 17 the Lord Jesus prayed, not for the apostles, but for the disciples. Furthermore, in chapter twenty of John, the Lord appeared on the day of His resurrection to the disciples. On the day of Pentecost one hundred twenty were together praying. The Spirit poured out on the day of Pentecost was poured out upon all the disciples, not just upon the apostles.

NO RANK AMONG THE BELIEVERS

In the New Testament economy there is no thought of hierarchy. On the contrary, God's economy in the New Testament makes all the believers of the same rank. This is the reason that the Lord Jesus said that we all are brothers and that only Christ is our Leader, Guide, Instructor, and Director. Although God's economy puts all believers in Christ on the same level, the natural concept is that in the church, as in any social group or organization, there should be a special class of leaders.

THE APOSTOLIC AGE

Due to the influence of this concept, a great mistake was made in the history of the church. According to the traditional view of church history, the first century is regarded as the apostolic age. This concept is erroneous. The apostolic age includes the entire New Testament age. Is the present age not part of the apostolic age? If it is not, then what age is it—the age of the clergy or the age of the hierarchy? If we are enlightened by the revelation in the New Testament, we shall see that the whole New Testament age is the apostolic age.

Some have said that the apostolic age is over and that it is impossible to have apostles today. In his early ministry, Brother Nee was not yet entirely free from the influence of this concept. In *The Assembly Life,* a book published in 1934, Brother Nee said that there are no official elders, only "unofficial" elders. Furthermore, he said that there are no apostles today, but that there is a group of people who are doing the work of apostles, such as preaching the gospel and establishing churches. Brother Nee admitted that those who do the work of apostles today do not have the holiness, the power, nor the victory of the apostles. Nevertheless, as Brother Nee remarked, God is using people to work for Him in every locality in a way similar to the way He used the apostles in the first century. In the past it was the apostles who established churches, but today it is those who are doing the work of the apostles who establish churches in various localities. Brother Nee pointed out that these ones are not worthy to be compared to the apostles nor even to be called apostles, but that they are nonetheless doing part of the work of the apostles. These are the people God is using in the midst of the degraded situation of the church today. In that book published in 1934 Brother Nee realized that certain people were doing the work of apostles, but he did not dare to call them apostles. However, he called them "unofficial" apostles who appointed "unofficial" elders in the local assemblies.

Three years later, in 1937, Brother Nee saw from the New Testament that it is erroneous to say that the apostolic age is over and that there can be no apostles today. Therefore, he published the book entitled *The Normal Christian Church Life,* where he boldly said that there are still apostles today. When this book was published about forty years ago, we had seen only part of the light on this matter and on matters related to it. Now, in the light of chapters three and four of Ephesians, we see that all the saints can do the same kind of work as the early apostles, prophets, evangelists, and shepherds and teachers did.

PERFECTING THE SAINTS

We have pointed out that the gifted persons in 4:11 are for the perfecting of the saints. What do you suppose the apostles, prophets, evangelists, and shepherds and teachers perfect the saints to do? The only reasonable and logical answer is that they perfect them to do the same thing that they themselves do. For example, a mathematics teacher trains his students in mathematics. His goal is to teach them to do what he himself is able to do. Eventually, through years of training, his students will also be able to become teachers of mathematics. But suppose a certain teacher has taught mathematics for many years without perfecting even one student. What a poor teacher he would be! Nevertheless, this is actually the situation that exists among many Christians today. Many Christians attend so-called church services year after year without being perfected in the least.

About twenty-five years ago, some brothers from the church in Manila went to a hospital to visit a certain brother who was sick. As they gathered around the brother's bed, each of them offered prayer to the Lord. Some other Christians were nearby and were greatly surprised to hear so many people praying. One of them said to our brothers, "In our church, the pastor is the only one who prays in a public way. We don't know how to pray. But look at you—every one is able to pray. What kind of church do you go to?" This is just one example of the shortage of a perfecting work among today's Christians.

I am very burdened about the situation among us in the Lord's recovery. I must honestly ask myself how many brothers and sisters have been perfected under this ministry. Just as we can earn a college degree by four years of diligent study, so we should show some marks of being perfected after several years in the Lord's recovery. But many have been with us for years, but they seem not to have been perfected very much. Because of this, certain aspects of the clergy-laity system have crept in among us. We cannot tolerate this. We are not here to have so-called services as in Christianity. What we do in the meetings must be for the perfecting of the saints. If we are faithful to perfect the brothers and sisters, then after three or four years everyone will be perfected to do the same kind of work as was done by the early apostles, prophets, evangelists, and shepherds and teachers.

In Acts 8 a persecution rose up against the church, and the believers were forced to scatter. The apostles, however, remained in Jerusalem. The disciples who were scattered spontaneously did the work of apostles, prophets, evangelists, and shepherds and teachers. Suppose today's Christians were scattered because of persecution. What would these scattered ones be able to do? We need to ask this question of ourselves. What would we be able to do if we were scattered? My hope is that many would be able to function as apostles, prophets, evangelists, and shepherds and teachers. Finding themselves in an unfamiliar place, some would become burdened for the Lord's interests there. Firstly, they would preach the gospel. Then they would care for those who are saved by shepherding them and teaching them. We all need to be perfected in order to do this work.

IN THE CHURCH AND UNDER THE MINISTRY

The practice of today's Christianity is not the Lord's way according to the New Testament. In Christianity seminaries are established to train people to serve the Lord. But those educated in the seminaries are not perfected according to God's New Testament economy. The genuine perfection of the saints must be in the church and under the ministry. Today the Lord's ministry is criticized, slandered, and scorned. If the eyes of the believers are opened, they will see what the ministry is and where it is today. In the church the ministry is needed to perfect the saints unto the work of ministry, unto the building up of the Body of Christ.

I am very concerned that little has actually been accomplished among us to perfect the saints unto the work of ministry. How much we have been under the influence of degraded Christianity! Many Christians today care mainly for the preaching of the gospel and somewhat for the teaching of the Bible. We all need to see clearly that today the Lord is doing one work—to perfect all the saints until we all arrive. We have seen that in Ephesians 4 Paul did not place himself in a separate category. Rather, he included himself with all the saints. We all, including Paul, need to hold the truth and grow up into Christ until we arrive at a full-grown man.

In these days I bear a very heavy burden concerning the perfecting of the saints. This burden cannot be discharged until I see that all the saints are able to do the same kind of work as was done by the early apostles, prophets, evangelists, and shepherds and teachers. I do not care merely to be a preacher or a teacher of the Bible. I desire to be perfected and to perfect others unto the building up of the Body of Christ.

LIFE AND FUNCTION

In order to be perfected, we must pay attention to life and to function. The way to be perfected is to grow in life and to become skillful in function. The Greek word rendered "perfecting" here also means completing, equipping, furnishing. To perfect a saint is to complete him, to equip him, and to furnish him. Only by growing in life can we be completed. Not until we become mature will we be completed. For example, a child of five is not a full-grown person. As long as, spiritually speaking, we remain underage, we shall not be complete. Mothers perfect their children by feeding them. Furthermore, parents equip their children and furnish them by training them to behave and to speak in a certain way. Thus, children are perfected by feeding and by training. The same is true with respect to perfecting the saints according to God's economy. The saints need to be fed and they need to be trained so that they may function with the proper skill.

Once when I was visiting a certain place which was regarded as being rather spiritual, I was asked why we conduct trainings in the Lord's recovery. I replied that as human beings we need to grow and we need also to learn. If we do not grow, we shall not have the stature required to do certain things. If we do not learn, we shall be "barbarians." For example, if a child is not taught to eat properly with the necessary utensils, he will be "wild" and unruly at the table. Do not think that as long as a person is spiritual in life, he requires no training. No, in spiritual things, as in physical things, there is the need of training. In spiritual things we need the maturity, the growth in life, and we also need the skill. The maturity comes from growth, and the skill comes from training. Therefore, in order to perfect the saints, we need to feed them with spiritual food that they may grow, and we also need to train them to develop certain skills.

THE NEED FOR THOROUGH TRAINING

To the present moment, I have not yet discharged my burden in the matter of training. We need to be trained for the practice of the church life. This means that the training should enrich and uplift our practice of the church life. Although the help given to the saints thus far is far from adequate, we cannot deny the fact that since coming into the Lord's recovery many saints have undergone some training. This is evident as we listen to them testify or pray in the meetings. However, the need remains for more thorough and complete training. My burden is that after a period of time, perhaps after three or four years, virtually all the saints in the Lord's recovery in this country will have been adequately trained.

To be trained is to have the rich supply of Christ ministered to us that we may grow, and it is to be equipped that we may be skillful in speaking, in contacting new ones, in shepherding, and in preaching and teaching. Do not say that you cannot speak because you are not a talented speaker. We all are able to speak for the Lord.

THE LORD'S WAY

Once the saints have been perfected, then wherever they go, they will be apostles, the ones sent to that place. They will also be prophets, evangelists, and shepherds and teachers. To perfect the saints to be such gifts to the Body is the Lord's way. If we do not follow this way, the Lord will not be able to get what He desires. How we thank Him that, in His mercy, He has shown us His way!

We have seen that in 4:13-15 Paul did not exclude himself. Rather, he said, "Until we all arrive...that we may be no longer babes...but holding to truth in love, we may grow up into Him in all things...." None of us should think that we have already been perfected. On the contrary, we all need more life supply and more training. If we are willing to grow and to be trained, then we shall not repeat the history of Christianity. If we are faithful to practice what the Lord shows us, the Lord will have a way among us. The Lord's way has never changed. His way is to perfect the saints to do the work of ministry for the building up of the Body of Christ. This is the way for the Lord to gain what He desires as the necessary preparation for His coming back.

LIFE-STUDY OF EPHESIANS

MESSAGE FORTY-TWO

ALL BUILDING MEMBERS WITHOUT RANK

Throughout the centuries Christians have held the natural concept that the church is merely a social organization. Actually the church is not an organization. As Paul says in his Epistles, the church is the Body of Christ. Our physical body, which is a picture of the mystical Body of Christ, is not an organization, but an organism. As an organism, it is altogether dependent upon life. When the life is gone, the body becomes a corpse, which could possibly be regarded as an organization.

AN ORDER OF FUNCTION, NOT OF RANK

The concept that the church is a social organization has caused a great deal of damage. In social organizations there is the need for certain members to be on the top, to be of the highest rank. In religion this may take the form of hierarchy. But there is no hierarchy in our physical body. No doubt, certain members are above others, but this is a matter of functional order, not of rank. For example, for the purpose of function, the nose is higher than the mouth. It would be absurd to say that the nose has a higher rank than the mouth has. In like manner, our fingers are below both our arms and shoulders. But this does not mean that the fingers have a lower rank. This is entirely a matter of order according to function. How could the fingers function if they were attached to the shoulders? Therefore, in the physical body, a picture of the living organism of the Body of Christ, there is no rank nor hierarchal order, but only order according to function.

In the past I have met some women who did not agree with Paul's word in Ephesians 5 about wives submitting to their husbands. Likewise, they could not accept Paul's word in 1 Corinthians 11 about the man being the head of the woman. Under the influence of the modern concept of female emancipation, they questioned why the woman had to be under the man. I answered them by pointing to the arrangement of the members in our physical body. I tried to show them that this arrangement is not a matter of rank, but a matter of function. For example, the nose is in the right place for its particular function. The same is true of all the members of the body. However, the fact that the nose is higher than the mouth in functional order does not mean that it is of a higher rank than the mouth. To consider the matter of rank with respect to the Body of Christ is to be under the influence of the fallen human concept. Many troubles and problems have been caused by this very concept.

As we consider the apostles, prophets, and elders spoken of in the New Testament, we need to drop the natural concept. If we hold to our natural concept, we shall automatically think that the apostles, prophets, and elders have a higher rank. The concept of rank is altogether a natural concept, a concept foreign to the Scriptures. The apostles, prophets, and elders carry out certain functions, but fulfilling these functions does not place them on a level above the other saints. In the Body there are many members, and these members have different functions. Although there is a difference of function, there is no difference of rank. In an organism there is no consciousness of rank. If our shoulders could speak, they would say that they have never thought of having any rank in our body; they would say that they have never regarded themselves as higher than the other members.

Some of the elders have been rather proud of their position and have expected the saints to give place to them. Other brothers have been ambitious to become elders. There is no room for such ambition in the church life. If we know the Bible, we shall realize that an elder is a slave. The thought of rank must be purged away. The apostles and elders are not high officials. On the contrary, they are those who serve Christ to the churches and to the saints.

THE PERFECTING OF THE SAINTS
UNTO THE WORK OF MINISTRY

My burden in this message is to point out that all the saints should be building members. Ephesians 4:11 says, "And He gave some apostles, and some prophets, and some evangelists, and some shepherds and teachers." These gifted ones are not high officials with a special rank. Rather, they are given for the perfecting of the saints (v. 12). The saints need to be perfected, equipped, furnished, unto the work of ministry. This work of ministry is the building up of the Body of Christ. Because so many saints are not yet doing the work of ministry, they need the gifted ones mentioned in verse 11 to perfect them, to equip them, that they may be qualified to carry out the work of ministry for the building up of the Body of Christ. The perfecting or equipping is related both to growth in life and to training in certain skills.

The light on these verses has never been as bright and clear as it is today. We have seen that the work of ministry is simply the building up of the Body of Christ. This work should be carried out not only by the apostles, prophets, evangelists, and shepherds and teachers, but by all the members. Hence, all the saints are building members. We are not only members who have been built up, but we are also members who build up the Body. Firstly, the apostles, prophets, evangelists, and shepherds and teachers perfect the saints. This means that they build up the saints. Then the perfected saints become the building members. In these days the saints are being perfected. But after another period of time I expect that the saints who are being perfected now will also become the building ones.

UNTIL WE ALL ARRIVE

Verse 13 says, "Until we all arrive at the oneness of the faith and of the full knowledge of the Son of God, at a full-grown man, at the measure of the stature of the fullness of Christ." Notice that in this verse Paul says "we," not "you." When Paul wrote this verse, he himself was already mature. However, he was waiting for the immature ones to grow up. In other words, he was waiting until we all arrive. Paul did not want to arrive at the destination ahead of the younger ones. Rather, he was waiting until we all arrive at three things: at the oneness of the faith, at a full-grown man, and at the measure of the stature of the fullness of Christ. In this verse there are three phrases beginning with the word *at*. The fact that there is no conjunction indicates that the second is in apposition to the first and that the third is in apposition to the second. Thus, the three phrases actually refer to one thing.

Paul expected all the saints to come up to his standard and to be the same as he was. Paul was a builder, and we all should be builders also. Paul was not some great official. At most, he was simply a member of the Body. The difference between him and most of us is that Paul was a building member, whereas most of us are just builded members. Nevertheless, the day is coming, perhaps after a few years, when we all shall be building members. Then we shall all arrive at the destination together.

GROWTH AND TRAINING

Verse 14 continues, "That we may be no longer babes tossed by waves and carried about by every wind of teaching in the sleight of men, in craftiness with a view to a system of error." A babe cannot be a building one. He first needs to become a builded one. For this, a spiritual babe needs to grow. If we would be a builded member and especially a building member, we must grow. Furthermore, we need to develop certain skills. In the foregoing message we pointed out that the way to perfect the saints is to feed them so that they may grow and to train them so that they may learn certain skills. The learning of skills is related to our growth in life. The more mature we are, the more we are able to be trained. For example, an older child is able to learn more skills in mathematics than a younger child. It is the growth in life that gives us the capacity to learn certain skills.

Not many Christians today pay attention to the growth in life. Furthermore, very few concentrate on the matter of training. Therefore, among most Christians today there is no growth and there is no training. This is the reason that one can attend so-called church services for many years and still remain a babe. Such a one can never do what the apostles and prophets were able to do, because he has been neither fed nor trained.

The situation in the Lord's recovery must be altogether different from this. We need to rise up and declare that we want to grow in life and that we want to develop the necessary skills to become building members. I hope that after a few years all the saints will become building members with the growth in life and with the skills. This is what it means to be perfected, completed, equipped, and furnished.

OUR POTENTIAL REALIZED BY GROWTH

Verse 15 says, "But holding to truth in love, we may grow up into Him in all things, Who is the Head, Christ." This verse clearly speaks of growth. Oh, how we need to grow! It is good to be encouraged by the word that we all can do the same kind of work as was done by the apostles, prophets, evangelists, and shepherds and teachers. We all have the potential for this, but this potential can be realized only by growth. Without growth, the potential does not mean anything. If we would grow, we need to get into the Word, feed on the Word, and exercise our spirit to pray and to receive the Lord each day. By feeding on the Word and by receiving the Lord, we shall receive the nourishment required for the growth in life.

THE OPERATION IN THE MEASURE OF EACH PART

The following verse, verse 16, reveals that the Body comes out of the Head: "Out from Whom all the Body, fitted and knit together through every joint of the supply, according to the operation in measure of each one part, causes the growth of the Body unto the building up of itself in love." This verse indicates that the Body causes the growth of the Body unto the building up of itself in love. Here "every joint of the supply" refers to the specially gifted persons, such as those mentioned in verse 11. But "each one part" denotes the members of the Body. There is an operation in the measure of every member. This indicates that every member is a building member. The building members in this verse are those who have grown in life and who have developed the skills in function.

THE NEED FOR TRAINING

I am extremely burdened that we all grow in life and that we all receive training in order to function. We are here to be absolute with the Lord. The church meetings are not a time for relaxation or entertainment. The Lord needs a people who are willing to grow, to be trained, and to be disciplined. Thus, every church should set aside one evening a week for training. If we are faithful to the Lord in this matter of training, after a few years all the saints will be useful in His hand. May we be willing to say, "Lord, we want to be trained. We want to know how to grow in life in a practical way, and we want to develop all the necessary skills."

We need training in how to speak, how to preach the gospel, and how to teach and shepherd others. Every proper Christian who is up to the Lord's standard should be one who is sent out, who speaks for God, who preaches the gospel, and who takes care of others. We should not be those who are merely saved and who are just waiting for heaven. Such believers are actually not very different from the people in the world. In contrast, we must be those who are continually sent out to speak for the Lord. We must preach the gospel and shepherd those who are saved through our gospel preaching. If we are like this, we shall be different both from the worldly people and from most Christians. We shall be a heavenly people carrying out a heavenly commission.

Do not wait for others to be raised up to be the Lord's servants or to do the work of ministry. We all must function as apostles, prophets, evangelists, and shepherds and teachers. We all must be and we all can be the building members. We do not care to have some vain title or empty position. We would like to be today's apostles and prophets in a practical way. We need to be genuine preachers of the high and rich gospel and also those who truly know how to shepherd the new ones. May we all go to the Lord in a desperate way and pray that He train us to be such members of His Body. I cannot be at rest until I see that all the saints in the Lord's recovery are being trained in such a way. Our burden is to perfect the saints unto the work of ministry, unto the building up of the Body of Christ.

MAKING A DEFINITE DECISION

I believe that the Lord has made this vision clear to us all. Now the crucial matter is how the saints will respond. I believe that all those among us are sincere and faithful to the Lord. The only thing remaining is that we make a definite decision before Him, even a vow, that we do not want to be left behind. Rather, we want to be those who answer the Lord's call, satisfy His desire, and make Him happy. If we are not for this, then our life on earth is meaningless.

Perhaps we can do little to help those Christians in today's religion, but by the Lord's mercy and grace we ourselves can be helped to become building members in reality and in practicality. We believe that even the weakest one among us can become a building member. On the one hand, the leading ones must endeavor to perfect the saints. On the other hand, the saints must make a definite decision with the Lord regarding their willingness to be trained to be building members. If we are faithful on both sides, then God will do superabundantly above all we ask or think for the sake of His economy concerning Christ and the church.

CHRIST, THE UNIQUE LEADER

Among the building members in the Body of Christ there should be no rank. In Matthew 23:10 the Lord Jesus said, "Neither be called leaders, because One is your Leader, the Christ." We all are brothers in the Lord, and there should be no leader among us. The Lord's clear word is that none of us should be called the leader, for He Himself is our unique Leader.

HELPS AND GOVERNMENTS

It is quite significant that in 1 Corinthians 12:28 Paul places "helps" before "governments." The helps refer to the service of the deacons, whereas governments denote the function of the elders. In this verse Paul purposely places the service of the deacons ahead of the function of the elders. He may have done this to impress the Corinthians with the fact that in the church there should be no concept of rank. We should not regard the governing of the elders as higher than the service of the deacons.

STEWARDS OF THE GRACE OF GOD

We have seen that in Ephesians 3 Paul said that he had been given the stewardship of the grace of God. He mentioned this with the intention of helping the saints to realize that they all are to be stewards of God's grace. The same thought is found in 1 Peter 4:10: "As every man hath received the gift, even so minister the same one to another, as good stewards of the manifold grace of God." Thus, all the saints, not just the apostles, should be stewards. The elders should not place themselves in a special category, but they should consider themselves stewards, just as all the saints are stewards.

NOT LORDING IT OVER THE CHURCH, BUT SETTING AN EXAMPLE

In 1 Peter 5:3 Peter encouraged the elders not to lord it over the church as if the church were their private possession. The church is the Body of Christ; it is not the personal property of the elders. The elders, therefore, should not regard the church as their own possession. However, in certain places I have known elders who had such an attitude. They kept the church in their "pocket" as their possession and conducted themselves as if they were the "boss." Such an attitude is utterly wrong. The elders must remember that they are stewards among a company of stewards.

As stewards, the elders should set an example for the saints to follow. In reading the Word, in prayer, in offering themselves to the Lord, in the growth in life, in the practical service of the church, and in all other things as well, they should be examples. The elders are not lords or kings; they are slaves, servants. They are also stewards of the grace of God. As such stewards, they should be models for the saints in shepherding, in teaching, and in preaching. If we are all clear about this, then there will be no problem among us as far as leadership is concerned.

MUTUAL SUBMISSION

Some have asked me whether or not they should submit themselves to the elders in their church. Certainly the saints should be submissive to the elders. In 1 Peter 5:5 Peter says, "Likewise, ye younger, submit yourselves unto the elder." However, in the very same verse Peter goes on to say, "Yea, all of you be subject one to another, and be clothed with humility." This indicates that not only should the younger ones submit to the older ones, but that the older ones should also submit to the younger ones. Both the older ones and the younger ones need to be clothed with humility. For the younger to submit to the elder is somewhat difficult, but for the elder to submit to the younger is even more difficult. Nevertheless, in the church life there should be such a mutual submission.

A QUESTION ABOUT AUTHORITY

Others have asked me if the elders have authority. This question springs from the natural concept concerning rank. If we were not under the influence of the natural concept, we would not raise this question. I repeat, in the church there is no such thing as rank. Rather, we all are stewards of the grace of God, and we submit ourselves one to another. If the Lord has placed you in the eldership, you should not be proud. Do not regard yourselves as higher than others, and do not lord it over the church as if the church were your possession. On the contrary, as a leading one, set an example for the saints to follow. When the saints see such examples established for them by the leading ones, they may say, "Lord, thank You for these good examples. We desire to follow them in praying, in reading the Word, in preaching and teaching, and in shepherding the saints." By the setting of the example and the following of the example, we all shall eventually serve together as stewards of the manifold grace of God. This is the proper church life, where there is no organization, no rank, no hierarchy, and no clergy-laity.

In order for the church to go on in a proper way, there is the need for some brothers to take care of the administrative affairs. But this does not make them high officials with all the other saints as their subordinates. This natural concept must be dropped. There is no place for it in the kingdom of God. In the church life, which is the kingdom of God in a practical way today, we have one King, the Lord Jesus Christ, and we all are His subjects.

LIFE-STUDY OF EPHESIANS

MESSAGE FORTY-THREE

ARRIVING AT THREE THINGS

Ephesians 4:13 says, "Until we all arrive at the oneness of the faith and of the full knowledge of the Son of God, at a full-grown man, at the measure of the stature of the fullness of Christ." This verse is the direct continuation of verses 11 and 12, which say that the apostles, prophets, evangelists, and shepherds and teachers have been given for the perfecting of the saints unto the work of ministry. We have pointed out that the gifted ones in verse 11 perfect the saints to do the same things that they themselves do. We all can be sent out and we all can speak for the Lord as prophets, preach the gospel as evangelists, and shepherd others and teach them as shepherds and teachers. If we love the Lord, we shall speak for Him as His witnesses. Furthermore, we need to preach the gospel, whether in season or out of season. This is not only the task of the leading evangelists, but of all the saints. Furthermore, we daily need to shepherd others and to teach them. The leading ones set the pattern for these functions, and we follow their example. Hence, all the saints can do the work of the apostles, prophets, evangelists, and shepherds and teachers.

The saints need to be perfected unto the work of ministry. In the New Testament there is a unique ministry: the dispensing of Christ into others for the building up of the Body. In order to carry on the work of ministry, the saints need to be perfected.

The building up of the Body of Christ is not accomplished directly by the leading ones. The direct work of building is carried out by the saints who have been perfected. How different this is from the situation in today's Christianity! The proper way is for the leading ones to set up a pattern and then train the saints to do what they do. After the saints have been perfected, the leading ones should step aside and allow the saints to do the direct work of building. Every leading one must learn when and how to step aside. Firstly, the leading ones must learn how to perfect others. After this work of perfecting has been accomplished, the leading ones must leave the direct work of building in the hands of all the members of the Body.

In verse 13 Paul did not say, "until *you* all arrive"; he said, "until *we* all arrive." This indicates that Paul included himself with all the saints. It is not good for a few to arrive at the destination and to leave so many others behind. On the contrary, we all should arrive together. Arriving at the three things spoken of in verse 13 is not a matter of a race; it is a matter of all arriving at the destination at the same time.

I. ARRIVING AT THE ONENESS

A. Of the Faith

The Greek word rendered arrive in verse 13 may also be rendered attain to. This indicates that a process is required for us to attain to or arrive at the practical oneness.

The oneness of the Spirit in verse 3 is the oneness of the divine life in reality, whereas the oneness in verse 13 is the oneness of our living in practicality. We already have the oneness of the divine life in reality. We only need to keep it. But we need to go on until we arrive at the oneness of our living in practicality. This aspect of oneness is of two things: the faith and the full knowledge of the Son of God. The faith does not refer to the act of our believing, but refers to what we believe in, such as the divine Person of Christ and His redemptive work for our salvation. The faith is used in this sense in Jude 3, 2 Timothy 4:7, and 1 Timothy 6:21.

B. The Full Knowledge of the Son of God

The full knowledge of the Son of God is the realization of the revelation concerning the Son of God for our experience.

The Son of God refers to the Lord's Person as life to us, whereas Christ refers to His commission to minister life to us that we, as members of His Body, may have gifts for function. The more we grow in life, the more we shall cleave to the faith and to the realization of Christ and the more we shall drop all the concepts concerning minor doctrines which cause divisions. Then we shall arrive at or attain to the practical oneness; that is to say, we shall arrive at a full-grown man, at the measure of the stature of the fullness of Christ.

Many Christians do not know the difference between the oneness of the Spirit and the oneness of the faith and of the full knowledge of the Son of God. The first is the oneness of reality, and the second is the oneness of practicality. Because the Spirit is the reality of our oneness, the oneness of the Spirit is the oneness of reality. Oneness is nothing less than the Spirit Himself. If there were no Spirit, then there would be no oneness. Although we have the oneness in reality, there is still the need for the oneness of practicality. This means that the oneness of reality must be practiced; that is, it must become the oneness in practice. Hence, in verse 13 Paul speaks of the oneness of practicality.

Between the oneness of reality and the oneness of practicality there is a distance. For this reason, there is the need to "arrive at" the oneness of practicality. The oneness of the Spirit is the beginning, whereas the oneness of the faith and of the full knowledge of the Son of God is the destination. This indicates that we must journey from the oneness of the Spirit to the oneness of the faith and of the full knowledge of the Son of God. In other words, we must travel from the oneness of reality until we arrive at the oneness of practicality.

As believers, we already have the oneness of reality. But we need to keep it. The best way to keep the oneness of reality is to go on, to proceed, toward the oneness of practicality.

We have pointed out that the faith in verse 13 does not refer to our act of believing, but refers to the object in which we believe. Every believer in Christ accepts this faith. When we first believed in the Lord Jesus, we were very simple. All we had was the faith. But afterward we became quite complicated by taking in various doctrines, teachings, and concepts, nearly all of which are divisive.

Several young men may be saved at the same time, through the preaching of the same evangelist. On the day they are saved, they all accept the faith. Afterward, however, they take in different doctrinal concepts. These concepts cause them to be divided from one another. In order for these believers to arrive at the oneness of the faith, they need to be perfected through the work of the apostles, prophets, evangelists, and shepherds and teachers. This work of perfecting will cause them to care for the oneness of the Spirit and to lay aside the divisive doctrines. As they arrive at the oneness of the faith, they no longer care for the various divisive doctrines, but care only for the unique faith concerning Christ and His redemptive work. By the perfecting work they also arrive experientially at the full knowledge of the Son of God. They do not pay attention to divisive doctrines or practices, but care only for Christ as the Son of God. They care for the full knowledge of the Son of God as life experientially. They desire more and more to experience Christ in their daily life. By arriving at the oneness of the faith and of the full knowledge of the Son of God, these believers have not only the oneness of reality, but also the oneness of practicality. Now they are able to come together without division and to enjoy oneness in a practical way.

The oneness in the Lord's recovery is such a practical oneness. Our oneness is the oneness of our unique faith and of the full knowledge of the Son of God in our daily experience of Him as our life. I believe that most of us in the Lord's recovery have arrived at the oneness of practicality. Therefore, we are one both in reality and in practicality.

Today many Christians who love the Lord, including a good number of pastors and ministers, have not seen the oneness of practicality. However, they do have the oneness of reality, which is the oneness of the Spirit. Many of these Christians say that as long as we are genuine believers in Christ and have the indwelling of the Spirit, we all can be one. In a sense, this is true. But this oneness is not yet the oneness of practicality. It is real, but it is not practical. Therefore, such Christians need to journey the distance between the oneness of reality and the oneness of practicality. I praise the Lord that so many of us have traveled from the beginning, the oneness of the Spirit, to the destination, the oneness of the faith and of the full knowledge of the Son of God. We have made the journey from the oneness of reality to the oneness of practicality.

II. ARRIVING AT A FULL-GROWN MAN

Verse 13 also says that we need to arrive at a full-grown man. A full-grown man is a mature man. Through regeneration the saints have become babes in Christ (1 Cor. 3:1). Now the saints need to grow into maturity (1 Cor. 3:6, Gk.; Heb. 6:1). Such maturity in life is needed for the practical oneness.

If we are still divided by doctrinal differences, it is an indication that we are childish. Such divisive doctrines are "toys." During the early stages of our Christian life, we may be fond of playing with such "toys." The more childish the saints are, the more "toys" they have. But as children grow up, they gradually lay aside their toys. When people become fully matured, they have no toys at all. In the first few years of my Christian life I dearly loved my doctrinal "toys." Because these "toys" meant so much to me, it took me a rather long time to drop them. But today I have no "toys." I have only Christ and the church.

In 1 Corinthians 13:11 Paul said, "When I was a child, I spake as a child, I understood as a child, I thought as a child: but when I became a man, I put away childish things." Here Paul indicates that certain things may be "toys." As the believers grow, they will drop these "toys." Eventually, by being perfected, they will all arrive at a full-grown man.

III. ARRIVING AT THE MEASURE OF THE STATURE OF THE FULLNESS OF CHRIST

According to verse 13, we also are to arrive at the measure of the stature of the fullness of Christ. The fullness of Christ is the Body of Christ (1:23), which has a stature with a measure. To arrive at the measure of the stature of the fullness of Christ is also a necessity for the practical oneness. Hence, to go from the oneness of reality to the oneness of practicality we need to press onward until we arrive at the three things mentioned in this verse.

The fullness of Christ is simply the expression of Christ. As Christ's fullness, the Body is Christ's expression. Christ's fullness, the Body, has a stature, and with this stature there is a certain measure. Hence, verse 13 speaks of the measure of the stature of the fullness of Christ.

To arrive at the measure of the stature of the fullness of Christ is to arrive at the full building up of the Body of Christ. It is to arrive at the full completion of the building up of the Body.

We have seen that we need to arrive at the practical oneness, at the full growth, and at the complete building up of the Body. If we would arrive at these three things, we need to do the work of ministry. As verse 12 indicates, the work of ministry is equal to building up the Body of Christ. Among us there is just one ministry. Although thousands of us may participate in the work of ministry, the ministry itself is unique. This ministry is strictly for the building up of the Body of Christ. No matter who we may be, leaders or followers, we all are working to carry out the ministry in the New Testament economy to build up the Body of Christ. We are not here to go on alone, but to go on with others, even to bring others on. As we ourselves go on, we need to bring others on. We take others on by speaking for Christ, by teaching, and by shepherding.

Once again I wish to point out the need in all the churches for some kind of practical training. We need to be trained in the matters of teaching, shepherding, and preaching the gospel. Through this training the saints will learn how to function as apostles, prophets, evangelists, and shepherds and teachers. As we function in all these ways, we have one goal: the building up of the Body of Christ. As we participate in the work of ministry for the building up of the Body, we arrive at the practical oneness, at full growth, and at the completion of the building up of the Body of Christ.

If our only goal is the building up of the Body, we shall spontaneously be regulated. As we carry on a particular work, it will be with the consciousness that this work is for the building up of the Body. Formerly, we may have preached the gospel without realizing that gospel preaching must be for the building up of the Body. Now we see that whatever we may do as apostles, prophets, evangelists, and shepherds and teachers must be for the unique goal of building up Christ's Body. If we have seen the goal, then we shall be burdened to help others arrive with us at the practical oneness, at the full growth, and at the full building up of the Body. If we are clear about this, then the Lord will have a way to come back, for He will have a way to obtain the Bride He desires.

The Lord's way to do this is found in three crucial verses —in Ephesians 4:11-13. These verses reveal that all those who have been captured by the Lord have been presented to the Body as gifts for the perfecting of the saints, so that the work of ministry may be carried out and that the building up of the Body of Christ may be accomplished. Then we shall all arrive together at our destination—at the oneness of the faith and of the full knowledge of the Son of God, at a full-grown man, and at the measure of the stature of the fullness of Christ. This is our goal, and we must diligently press toward it until we all reach it together.

LIFE-STUDY OF EPHESIANS

MESSAGE FORTY-FOUR

BABYISHNESS AND THE WINDS OF TEACHING

Ephesians 4:13 says that we need to arrive at the oneness of the faith and of the full knowledge of the Son of God, at a full-grown man, and at the measure of the stature of the fullness of Christ. It is difficult to define these items adequately because they are all related to life and life is very mysterious. The real oneness in practicality is a matter of life. Likewise, the full-grown man and the measure of the stature of the fullness of Christ are matters of life. Only after our experience of life has reached a certain degree can we understand such a verse as 4:13.

In 4:13 Paul begins with the oneness of the faith. From my limited experience, I can say that the faith here refers to Christ with His redemptive work. Hence, the object of our Christian faith is the living Christ with His work.

Verse 13 also speaks of the full knowledge of the Son of God. Apparently there is little relationship between the faith and the full knowledge of the Son of God. According to our experience, however, the two are actually one, for both refer to Christ. The full knowledge of the Son of God is a matter of knowing Christ as life and everything to us. In the New Testament the Lord is called the Son of God in relation to life, but in relation to His commission He is called Christ. When Peter received the revelation regarding Christ, he said that the Lord Jesus was the Christ, the Son of the living God (Matt. 16:16). Furthermore, in the Gospel of John we are told that we need to believe that Jesus is the Christ, the Son of God (John 20:31). This means that we believe in the Lord Jesus for life and for His commission. To know the Lord's commission is rather easy, but to know Him as our life is quite difficult. This comes not by mere objective knowledge, but by experience. When we experience Christ as our life, we know Him as the Son of God. Then we have the experiential and practical oneness, that is, the oneness of the faith and of the full knowledge of the Son of God.

God desires that Christ be everything to us. Christ is the object of our faith, and He is also our life. If we see this, we shall begin to lay aside whatever distracts us from Christ; we shall drop everything other than Christ Himself. How much we drop depends on our experience of Christ. The more we experience Christ as life, the more things we shall lay aside. In this way we arrive at the oneness of the faith and of the full knowledge of the Son of God.

Today, because we are still short of the experience of life, we do not have the full realization of this practical oneness. But we are growing. We cannot say that we have arrived at the oneness of the faith and of the full knowledge of the Son of God, at a full-grown man, or at the measure of the stature of the fullness of Christ. Nevertheless, we thank the Lord that, in His recovery, we are on the way toward this goal.

I. BABES IN CHRIST

Verse 14 says, "That we may be no longer babes tossed by waves and carried about by every wind of teaching in the sleight of men, in craftiness with a view to a system of error." This verse is the continuation of verse 13. The word "that," which may also be rendered "in order that," indicates that the result of arriving at the three things in verse 13 is that we are no longer babes tossed by waves and carried about by every wind of teaching. Therefore, arriving at the three things in verse 13 has a purpose, and this purpose is that we be no longer babes.

A. Those Lacking Maturity in Life

Babes are those believers who are young in Christ, who lack maturity in life (1 Cor. 3:1; 13:11; Heb. 5:13). In the first stage of our spiritual life, we Christians are all babes.

B. Tossed by Waves and Carried About by Winds

Verse 14 indicates that the babes are tossed by waves. The Christian life is like a journey on the sea, where there are many storms. As Christians, we should not expect our journey to be calm, with no waves or winds. The waves and the storms come not only upon individual believers, but even upon the church. There are times when the church experiences waves and is in the midst of storms. Paul's concept here is not that we can avoid the waves and winds, but that we can be kept from being tossed by waves and carried about by winds.

Difficulties and hardships are different from waves and storms. Hardships are like rocks, and difficulties are like heavy weights that we must bear. Waves, on the contrary, often come in a pleasant, appealing way and even with a sweet, loving appearance. Most of those who are tossed by waves are not tossed against their will, but are tossed willingly by waves that seem most pleasant and enjoyable to them. As they are being tossed by the waves, they have no sense of danger. Rather, they may have a sense of excitement or enjoyment. Because waves may have such a pleasant appearance, they are quite different from hardships or difficulties. Actually, few Christians are tossed by difficulties, but many are tossed by waves and carried away by winds.

Perhaps you are wondering what the waves and the winds are. They are the various teachings, doctrines, concepts, and opinions. As the church is journeying on the sea, Satan will seek an opportunity to send in some appealing teachings, concepts, and opinions to entice the believers. His purpose in doing so is to carry them away from Christ and the church.

At the time of Paul, certain Judaizers taught the Old Testament in an enticing manner. Their teaching was related to certain practices that had been ordained by God in the Old Testament. It was difficult for the babes in Christ to discern the subtleties of these appealing teachings. The principle is the same today, but now there are even more distracting teachings, concepts, and opinions. All these have a pleasant and positive appearance. Otherwise, no one could be cheated by them. Thus, many today are being tossed by waves and carried about by winds of teaching.

A babe can easily be deceived or led astray. For example, children can be led away from home by someone who offers them candy or gum. Their love for candy causes them to forget everything else. Because many Christians are still babyish, desiring sugar-coated teachings, they are easily deceived.

The only way to escape from the waves and the winds is to grow in life. As you are growing, you need to hide under the covering of your parents in the Lord. Do not care for spiritual candies, but care for the way your parents in Christ are taking. In this way you will be preserved and safeguarded.

In the church life the young ones should hide under the shelter provided by the older ones. This covering is the best hiding place. On your own do not take in any concept, no matter how sweet it may seem. Whenever you are tempted in this way, you should say, "I don't care for these sweet things. I care for Christ, for the church, and for the shelter of the older ones." If you take in the candy, you will discover that there is poison under its sugar coating.

By reading verse 14 in its context we see that the most reliable test to expose any deceptive teaching is Christ and the church. In his subtlety, the enemy, Satan, uses waves and winds to distract the saints from Christ and the church. At times, Satan will even use the Bible to do this. This indicates that even scriptural teachings may be used by Satan to carry us away from God's purpose. Satan can use almost anything to distract us from Christ and the church. He used even the words of Scripture to tempt the Lord Jesus in the wilderness. There is no better safeguard than Christ with the church. Do not accept any teaching that cannot pass the test of Christ and the church.

Satan may even come to you with a teaching under the pretense that this teaching will help you to enjoy the church life more. However, when you take in such a teaching, you find that your appetite for the church life is actually nullified. Before you accepted that teaching, you were absolute for the church and for the church testimony; you desired to attend the meetings of the church and had a high regard for the ground of the church. But the subtle satanic teaching kills your desire for the meetings, dilutes your absoluteness for the church life, and causes you to disregard the church ground. As this teaching does its damaging work within your being, no longer do you care for the genuine testimony of the church; yet all the while you are convinced that, through the concept you have absorbed, you are on the way to a better church life. This is the most subtle doctrine of all! This subtle wind carries you away from the church life.

This kind of subtle teaching also causes you to lose your appetite for Christ. Through its influence, you are no longer as hungry and thirsty for Christ as you once were. You come to feel that it is religious or legal to love the Lord in an absolute way. All this is evidence that the poisonous essence of this satanic teaching has entered into your being and corrupted it, causing your spiritual senses to become dull. This is the most subtle way for a believer to be carried away from Christ and the genuine church life.

The only way to grow, to be protected, and to be covered is to stay in the proper church life. Do not place so much confidence in your personal sense about any situation. Certain teachings may cause you to feel that the church life is not very good or that it is even unnecessary. Through the years I have learned that we must always be on guard against any thought that the church is poor, wrong, or unnecessary. Such a thought is a clear sign that a wind of teaching is approaching. I do not claim that the church today is perfect. However, I do say that any negative thought about the condition of the church is an indication of the working of a subtle teaching. Such a teaching does not first appear to be threatening. It is usually concealed beneath a pleasant appearance. The color may at first be very appealing, but after this teaching enters into you, its color becomes darker as time goes by.

This is a sign that this teaching is exerting a poisonous influence within you.

I say again that the only way to escape the waves and the winds is to grow. However, we cannot grow up overnight like a mushroom. Rather, we grow gradually little by little and day by day. As we are slowly growing in the Lord, we need to remain under the protective covering of the church. Trust the church, not your individual, subjective feeling. Look to the Lord that He will cause you to place your trust in Him and in the church. This is necessary especially when, according to your feeling, the church is not so good. At the very time you feel the condition of the church is not positive, you should place your trust in the church all the more.

II. WINDS OF TEACHING

A. A Teaching That Differs from God's Economy

In verse 14 Paul does not speak of the wind of heresy, but he speaks of the wind of teaching. Any teaching, even a scriptural one, that distracts believers from Christ and the church is a wind that carries them away from God's central purpose. First Timothy 1:3 and 4 reveal that some in Paul's time were teaching differently. This does not mean that they were teaching heresy; it means that they were teaching something different from God's New Testament economy. Their teaching was not the teaching of the New Testament ministry. In the New Testament there is one ministry. This ministry is the dispensing of the Triune God into the believers for the building up of the churches. We must beware of any teaching or supposed ministry that teaches something different from God's economy, that is, that teaches something other than God's dispensation for the building up of the churches.

As a whole, Christians today have been carried away by various winds of teaching. Every denomination or independent group is under the influence of some kind of doctrinal wind. What Christians today are not being tossed by waves or carried about by winds? We need to ask ourselves whether we are still under the influence of such waves and winds. I can strongly proclaim that I am not tossed by any waves or carried about by any winds, because I care only for Christ and the church. Some have asked me about pray-reading. I have answered that I am not for pray-reading, but that I am for Christ and the church. As a result, I do not make myself different from other Christians. However many Christians have made themselves different from me.

For example, some strongly disagree with immersion and advocate sprinkling. I can say to such a one, "Brother, I don't care for sprinkling, but I certainly care for you. I simply receive you as my brother in the Lord." By receiving him in this way, I am the same as he. But by insisting on sprinkling, he makes himself different from me. Therefore, he, not I, must bear the responsibility for any difference between us.

Before you came into the Lord's recovery, you were probably concerned about certain things besides Christ and the church. You may have cared for a particular doctrine, practice, or work. But in the church life in the Lord's recovery, we care only for Christ and the church. It is crucial that we have the clear vision that the New Testament economy is for nothing other than the dispensing of the Triune God into people for the building up of the Body of Christ. This is our goal and our testimony. It is also God's recovery. If we have this goal always before us, we shall not receive any teaching, concept, or opinion that distracts us from the central lane of God's economy.

B. In the Sleight of Men

In verse 14 Paul speaks of the "sleight of men." The Greek word for sleight signifies the cheating of dice players. The teachings that become winds, carrying believers away from the central lane of Christ and the church, are a deception instigated by Satan in his subtlety and utilizing the sleight of men, in order to frustrate God's eternal purpose to build up the Body of Christ. No matter how good a teaching may appear to be, if it distracts us from Christ and the church, it is something of the sleight of men. The sleight of men is even worse than deceit, for not only is it false, but it also involves an evil plot. Even if a doctrine is scriptural, it may be utilized in such a wicked plot.

C. In Craftiness

In this verse Paul also mentions craftiness. This word indicates that a certain evil skill is involved. Hence, the sleight of men involves both the formulation of a plot and the use of skill to deceive.

D. With a View to a System of Error

Finally, Paul says, "with a view to a system of error." These teachings that divide are organized and systematized by Satan to cause serious error and thus damage the practical oneness of the Body life. The plot is apparently of man, but the system is of Satan. We have seen that God's economy is to dispense the Triune God into us for the building up of the Body of Christ. Satan hates this. Therefore, he uses teachings, concepts, doctrines, and opinions in craftiness as part of an evil plot to carry people away and eventually to lead them into a system of error. How devilish! May the Lord expose the subtlety of the enemy so that we may detect the system of error related to the deceitful teachings that are designed to distract the saints from Christ and the church life.

LIFE-STUDY OF EPHESIANS

MESSAGE FORTY-FIVE

THE GROWTH OF THE MEMBERS
FOR THE BUILDING UP OF THE BODY

In this message we come to 4:15 and 16. Verse 15 says, "But holding to truth in love, we may grow up into Him in all things, Who is the Head, Christ." The fact that Paul begins this verse with the word "but" indicates that the truth in verse 15 is in contrast to the sleight of men, the craftiness, and the system of error in verse 14. Holding to truth in love is in contrast to the sleight of men and error in verse 14. To be carried away by the winds of teaching in the sleight of men unto a system of error is not holding to truth.

I. HOLDING TO TRUTH IN LOVE

There is some disagreement among translators concerning the rendering of the Greek word for "holding to." Some prefer the translation "speaking." Those who advocate this translation regard truth in verse 15 as that which is opposed to a lie. Hence, to them speaking the truth is in contrast to telling lies. I do not say that this understanding is wrong. However, if we consider this verse in its context, we shall see that in its spiritual meaning a great deal more is involved here than merely speaking truth instead of lies.

A. Truth

Truth here means things that are true. According to the context, it refers to Christ and His Body. Both are true things. We should hold to these true things in love so that we may grow up into Christ.

To hold the truth in love is to handle the truth in love. The word truth in verse 15 denotes that which is real. In this universe the real things, the true things, are Christ and the church. Only by speaking concerning Christ with the church do we actually handle the truth. This means that although we may refrain from telling lies, we still may not be speaking the truth. For example, certain reports in the newspapers may not be lies; however, these reports are not the truth, the reality. On the contrary, they are vanity. Anything apart from Christ with the church is a vanity and a falsehood. If I am a person without Christ, my very being is vanity. A person may be extremely wealthy and possess an abundance of material things, but if he does not have Christ, all those riches and material items are nothing but vanity. The book of Ecclesiastes says that all is vanity (1:2). Apart from Christ with the church, nothing is true, nothing is real. To those who love the Lord Jesus and who are for today's church life, the only reality in the universe is Christ with the church. Day by day, we may talk about many things. But if we do not speak concerning Christ and the church, we are handling vanity; we are not handling the truth.

Instead of being carried about by winds of teaching, we should handle the truth and embrace it. Suppose someone comes to you advocating a particular doctrine, such as the doctrine of foot-washing. Although his particular teaching may be true, even this true teaching can distract you from Christ and the proper church life. Thus, even something such as foot-washing may become a falsehood, a vanity. I know of a brother who became distracted and eventually dissenting over this very thing. This indicates that we may talk about scriptural doctrines but still not be handling the truth.

The entire fourth chapter of Ephesians is a chapter of truth. The first item of truth in this chapter is the oneness in two aspects: the oneness of the Spirit and oneness of the faith and of the full knowledge of the Son of God. If you truly desire to handle the truth and to speak the truth, you must care for the oneness of the Spirit and the oneness of the faith and of the full knowledge of the Son of God. Furthermore, you must take care of Christ, who is the center of God's New Testament economy. God's economy today is nothing less than Christ with His Body. However, many Christians care neither for the Head nor for the Body. Instead, they are occupied by secondary teachings. To neglect Christ as the Head and the church as the Body and to speak about secondary matters is not handling the truth. This is not the speaking of the truth; it is the speaking of vanity.

Holding to truth in love means to handle, embrace, and speak Christ with the church. Others may teach differently, emphasizing doctrines or opinions that distract people from Christ and the church. However, we should not speak in such a way. Rather, we should speak those things that bring us into contact with Christ and that build us up as the Body of Christ. To speak in this way is to handle the truth.

According to verse 14, the babes are tossed to and fro by waves and carried about by winds of teaching. No doubt these waves and winds refer to various teachings and practices. Although these teachings may be scriptural or fundamental, they do not minister Christ to people. Their effect is to distract people from Christ and the church. Others may be tossed or carried about by such teachings, but we must hold to the truth in love; that is, we must hold to Christ and the church. This is what we speak, and this is our fellowship. It should even be the focal point of our prayer.

B. Love

In verse 15, Paul says that we should hold to truth in love. This is the love of Christ in us, by which we love Christ and the fellow-members of His Body. The love here is not our love, but the love of God with which He first loved us. Now with the very love with which God has loved us, we love the Lord and one another. It is in such a love that we hold to the truth, that is, to Christ with His Body.

If we speak about things other than Christ and the church, we are not acting in love. We may not only waste time, but also bring in elements that are foreign to the Body. If we truly love others, we shall be exercised to hold the truth and speak concerning Christ and the church. Instead of being influenced by the winds of teaching, we shall hold to Christ and the church in love.

II. GROWING UP

A. Into the Head, Christ

By holding to truth in love we grow up into Christ in all things. To be no longer babes (v. 14) we need to grow up into Christ. This is to have Christ increase in us in all things until we attain to a full-grown man (v. 13). The word Head here in verse 14 indicates that our growth in life with Christ should be the growth of the members in the Body under the Head.

The fact that we grow in Christ by holding to truth in love proves that holding to truth involves more than not telling lies. Do you believe that you can grow in Christ simply by telling the truth instead of lies? This is not what enables us to grow in Christ. There are a good number of unbelievers who are honest and who do not tell lies. Nevertheless, their speaking of the truth does not cause them to grow up in Christ.

To grow up into the Head means that we care only for Christ and the church. We grow by caring only for Christ and the church, that is, by handling truth in love. We do not grow by some kind of honesty or sincerity related to ethical behavior.

In this verse the matter of growth is specifically related to growing up into Christ, the Head, in all things. Verses 13 and 14 both point to the need for growth. If we would be a full-grown man, we need to grow. Likewise, if we would be no longer babes tossed to and fro and carried about, we also need to grow. But we should grow up into Christ, not up into ourselves or into something else apart from Christ.

Paul clearly says that we are to grow up into the One who is the Head. This indicates that our growth must be in the Body. In order to grow into the Head, we must surely be in the Body. Many Christians are apparently growing spiritually; however, their supposed growth is not in the Body. I have known some Christians who have actually become more dissenting as they have had this kind of growth. It seems that the more they grow, the more critical they become. When they have relatively little growth, they are no problem in the church life. But as they grow, they become troublesome. This is an indication that their growth is not growth into the Head. As long as anyone's growth is not into the Head, it is not growth in the Body.

It is of great importance that Paul does not tell us to grow up into the Savior, into the Master, or into the Lord. He says specifically that we are to grow up into the Head. This can take place only in the Body. If you do not remain in the Body, you may have a certain kind of growth, but it will not be the growth into the Head.

B. In All Things

In verse 15 Paul tells us that we must grow up into the Head in all things. In certain aspects you have grown up into the Head, but in other aspects you probably have not. According to my experience, the most difficult matter in which to grow up into Christ, the Head, is in our talking. Psalm 141:3 says, "Set a watch, O Lord, before my mouth; keep the door of my lips." Because it is so hard for us to control our speaking, we should make this our prayer also. Whether you are young or old, a brother or a sister, this is an area in which all of us desperately need to grow up into Christ as the Head.

If we bring to the Lord this matter of growing up into Him in all things, we shall see that there are many small things in which we have not yet grown up into the Head. How much we still need to grow up into Christ! May this need for growth touch our heart and turn us afresh to the Lord.

III. OUT FROM THE HEAD

Verse 16 says, "Out from Whom all the Body, fitted and knit together through every joint of the supply, according to the operation in measure of each one part, causes the growth of the Body unto the building up of itself in love."

Our growth in life is to grow into the Head, Christ, but our function in the Body is to function out from Him. Firstly, we grow up into the Head. Then we have something which is out from the Head.

Verse 16 indicates that growth is not for individuals, but for the Body. Any growth that is not for the Body is not genuine. The words "each one part" refer to every member of the Body. Every member of the Body of Christ has its own measure, and this measure works for the growth of the Body. The Body causes the growth of itself through the supplying joints and working parts. Both the joints of the supply and every single part with its measure are needed for the church to build itself up. The growth of the Body is the increase of Christ in the church. This results in the Body building itself up.

A. Every Joint of the Supply

In this verse Paul speaks of "every joint of the supply." This refers to the specially gifted persons, such as those mentioned in verse 11. The article before the Greek word rendered "supply" is emphatic. It indicates that the supply should be a particular supply, the supply of Christ. As the leading ones, the apostles, prophets, evangelists, and shepherds and teachers have *the* supply, the particular supply. Yes, we all can be today's sent ones. Nevertheless, among the saints there are those who have the particular supply. This supply is not common to all.

Once again we see the twofoldness of the truth in the Scriptures. It is correct to say that all the saints can do the work of the apostles, prophets, evangelists, and shepherds and teachers. However, not all have the particular supply spoken of in this verse. In the Body the leading ones are the joints with the particular supply.

B. Causing the Growth of the Body

If we read verse 16 carefully, we shall see that it says that all the Body causes the growth of the Body. This means that the Body grows by the Body itself. The Body makes the growth of the Body. It is not wrong for churches to invite certain ones to come to minister the Word to them. However, a local church is not built up in this way. A local church must grow by the local church itself. For example, it is the church in Anaheim that makes the growth of the church in Anaheim. Even a very small church must grow by itself. If you cannot cause the church in your locality to grow, then you should not be there as the church. Do not expect that visits from those brothers who share in the ministry of the Word will cause the growth of the church in your locality.

Verse 16 speaks of the growth of the Body unto the building up of itself in love. This indicates that a local church must build itself up in love through every joint of the supply and according to the operation of the measure of each one part. Those with the particular supply are not only in the Body as a whole, but also in the local churches, which are the practical expression of the one Body. Even if the number of saints in a church is very small, perhaps only fifteen, there will still be some with the particular supply. This should be an encouragement to every local church. Through the particular supply of the leading ones and through the operation in each part, the church will cause the growth of itself in love. In this way we shall see the growth of the members for the building up of the Body of Christ.

LIFE-STUDY OF EPHESIANS

MESSAGE FORTY-SIX

LEARNING CHRIST AS THE TRUTH IS IN JESUS

In this message we shall consider 4:17-21, with special attention to verses 20 and 21, which speak of learning Christ as the truth is in Jesus.

I. THE THIRD ITEM
OF A WALK WORTHY OF GOD'S CALLING

In 4:1 Paul beseeches us to walk worthily of the calling with which we are called. The first item of a walk worthy of God's calling is to keep the oneness, and the second is to grow up into Christ the Head. The third item is to learn Christ as the truth is in Jesus.

Verse 17 of chapter four begins a new paragraph. The first two items of a worthy walk are put together in the first paragraph in this chapter. The reason for this is that growth in Christ is intimately related to the keeping of the oneness; they cannot be separated. In verses 1 through 16 the living and the function of the Body are dealt with. Now in verses 17 through 32 the daily life is touched. Verses 17 through 24 give us the principles of our daily walk, and verses 25 through 32 give us the details.

II. NO LONGER WALKING AS THE NATIONS

Verse 17 says, "This therefore I say and testify in the Lord, that you no longer walk as the nations also walk, in the vanity of their mind." This word indicates that what the apostle is about to say is not only his exhortation, but also his testimony. What he exhorts is what he lives. Because he himself lives the kind of life he intends to describe, in his teaching he gives us a testimony.

A. Walking in the Vanity of Their Mind

Paul's exhortation is to "no longer walk as the nations...walk in the vanity of their mind." The nations, the Gentiles, are the fallen people, who have become vain in their reasonings (Rom. 1:21). They walk without God in the vanity of their mind and are controlled and directed by their vain thoughts. Whatever they do according to their fallen mind is vanity; it is all without reality. The life of fallen mankind is a walk in the vanity of the mind. All the worldly people today walk in such vanity. In the eyes of God and in the eyes of the Apostle Paul, whatever the people in the world think, say, and do is nothing but vanity. None of those things is real or solid—everything is empty. As believers, we should no longer walk in the vanity of the mind. Instead, we must walk in the reality of our spirit.

B. Darkened in Their Understanding

According to verse 18, the nations who walk in the vanity of the mind are "darkened in their understanding." When the mind of fallen people is filled with vanity, their understanding is darkened regarding the things of God.

C. Estranged from the Life of God

The nations are also "estranged from the life of God" (v. 18). This life is the uncreated, eternal life of God, which man did not receive at the time of creation. After being created, man with the created human life was placed before the tree of life (Gen. 2:8-9) to receive the uncreated divine life. But man fell into the vanity of his mind and became darkened in his understanding. In such a fallen condition, man is not able to touch the life of God until he has his mind turned to God, until he repents and believes in the Lord Jesus to receive God's eternal life (Acts 11:18; John 3:16).

God's intention in His creation of man was that man would partake of the fruit of the tree of life and thereby receive the eternal life of God. But in the fall, Satan's evil nature was injected into man. As a result, man had to be barred from the tree of life. According to Genesis 3:24, the

Lord "drove out the man: and he placed at the east of the garden of Eden cherubim, and a flaming sword which turned every way, to keep the way of the tree of life." Thus, man was estranged from the life of God. The cherubim, the flame, and the sword signify God's glory, holiness, and righteousness. These three things kept sinful man from receiving eternal life. When the Lord Jesus died on the cross, He fulfilled all the requirements of God's glory, holiness, and righteousness. Therefore, through the redemption of the Lord Jesus, the way has been opened for us to contact the tree of life once more. This is the reason Hebrews 10:19 says that we have "boldness for entering the Holy of Holies by the blood of Jesus." The tree of life is in the Holy of Holies. As believers in Christ, we have been brought back to the tree of life. Now the divine life in the Holy of Holies may be our daily enjoyment. The nations, however, are still estranged from the life of God.

1. Because of the Ignorance Which Is in Them

One reason for this estrangement is "the ignorance which is in them" (v. 18). Ignorance here means not only lack of knowledge, but also not wanting to know. Fallen man does not approve of knowing the things of God (Rom. 1:28) because of the hardness of his heart. Due to this, his understanding is darkened that he cannot know God.

The unbelievers have no knowledge of God or of spiritual things. Furthermore, they are not willing to gain this knowledge. What a mercy that we not only have the proper knowledge, but also have the desire to know! It is a great blessing to have within us the desire to know God, to know life, and to know spiritual things. Before we were saved, we did not have this desire. We, like the nations, lacked both the knowledge and the willingness to know. But now we hunger and thirst to know God. The more we can know of Him and of the divine life, the better it is. Any Christian who does not seek to know the Lord cannot be happy or satisfied. To seek the Lord and to seek to know life and the things of God is a source of great happiness. This is the reason we are so happy in the church meetings. It is also the reason that I have an inward joy when I minister the Word to the Lord's people. Something of the Lord has been sown into us to give us the desire to know Him.

2. Because of the Hardness of Their Heart

Another reason the nations are estranged from the life of God is the hardness of their heart. The hardness of fallen man's heart is the source of the darkness in his understanding and the vanity of his mind. Before we were saved, we also were hard of heart. We seemed to be impenetrable, and God's words could not enter into us. This is the situation of unbelievers today.

D. Having Ceased from Feeling

Furthermore, in his thorough diagnosis of the condition of fallen man, Paul points out that the nations have "ceased from feeling" (v. 19). The word feeling here refers mainly to the consciousness of the conscience. Hence, "having ceased from feeling" means not to care for the conscience. After man's fall, God ordained that man should be under the rule of his conscience. But rather than regard his conscience, fallen man gave himself over to unsatisfied lust. Because the unbelievers refused to care for the feeling of their conscience, eventually the conscience stopped functioning. Therefore, the feeling within them ceased.

E. Having Given Themselves Over to Lewdness

Moreover, they give "themselves over to lewdness to work all uncleanness in greedy unsatisfied lust" (v. 19). They are given over to lusts that cannot be satisfied. If we look at the situation in the world today, we shall see that unbelievers have given themselves over to lewdness to work uncleanness in their unsatisfied lust.

III. LEARNING CHRIST

Verses 17 through 19 are a dark background for what Paul says in verse 20: "But you did not so learn Christ." The New Testament strongly indicates that we should live Christ. In Philippians 1:21 Paul declares, "To me to live is Christ." But here in Ephesians 4:20 we are told that we have learned Christ. Notice that Paul uses the past tense in speaking of our learning Christ. He also uses the past tense in the next verse, which says, "Since indeed you have heard Him and been taught in Him as the truth is in Jesus." This matter of learning Christ as the truth is in Jesus is difficult to comprehend, and we need to consider it very carefully.

Christ is not only life to us, but also an example (John 13:15; 1 Pet. 2:21). We learn from Him (Matt. 11:29) according to His example, not by our natural life, but by Him as our life. According to the New Testament, the Lord Jesus did not come into us as life directly. Rather, after living on earth for thirty years, He ministered for another three and a half years. During the thirty-three and a half years of His life on earth, He set up a pattern, a mold, a model. This is a matter of great significance. One reason the four Gospels were written was to show the pattern of the life that God desires, the mold of the life that can satisfy God and fulfill His purpose. For this reason, the New Testament gives us a unique biography, the biography of the Lord Jesus, written from four directions. After the Lord Jesus set up the pattern revealed in the Gospels, He was crucified on the cross and then He entered into resurrection. It is in resurrection that He comes into us to be our life.

According to the New Testament, to be saved is to be put by God into Christ. First Corinthians 1:30 says, "But of him are ye in Christ Jesus." When God put us into Christ, He put us into the mold. Just as a sister shapes dough into the form of a mold, so God intends to form us into the mold of Christ. Hence, Romans 8:29 indicates that we are to be conformed to the image of Christ, the Firstborn among many brothers. To be conformed is to be molded. The Firstborn is the pattern, and the many brothers of the Firstborn are those who are to be conformed to this pattern. To learn Christ is simply to be molded into the pattern of Christ, that is, to be conformed to the image of Christ.

By means of baptism God has put us into Christ, who is the pattern. To be baptized is to be placed into Christ as the mold. Both Romans 6:3 and Galatians 3:27 speak of being baptized into Christ. To be baptized into Christ is to be buried into Him. The tomb of this baptism is the pattern, the mold. In God's eyes, we were put into this mold when we were baptized. Through being placed into the mold we have put off the old man and have put on the new man. By being buried into Christ, we have been brought out of Adam and the old creation. By baptism we have been put into Christ, who is both our life and our pattern. This explains why Paul uses the past tense in speaking about learning Christ. We learned Christ when we were buried into Him in baptism. This means that to learn Christ is to be put into Christ as the mold. It is to be molded into the pattern set up by Him during His years on earth.

After Christ established the pattern, He was crucified and then He entered into resurrection, becoming in resurrection the life-giving Spirit (1 Cor. 15:45). It is as the Spirit that He comes into us to be our life. We have pointed out that at the time we believed in Christ and were baptized in Him, God put us into Him as the pattern, the mold. Therefore, Paul could tell the Ephesians that they "did...learn Christ." According to the light of the New Testament and according to our experience, to learn Christ is to be placed into Christ by God. On God's side, He has put us into Christ. On our side, we have learned Christ by being put into Him.

After a person is saved, deep within him he desires to live a life in the pattern established by the Lord Jesus. However, many either ignore this desire or cultivate it in a mistaken way, thinking that by self-effort they can succeed in imitating Him. It is a mistake to think that we can imitate Christ by the exercise of our natural life. The believers in Christ should imitate Him, but they should not do so according to their natural life.

The truth in Jesus is the real situation of the life of Jesus as recorded in the four Gospels. In the godless walk of the nations, the fallen people, there is vanity. But in the godly life of Jesus there is truth, reality. Jesus lived a life always doing things in God, with God, and for God. God was in His life, and He was one with God. This is the truth in Jesus. We, the believers, regenerated with Christ as our life and taught in Him, learn from Him as the truth is in Jesus.

We have pointed out that it is a mistake to endeavor to imitate Christ by the efforts of our natural life. We have also seen that when we believed in the Lord Jesus and were saved, God put us into Christ as the mold. This mold is the life of Jesus recorded in the four Gospels, a life absolutely according to truth. Truth is the shining of light, the expression of light. Since God is light (1 John 1:5), truth is the expression of God. Every aspect of the life of Jesus recorded in the Gospels is an expression of God. In everything He said and did, He expressed God. This expression of God is the shining of light; hence, it is the truth. This life of Jesus according to truth is the pattern in which God has placed us. In this pattern we have learned Christ as the truth is in Jesus. This means that we have learned Christ according to the truth shown in the Gospels, that is, according to the life of the Lord Jesus, which was wholly according to God's truth. This life is the shining of light. The shining of the light is truth, and truth is the expression of God. Therefore, in the life of Jesus there is truth. The essence of the pattern set up by the Lord Jesus is truth. This means that the essence of the life of Jesus is truth. We have learned Christ as the truth is in Jesus.

The truth, the reality, in Jesus in verse 21 is in contrast to the vanity of the mind in verse 17. The nations walk in the vanity of their mind, but we believers live a life as the truth is in Jesus. When the Lord Jesus was living on earth, He never walked in vanity. Rather, He always walked in truth, that is, in the shining of the divine light. This means that the Lord Jesus lived and walked in the expression of God. We have learned Christ according to this very truth that is in Jesus.

LIFE-STUDY OF EPHESIANS

HAVING PUT OFF THE OLD MAN
AND HAVING PUT ON THE NEW MAN

In His thirty-three and a half years on earth, the Lord Jesus formed the mold, the pattern, to which all those who believe in Him are to be conformed. According to the record of the four Gospels, the life of the Lord Jesus was a life of truth. Truth is the shining of light. Light is the source, and truth is its expression. As Hebrews 1:3 says, the Lord Jesus is the effulgence of God's glory. This means that He is the shining of God who is light. Because in every aspect of the Lord's living on earth there was the shining of light, His life was a life of truth, a life of the shining of God Himself. That life of truth was the very expression of God. For this reason Paul says that we learn Christ as the truth is in Jesus. In other words, we learn Christ according to the mold of the life of Jesus. The mold of the life of Jesus is the truth.

After Christ established this mold, He passed through death and resurrection, and in resurrection He became the life-giving Spirit. As such a Spirit, He comes into us to be our life. When we believed in Him and were baptized, God put us into Him as the mold, just as dough is placed into a mold. By being put into the mold we learned the mold. This means that by being put into Christ, we learn Christ. On the one hand, God put us into Christ; on the other hand, Christ has come into us to be our life. Now we may live by Him according to the mold in which we have been placed by God.

Not many of us may realize the influence the four Gospels have on us. When we read in the Gospels of the mold formed by the Lord Jesus, that mold spontaneously influences our living. As we love the Lord, contact Him, and pray to Him, we automatically live Him according to the mold described in the Gospels. In this way we are shaped, conformed, to the image of this mold. This is what it means to learn Christ.

Learning Christ in this way is altogether different from taking Him as an objective example and endeavoring in our natural life to imitate Him. God has put us into the mold formed by the life of Jesus on earth. Simultaneously, Christ as the life-giving Spirit has come into our being as life. The more we love Him and contact Him, the more we live Him according to this mold. As a result, we are spontaneously conformed to the image of that mold. Therefore, with Paul we can say, "For to me to live is Christ" (Phil. 1:21). We live Christ in the form of His own life, in the form recorded in the Gospels.

We must distinguish this kind of living from that according to the modernistic teaching regarding imitating Christ as our example. The modernists falsely teach that Christ is not God, but a man who established the highest standard for us to follow. This teaching requires that we exercise our natural life to imitate Christ and to live up to His standard. Such a teaching is heretical. It has absolutely nothing to do with the truth as it is in Jesus. It denies the fact that a true believer is in Christ and has Christ in him. In contrast to this heretical, modernistic teaching, we say according to the New Testament that when a sinner repents and believes in Christ and is baptized into Christ, God puts this one into Christ as the mold. At the same time, Christ as the life-giving Spirit comes into him to be his life. Thereafter, this believer is to live by Christ as his life according to the mold. The more he lives by Christ, the more he will be spontaneously shaped into the form of the mold. This is a life in Christ and also a life of Christ in us. We are in Christ as the mold, and He is in us as our life. In this way we learn Christ as the truth is in Jesus.

Ephesians 4 covers three items concerning a life worthy of God's calling: keeping the oneness (vv. 1-14), growing up into the Head (vv. 15-16), and learning Christ as the truth is in Jesus (vv. 17-32). Concerning the learning of Christ as the truth is in Jesus, Paul firstly exhorts us and testifies to us that we should no longer walk as the Gentiles walk, in the vanity of their mind (v. 17). Instead, we should walk in the life that is according to the truth in Jesus. The Gentiles walk in the vanity of their mind, but we walk in the reality expressed in the life of Jesus recorded in the Gospels. In His life we see reality, truth, the shining of light, the expression of God. As the believers in Christ, we are to walk in such a reality.

Verse 21 says that we have been taught in Christ as the truth is in Jesus. Verses 22 and 24 show us what we have been taught: that we have put off the old man and have put on the new man. We were taught this when we were put into the mold, that is, when we were baptized. In baptism we were taught that our old man has been crucified and that he is to be buried by baptism. Furthermore, we were taught that as we come out of the water, we are resurrected into the new man. Therefore, by baptism we were taught that we have put off the old man and have put on the new man.

At this point we need to consider Romans 6:3-5. Verse 3 says, "Are you ignorant that as many as have been baptized into Christ Jesus have been baptized into His death?" To be baptized into Christ Jesus means to be put into Him. Furthermore, through baptism we have been buried into Christ's death. In verses 4 and 5 we see the mold. These verses indicate that through baptism we were taught that we have put off the old man and have put on the new man. This is the normal Christian experience.

Normally, as we preach the gospel to sinners, we tell them of the life, death, and resurrection of the Lord Jesus. Then we encourage those who are willing to believe in Christ to receive Him into them as their life. The next step is to baptize them. This indicates that we put them into Christ as the mold. Thereafter, they are to live by Christ according to the mold. By baptism they have been taught that they have put off the old man and have put on the new man. By being buried through baptism, they learned Christ as the truth is in Jesus.

We should not try to understand verses such as 4:20-24 through the exercise of our natural mind. Rather, we need to consider them in the light of our Christian experience. If we do this, the light will gradually shine upon us, and we shall see the truth. The truth here is that when we were baptized, we were taught that we have put off the old man and that we have put on the new man. Notice that Paul does not say that we have been taught *to* put off the old man and *to* put on the new man. No, we have already put off the old man and have put on the new man. Our old man was buried in the waters of baptism. Hence, we have put off the old man. Furthermore, as we rose up from the water in resurrection, we were clothed with the new man. Hence, we have also put on the new man. Therefore, we have been taught in Christ as the truth is in Jesus that we have put off the old man and put on the new man.

I. A CONDITION OF LEARNING CHRIST

Having put off the old man and having put on the new man is a condition of learning Christ. This is utterly different from the devilish, modernistic teaching which says that Christ established the highest standard of human living and that we must endeavor to copy Him and to live up to this standard. If we would learn Christ as the truth is in Jesus, we must fulfill the condition of having put off the old man and of having put on the new man. This is not a superficial truth.

II. HAVING PUT OFF THE OLD MAN

A. As Regards Our Former Manner of Life

Verse 22 says that we have put off, as regards the former manner of life, the old man. The former manner of life was a walk in the vanity of the mind. Such a manner of life has been terminated and put away.

B. The Old Man

Verse 22 also says that the old man "is being corrupted according to the lusts of the deceit." The old man is of Adam, created by God, but fallen through sin. The article before the word deceit is emphatic and indicates that the word deceit is personified. Hence, deceit here refers to the deceiver, the Devil, from whom are the lusts of the corrupted old man. The old man is corrupted according to the lusts of the Devil, the deceiving one. Outwardly, the manner of life of the old man is a walk in the vanity of the mind. Inwardly, the old man is corrupted according to the lusts of the Devil, the lusts of the deceit.

This old man was crucified with Christ (Rom. 6:6) and was buried in baptism (Rom. 6:4). Hallelujah, we have put off the old man in baptism!

III. BEING RENEWED

Between the word regarding the putting off of the old man and the putting on of the new man, Paul wedges in the thought of being renewed in the spirit of our mind (v. 23). Based upon the accomplished facts of the putting off of the old man and the putting on of the new man, verse 23 tells us to be renewed in the spirit of our mind. To be renewed is for our transformation to the image of Christ (Rom. 12:2; 2 Cor. 3:18). The spirit here is the regenerated spirit of the believers mingled with the indwelling Spirit of God. Such a mingled spirit spreads into our mind, thus becoming the spirit of our mind. It is in such a spirit that we are renewed for our transformation. In this way our natural mind is conquered, subdued, and put under the spirit. This, of course, implies a process of metabolic transformation. As this process takes place, the mingled spirit enters our mind, takes over our mind, and becomes the spirit of our mind.

By the spirit of the mind we are renewed to fulfill in experience what was accomplished in the putting off of the old man and the putting on of the new man. The putting off of the old man and the putting on of the new man are accomplished facts. Now we must experience and realize these facts by being renewed in the spirit of our mind. As these facts are realized in experience, we live a life that corresponds to the life of Jesus. This means that we live a life of truth, a life in the shining of light and in the expression of God. When we are renewed in the spirit of our mind to execute the fact of having put off the old man and having put on the new man, we live a life according to the truth that is in Jesus.

IV. HAVING PUT ON THE NEW MAN

A. Corporate

The new man is of Christ. It is His Body, created in Him on the cross (2:15-16). It is not individual, but corporate (Col. 3:10-11). The fact that the new man is created of two peoples proves that it is corporate. Furthermore, Colossians 3:10 and 11 reveal that the new man is a composition of many different peoples. In this corporate new man there is no Greek or Jew, no bond or free, no barbarian or Scythian, but Christ is all and in all. In Colossians 3:11 the word "all" refers to people. This means that in the new man Christ is all the people and is in all the people. Therefore, in the corporate new man Christ is all and in all.

The book of Ephesians reveals that the church is the Body of Christ (1:22-23), the kingdom of God, the household of God (2:19), and the temple, the dwelling place of God (2:21-22). It reveals further that the church is the new man. This is the highest aspect of the church. The Greek word for church, *ekklesia,* means those called out for a gathering, hence, an assembly. This is the initial aspect of the church. From this the apostle goes on to the aspects of fellow-citizens of the kingdom of God and members of the household of God. These are higher than the initial aspect, but not as high as the aspect of the church as the Body of Christ. Yet the new man is still higher than the Body of Christ. Thus, the church is not just an assembly of believers, a kingdom of heavenly citizens, a household of God's children, nor even a Body for Christ. It is in its uttermost aspect a new man to accomplish God's eternal purpose. As the Body of Christ, the church needs Christ as its life; whereas as the new man, the church needs Christ as its person. This new corporate person should live a life as Jesus lived on earth, that is, a life of truth, expressing God and causing God to be realized as the reality by man. Hence, the new man is the focus of the apostle's exhortation in this section (vv. 17-32).

B. Created according to God

Verse 24 says that the new man was created according to God. The old man was created according to the image of God outwardly, without God's life and nature (Gen. 1:26-27). But the new man was created according to God Himself inwardly, with God's life and nature (Col. 3:10).

C. In Righteousness and Holiness of the Truth

Furthermore, the new man was created in righteousness and holiness of the truth. Righteousness is being right with God and with man according to God's righteous way, whereas holiness is being separated unto God from anything common and being saturated with God's holy nature. Righteousness refers to the outward acts, whereas holiness refers to the inward nature. Outwardly everything related to the new man is righteous; and inwardly everything related to the new man is holy.

The righteousness and holiness of the new man are of the truth. The article before truth in verse 24 is emphatic. As the deceit in verse 22, related to the old man, is the personification of Satan, so truth here, related to the new man, is the personification of God. This truth was exhibited in the life of Jesus, as mentioned in verse 21. In the life of Jesus righteousness and holiness of truth were always being manifested. It was in the righteousness and holiness of this truth, which is God realized and expressed, that the new man was created.

Deceit is the Devil, and truth is God. The old man is according to the lusts of the Devil, but the new man is in the righteousness and holiness of God. It is a serious mistake to render the Greek word for truth here as an adjective. The King James Version made such a mistake in adopting the rendering "true holiness." Here Paul's concept is not that of true holiness but that of the holiness of the truth. Holiness here is the holiness of the divine Person. The new man was created according to God in the righteousness and holiness of God Himself.

In order that we might learn Christ, Paul presents a sharp contrast between the old man and the new man, between the Devil and God, and between lusts, on the one hand, and righteousness and holiness, on the other. We have been taught that we have already put off the old man and have put on the new man. This means we have put off the lusts and the falsehood of the Devil and have put on the righteousness and holiness of God. This God is the truth, and this truth is seen in the living of Jesus on earth. The human living of Jesus was according to the truth, that is, according to God Himself, full of righteousness and holiness. Praise the Lord that we have learned Christ as the truth is in Jesus!

If we learn Christ by putting off the old man and by putting on the new man, we shall be in the church life, for the new man actually is the church. If we learn Christ as the truth is in Jesus, then we can have a genuine, proper, and practical church life.

LIFE-STUDY OF EPHESIANS

MESSAGE FORTY-EIGHT

A LIVING THAT DOES NOT GRIEVE
THE HOLY SPIRIT OF GOD

In this message we come to 4:25-32. In 4:17-24 Paul gives us the basic principles for the living needed in our daily walk. In verses 22 and 24 we see that the condition for learning Christ is having put off the old man and having put on the new man. Once this condition is met, it is possible for us to live a life of truth, which is the expression of God in the shining of light.

I. A LIVING OF LEARNING CHRIST

In verses 25 through 32 we have a description of the practical daily life in the learning of Christ. In covering the daily life of learning Christ, Paul goes into a lot of detail. He mentions things such as anger, stealing, bitterness, wrath, clamor, evil speaking, malice, tenderheartedness, and forgiveness. Although these details are easy to see, it is more difficult to discern two important matters that Paul's speaking is based upon. These matters are truth and grace. The apostle's exhortation in verses 17 through 32 takes truth and grace as its basic elements (vv. 21, 24, 25, and 29). He wants us to live as Jesus did, a life full of grace and truth (John 1:14, 17). Grace is God given to us for our enjoyment, and truth is God revealed to us as our reality. When we live and speak truth (Eph. 4:21, 24), we express God as our reality, and others receive God as grace for their enjoyment (v. 29).

In the New Testament grace and truth are a pair. John 1:14 says that the Word became flesh and tabernacled among us, full of grace and truth, and verse 17 says that grace and truth came through Jesus Christ.

Just as grace and truth are a pair, so love and light are also a pair. In the Gospel of John we have grace and truth, but in the First Epistle of John we have love and light (4:16; 1:5). Grace is the expression of love, and love is the source of grace. In the same principle, truth is the expression of light, and light is the source of truth. In God's heart there is love. When this love is expressed, it becomes grace. Likewise, with God there is light. When the light shines forth, it becomes truth. When we trace grace and truth back to their source in God, we are in love and light.

We have pointed out that Paul's exhortation in 4:17-32 covers both truth and grace. Truth is clearly mentioned, but grace is somewhat hidden, being especially implied in Paul's mention of the details related to daily living. If we are short of grace, we cannot meet the standard in relation to these details. The principles for our learning of Christ are related to the truth, whereas the details are related to grace. If we would be conformed to the image of Christ, that is, if we would learn Christ, we need both the principles and the details. If we have the truth, we have the principles. If we have grace, we shall succeed in meeting the standard in all the details.

Paul says that we learn Christ as the truth is in Jesus (4:21). The pattern, the mold, set up by the Lord Jesus is the truth. The truth is the principle, the principle is the pattern, and the pattern is a matter of having put off the old man and of having put on the new man. In verses 17 through 24 we have the principle of our renewed daily living for the learning of Christ. This principle is the truth, the living of the Lord Jesus when He was on earth. The Lord's living was that of always putting off His own life and of putting on the Father's life. This is the life of Jesus, and this life is the truth that is the principle of a life of learning Christ. According to this principle, we have put off the old man and have put on the new man.

Every aspect of our daily living should be governed by this principle, not by a standard of ethics. For example, our conversation should be governed not by a standard of ethics, but by the New Testament principle of having put off the old man and of having put on the new man. Even how much we laugh or cry should be determined by the principle of having put off the old man and of having put on the new man. This principle is much higher than any ethical standard.

In baptism we put off the old man and put on the new man, which is the church life. Now our daily living in the church life is to be according to the principle of truth, according to the pattern of the life of truth set up by the living of the Lord Jesus. We have been taught according to this principle as the truth is in Jesus.

The details of our daily living are related to grace. In every aspect of our daily living, we need grace. Grace is God Himself in Christ as our enjoyment. We need to allow this enjoyment to remove from us the negative elements mentioned in verse 31. One of these negative elements is bitterness. Without grace, we cannot let go of our bitterness. But when we have God in Christ as our enjoyment, our bitterness will disappear. When we have sufficient grace, we can say, "I am filled with Christ as my enjoyment. Because I am filled to the brim with grace, there is no room in me for bitterness of any kind."

Only when we are filled with grace will the negative things be removed from us. Take gossip as an example. We enjoy gossiping because we are short of grace. If we are filled with grace, we shall not seek satisfaction in gossiping. On the contrary, we shall be content with the satisfaction that is in Christ. When we are filled with grace and when Christ is everything to us, we have no need to find satisfaction in other things.

Only by grace can we have a life that is according to the divine standard in all the details mentioned by Paul in these verses. If we are filled with grace, then in the place of bitterness, wrath, anger, and clamor, we shall have kindness, patience, mercy, forgiveness, and love. These qualities come not from self-effort, but from Christ as our enjoyment. When Christ is our enjoyment, we have no appetite for bitterness, wrath, anger, or clamor. Instead, we desire to have kindness, patience, endurance, gentleness, mercy, love, and various other virtues and qualities. What a difference it makes in our daily living when we are happy and satisfied through the enjoyment of God in Christ as grace!

II. HAVING PUT OFF THE FALSEHOOD

Let us now consider the details of a living of learning Christ. In verse 25 Paul says, "Wherefore, having put off the falsehood, speak truth each one with his neighbor, for we are members one of another." Falsehood here refers to anything that is false in nature. As we have put off the old man, we have also put off everything false. If we have the enjoyment of Christ, then in a practical way in our daily living we shall put off every false thing. The most honest and faithful people are those who have the full enjoyment of Christ. When we are filled to the brim with Christ, all falsehood will be put away from us.

III. SPEAKING TRUTH EACH ONE WITH HIS NEIGHBOR

Having put off the falsehood, we should speak truth each one with his neighbor. When we are filled with Christ, our speaking will be of things that are true. In our speaking there will be no lies and no vanity.

IV. BEING ANGRY AND NOT SINNING

Verses 26 and 27 say, "Be angry, and do not sin; do not let the sun go down on your indignation, neither give place to the Devil." Anger itself is not sin, but it is dangerously close to sin. We should not continue in anger, but rather relinquish our anger before the sun sets.

According to the four Gospels, the Lord Jesus sometimes was angry. But His anger was always under control. Hence, He could be angry and not sin. It must be the same with us in our daily living. Our anger must be under control. Otherwise, serious damage will result. In order to control our anger, we need much grace. The more we enjoy Christ, the more our anger will be limited and controlled.

A. Not Letting the Sun Go Down
on Our Indignation

In verse 26 Paul tells us not to let the sun go down on our indignation. We should be slow to become angry, but we should be quick to relinquish our anger. According to this verse, we should not keep it past the setting of the sun. We should not let our anger carry over into the next day. According to the Scriptures, we must relinquish our anger before the sun goes down. We all need to practice this. For such a practice, we need God in Christ as grace. If we have the supply of grace, we shall be slow to anger, and we shall not remain angry very long when we do become angry. If we have grace, our anger will not linger.

B. Neither Giving Place to the Devil

Verse 27 says, "Neither give place to the Devil." According to the context, to continue in anger is to give place to the Devil. In nothing should we give any place to him. If we hold on to our anger, we are actually welcoming the Devil. But if we relinquish our anger, we close the door to the Devil and give him no place.

V. LETTING HIM WHO STEALS STEAL NO MORE

Verse 28 continues, "Let him who steals steal no more, but rather let him labor, working with his own hands that which is good, that he may have to share with him who has need." In a book of such high revelation, the apostle still touches things on a practical level, even such low things as anger and stealing. Stealing is due mainly to slothfulness and greed. Hence, the apostle charges him who steals to labor instead of being slothful and to share what he gains with others instead of being greedy.

VI. LETTING NO CORRUPT WORD
PROCEED OUT OF THE MOUTH

Verse 29 says, "Let no corrupt word proceed out of your mouth, but only that which is good for needful building up, that it may give grace to those who hear." The Greek word for corrupt signifies something that is noxious, offensive, or worthless. Our conversation should not corrupt others, but should build them up. The church and every member of the church need the proper building up. This building up is accomplished primarily by our speaking. What proceeds out of our mouth should be that which is good for the building up of the church and all the saints.

Furthermore, the word out of our mouth should give grace to those who hear. Grace is God embodied in Christ as our enjoyment and supply. Our word should convey this as grace to others. The word that builds up others always ministers grace to the hearers. Our word should communicate God in Christ as enjoyment, imparting Christ to others as their life supply.

VII. NOT GRIEVING THE HOLY SPIRIT OF GOD

In verse 30 Paul says, "And do not grieve the Holy Spirit of God, in Whom you were sealed unto the day of redemption." The word "and" at the beginning of this verse indicates that in addition to all the things mentioned in verses 25 through 29, one crucial thing is needed, that is, that we should not grieve the Holy Spirit. To grieve the Holy Spirit is to displease Him. The Holy Spirit abides in us forever (John 14:16-17); He never leaves us. Hence, He is grieved when we do not walk according to Him (Rom. 8:4). If we have a life according to the principle of truth with grace for the details of our daily walk, we shall not grieve the Holy Spirit of God. However, if we do not live this way, the Spirit within us will be grieved.

For the Holy Spirit to be grieved means that He is not happy with us. Often when we feel unhappy, that feeling of unhappiness is actually the feeling of the Holy Spirit. However, when He feels happy within us, we are happy also. A proper life according to truth and in grace will always make the Holy Spirit happy and give us the joy of the Spirit.

In the apostle's exhortation in verses 17 through 32, there are not only grace and truth as the basic elements, but there are also the life of God (v. 18) and the Spirit of God as the basic factors on the positive side and the Devil (v. 27) on the negative side. It is by the life of God in the Spirit of God, with no place given to the Devil, that we can live a life full of grace and truth as the Lord Jesus did.

VIII. LETTING VARIOUS EVILS BE REMOVED FROM US

In verse 31 Paul says, "Let all bitterness and wrath and anger and clamor and evil speaking be removed from you, with all malice." All the evil things mentioned in this verse can be removed from us if we enjoy God in Christ as our grace. For example, there will be no clamor in our daily living, and there will be no evil speaking. No one who lives by the principle of truth and in grace will speak evil of others.

IX. BEING KIND ONE TO ANOTHER

Finally, verse 32 says, "And be kind to one another, tenderhearted, forgiving one another, as also God in Christ forgave you." Only the enjoyment of Christ as our life supply and as our joy can make our hearts tender. If we are tenderhearted, we shall forgive others. In our daily walk, we need both to forgive others and to ask others to forgive us. This is necessary because we are easily offended and we easily offend others. If we have offended someone, we need to ask for forgiveness. But if we have been offended, we need to extend forgiveness to others, even as God in Christ has forgiven us.

In his exhortation in this section, the apostle presents God as the pattern of our daily life. By the life of God, in His Spirit, we can forgive as God forgives. If this is our daily living, we shall not grieve the Holy Spirit of God. To have such a living, we need to live according to truth and by God in Christ as our grace.

LIFE-STUDY OF EPHESIANS

MESSAGE FORTY-NINE

A SUMMARY OF LEARNING CHRIST

In previous messages we have covered the condition of learning Christ and the living of learning Christ. The condition is a matter of having put off the old man and of having put on the new man. The living of learning Christ is a matter of applying the principle of truth and of living according to grace. In this message we shall present a summary of learning Christ. This summary includes truth (4:21, 24, 25) and grace (v. 29) as the basic elements and the life of God (v. 18), the Spirit of God (v. 30), and the Devil (v. 27) as the basic factors.

I. BASIC ELEMENTS

In the foregoing message we pointed out that in the New Testament grace and truth are a pair and that love and light are another pair. These pairs are revealed mainly in the writings of John. His Gospel speaks of grace and truth, and his First Epistle speaks of love and light. The Gospel of John tells how God came to us in the Son so that we may receive Him as grace and realize Him as truth. Then 1 John reveals that after we have received God in the Son, we may come to God the Father to enjoy Him as love and light. Thus in the Gospel of John God comes to us as grace and truth, but in the First Epistle of John we go to God to enter into His love and light in fellowship. This indicates that there is traffic between God and us and between us and God. According to the book of Revelation, the issue, the result, of this divine traffic is the golden lampstands in this age and the New Jerusalem in eternity.

John 1:17 says that the law was given through Moses and that grace and truth came through Jesus Christ. This means that before the coming of Christ grace and truth had not come to God's people. Yes, there were shadows of grace and truth in the Old Testament age, but there was not the reality of grace and truth until Jesus Christ appeared. When Christ came, grace and truth came also.

The Gospel of John reveals how God came to man through incarnation. The Word which was with God and which was God became flesh and tabernacled among us (John 1:1, 14). Verse 14 says that this incarnated One was full of grace and truth. It does not say that He was full of power and authority, majesty and sovereignty, or love and light. Many Christians quote John 1:14 without knowing the meaning of grace and truth. Grace and truth are intimately related to God Himself. Grace is something sweet, and truth is something real. Grace is actually the sweet Person of the Lord Jesus, who is the embodiment of the fullness of God and the effulgence of the divine glory (Col. 2:9; Heb. 1:3). This means that He is the expression of God.

The Gospel of John speaks a great deal about life. John 10:10 says that the Lord came that we may have life and may have it abundantly. The sweet and lovely Person of Jesus is the shining forth of God Himself, His very expression. As such a One, He is life to us. Life is the essence, whereas grace is the enjoyment that comes by tasting life. When we taste the sweetness of life, we experience grace as our enjoyment. Thus, life is the substance, and grace is the enjoyment.

This is confirmed in the writings of Paul. Paul suffered from "a thorn in the flesh" (2 Cor. 12:7). This thorn may have been a physical ailment or defect. Paul prayed to the Lord three times that this thorn might depart from him (2 Cor. 12:8). The Lord answered him by saying, "My grace is sufficient for thee: my power is made perfect in weakness" (2 Cor. 12:9, Gk.). The Lord allowed the thorn to remain so that Paul could have an opportunity to enjoy His grace. In Paul's weakness God's power, His sufficient grace, was made perfect.

Grace is the enjoyment of the Triune God in all that He is to us. When He is life to us, that is grace. When He is power to us, that also is grace. Grace is whatever Christ is to us subjectively as our enjoyment. We need grace daily, even hourly. We need the enjoyment of Christ as our life, our power, and everything to us. Grace is the Triune God becoming our enjoyment. He has come to us so that we may gain Him, experience Him, and enjoy Him. When we experience Him as our enjoyment, He becomes grace to us.

We come now to the matter of truth. Because our mind may be preoccupied with natural concepts of truth, we may find it difficult to understand the meaning of truth according to the New Testament. Many regard truth merely as doctrine. Whenever they see the word truth in the Bible, they automatically interpret it as doctrine. However, in the New Testament, truth does not denote doctrine. If you want proof of this, try substituting doctrine for truth in various verses where truth is mentioned. John 1:14 would then say that the Word became flesh, full of grace and doctrine; John 1:17, that grace and doctrine came through Jesus Christ; and John 14:6, that the Lord is the way, the doctrine, and the life. How ridiculous! It is absurd to say that we have learned Christ as the doctrine is in Jesus. Nevertheless, in the concept of many believers, truth means nothing more than doctrine. Others regard truth as sincerity. According to this understanding, to speak in truth is to speak in sincerity.

If we would know the meaning of truth in the New Testament, we need to lay aside these definitions. Truth is God revealed. How much different this is from saying that truth is doctrine or sincerity! In principle, because grace and truth have come through Jesus Christ, they must be something of God Himself. Jesus is God coming to us. When God comes to us, He does not come as doctrine or sincerity. When He comes, everything related to His being also comes. God comes to us for our enjoyment. This is grace. God also comes to reveal Himself to us. This is truth. In other words, when God is enjoyed by us, He is grace. But when God is revealed to us, He is truth. Truth, therefore, is God revealed to us.

These definitions of grace and truth can be applied to almost every case recorded in the four Gospels, especially to those cases found in the Gospel of John. Let us consider two such cases, one in John 4 and the other in John 8. In both chapters truth is mentioned (4:23-24; 8:32). As the Lord Jesus was going from Judea into Galilee, "He had to pass through Samaria" (John 4:4) in order to meet a certain immoral Samaritan woman, who came to the well to draw water. Wearied from His journey, the Lord sat down by the well and waited for this Samaritan woman to appear. When the Lord Jesus asked her for a drink, she was surprised that a Jew would ask a drink from a Samaritan woman. The Lord replied, "If you knew the gift of God, and Who it is that says to you, Give Me a drink, you would have asked Him, and He would have given you living water" (v. 10). After she questioned Him further, the Lord answered, "Everyone who drinks of this water shall thirst again, but whoever drinks of the water that I shall give him shall by no means thirst forever; but the water that I shall give him shall become in him a spring of water welling up into eternal life" (vv. 13-14). What grace He showed toward her! After the Samaritan woman tasted the grace of God, she came to realize something of who the Lord Jesus was. Thus God was not only enjoyed by her, but also revealed to her. When the Lord Jesus contacted the Samaritan woman, He was the embodiment of grace and truth.

In John 8 the Lord contacted another sinful woman, a woman caught in adultery. Through His contact with her, God became her enjoyment and was also revealed to her. The Lord helped her to receive Him as grace and to know Him as God revealed.

According to the Gospels, all who contacted the Lord Jesus in a positive way received grace and saw truth. The grace they received was God Himself, and the truth they beheld was also God. Therefore, John tells us that of His fullness we have all received grace upon grace (1:16). We have received from Him the riches of what God is. This is God received, experienced, and enjoyed. This is grace. Following this, God is seen and realized by us. This is truth.

When I was young, I was bothered by the fact that John

puts grace before truth. I thought that the revelation of God should precede the enjoyment of God. One day I saw that the Lord Jesus firstly comes to us as grace and then as truth. As I looked back on my experience, I realized that I enjoyed Christ as grace long before I knew Him as truth. Many of us enjoyed Christ as grace before we knew Him as truth. This means that we enjoyed Him without realizing what He is. This indicates that enjoyment comes before realization, that grace comes before truth.

We have pointed out that in the Gospel of John God comes to us, but that in the First Epistle of John we go to God. As we go to God, we enter into the inner chamber to contact the Father through the Son under the cleansing of the blood of Jesus. Here in this inner chamber we experience not grace and truth, but love and light. For this reason, in 1 John we have love instead of grace and light instead of truth. When God comes to us, we receive Him as grace and truth. But when we go to God, we meet Him as love and light. This is deeper and more inward than the experience of grace and truth.

When we have fellowship with the Father in the inner chamber and enjoy Him as love and light, we then have grace and truth for our practical daily living in the world. In our fellowship with the Father we have love and light, but at home or in our place of employment we have grace and truth. Through grace and truth we have the kind of daily living Paul exhorts us to have in Ephesians 4. Although we may be under pressure at work or at home, we can still live according to truth and by the supply of grace. If others are not pleasant toward us, we have the grace to bear it. Then others will see that God is with us. In this way our daily living will be of grace and truth.

The church life is the issue of God coming to us as grace and truth and of our going to God to meet Him as love and light. Out of this traffic come the seven lampstands in the book of Revelation. Ultimately, the issue of this heavenly traffic will be the New Jerusalem as God's eternal testimony. Both the lampstands and the New Jerusalem come out from the traffic between God and us and between us and God. In this traffic God comes to us to be our grace and truth, and we go to God to experience Him as our love and light.

A. Truth

We may apply this now to the book of Ephesians. We have seen that the basic elements in the learning of Christ are truth and grace. In contrast to the Gospel of John, in Ephesians 4 truth precedes grace. Truth is not the supply; it is the shining of light. Hence, truth is the principle, the pattern, the standard. As members of the Body of Christ under the Head, we are learning Christ as the truth is in Jesus.

Before he mentions grace here, Paul presents the principle, the pattern, the standard; that is, he presents the truth. We all have been baptized not into grace, but into the mold, into the pattern, which is the life of truth in Jesus. We have been placed by God through baptism into the pattern, the standard, the principle, set up by the living of the Lord Jesus on earth. This is the truth in Ephesians 4.

B. Grace

In order to live out such a standard, we must have grace. In verse 29 Paul relates grace to our speaking. This indicates that we need grace for the details of our daily life, not just for what we regard as important matters. We may have grace in big matters, but not in small matters. For example, a brother may have grace to minister the Word, but he may lack grace in speaking to his wife. Furthermore, in the prayer meeting we may all have grace, but in our daily conversation we may be devoid of grace. In no area of our daily life do we require grace more than in our conversation. If we have grace in this aspect of our living, we shall have grace in every other aspect.

In all things we need grace to live a life according to the truth that is in Jesus and to be molded into the image of Christ. Grace is our rich supply and enjoyment. If we have this supply and enjoyment, we shall be able to live according to the standard of the principle of truth. For this reason Paul takes truth and grace as the basic elements in his exhortation in chapter four.

II. BASIC FACTORS

A. On the Positive Side

Along with these basic elements, there are also some basic factors. On the positive side, these factors are the life of God (v. 18) and the Spirit of God (v. 30).

1. The Life of God

In contrast to the Gentiles, we are not strangers to the life of God. Instead of being alienated from the life of God, we are attached to the source of life. The life of God has become a fountain within our very being. Hallelujah for the life supply within us!

2. The Spirit of God

We also have the Spirit of God. The Spirit of God is the Person of God. God Himself in the Person of the Spirit dwells within us. We must be careful, therefore, not to grieve Him. Rather, we should obey Him, honor Him, respect Him, and be one with Him at all times.

B. On the Negative Side

The basic factor on the negative side is the Devil. In verse 27 Paul exhorts us not to give place to the Devil. Although we have the life of God and the Spirit of God within us, the enemy is still lurking about us; he is always seeking an opportunity to gain an advantage over us or to damage us. We need to be on the alert for this crouching enemy.

LIFE-STUDY OF EPHESIANS

MESSAGE FIFTY

LIVING IN LOVE AND LIGHT

In this message we come to 5:1-14. This portion of Ephesians covers the matter of living in love and light, the fourth item of a walk worthy of God's calling.

I. AS BELOVED CHILDREN,
BECOMING IMITATORS OF GOD

Verse 1 says, "Become therefore imitators of God, as beloved children." Paul's word here is an imperative, a command. He commands us to become imitators of God. What a glorious fact that since we are His beloved children, we can be imitators of God! As the children of God, we have His life and nature. We imitate God, not by our natural life, but by His divine life. It is by our Father's life that we, His children, can be perfect as He is (Matt. 5:48).

According to the New Testament, the believers in Christ are children of God. As God's children, we have God's life. John 1:13 says that we have been born of God. To be born of God is to have the life of God. Furthermore, 2 Peter 1:4 says that we are partakers of the divine nature. Because we have the divine life and the divine nature, we can be imitators of God. Imitating God in this way is much different from training a monkey to imitate a man. A monkey does not have human life or human nature. But we have the divine life and the divine nature. Therefore, we can be imitators of God.

II. WALKING IN LOVE

In verse 2 Paul issues another commandment: "Walk in love." As grace and truth are the basic elements in 4:17-32, so love (5:2, 25) and light (5:8, 9, 13) are the basic elements in the apostle's exhortation in 5:1-33. Grace is the expression of love, and love is the source of grace. Truth is the revelation of light, and light is the origin of truth. God is love and light (1 John 4:8; 1:5). When God is expressed and revealed in the Lord Jesus, His love becomes grace and His light becomes truth. After we have, in the Lord Jesus, received God as grace and realized Him as truth, we come to Him and enjoy His love and light. Love and light are deeper than grace and truth. Hence, the apostle firstly takes grace and truth as the basic elements for exhortation and then love and light. This implies that he wants our daily life to grow deeper, from the outward elements to the inward.

Love is the substance of God within, whereas light is the element of God expressed. It is possible to sense the love of God inwardly, and it is possible to see the light of God shining out. Our walk in love should be constituted of both the loving substance and the shining element of God. This should be the inner source of our walk. It is deeper than grace and truth.

Paul commands us to walk in love, even as Christ also loved us and "gave Himself up for us, an offering and a sacrifice to God for a sweet-smelling savor" (5:2). In 4:32 the apostle presents God as the pattern for our daily walk. Here he sets forth Christ as the example for our living. There it is God in Christ as our pattern since, in that section, God's grace and truth expressed in the life of Jesus are taken as the basic elements. According to 4:32, we are to forgive others as God in Christ has forgiven us. This means that God is the pattern of forgiveness. But in chapter five Christ Himself is our example since, in this section, love expressed by Christ to us (vv. 2, 25) and light shined by Christ upon us (v. 14) are taken as the basic elements. Here Christ, who loved us and gave Himself up for us, is the example of walking in love.

Paul says that Christ "gave Himself up for us, an offering and a sacrifice to God for a sweet-smelling savor." In the Bible there is a difference between an offering and a sacrifice. An offering is for fellowship with God, whereas a sacrifice is for redemption from sin. Christ gave Himself up for us both as an offering to have fellowship with God and as a sacrifice to redeem us from sin.

In loving us Christ gave Himself up for us. It was for us, but it was a sweet-smelling savor to God. In following His example, our walk in love should not only be something for others, but also a sweet-smelling savor to God.

III. THINGS NOT FITTING FOR SAINTS

In verses 3 and 4 Paul lists certain things not fitting for saints: "But fornication and all uncleanness or unbridled greedy lust, let it not even be named among you, as is fitting for saints; and filthiness and foolish talking or coarse jesting, which are not becoming, but rather giving of thanks." Nothing is more damaging to mankind than fornication. Unbridled greedy lust is a lust full of greed and uncontrolled. Such evil things should not even be named among us, as is fitting for saints, for persons separated unto God and saturated with God, living a life according to God's holy nature.

Instead of foolish talking or coarse jesting, there should be the giving of thanks. To give thanks to God is to speak God as truth, whereas foolish talking or coarse jesting is to speak the Devil as falsehood.

IV. NO INHERITANCE IN THE KINGDOM
OF CHRIST AND OF GOD

Verse 5 says, "For this you know, knowing that every fornicator or unclean person or person of unbridled greedy lust, who is an idolater, has no inheritance in the kingdom of Christ and of God." The Greek word rendered know is *oida* and signifies subjective knowledge, whereas the Greek word rendered knowing is *ginosko* and signifies objective knowledge. What Paul speaks in verse 5 we are to know both subjectively and objectively. We must realize that no fornicator or unclean person or person of unbridled greedy lust has any inheritance in the kingdom of Christ and of God. In the eyes of God, a person of unbridled greedy lust is actually an idolater, one who worships idols.

In this verse Paul speaks of the kingdom of Christ and of God. The kingdom of Christ is the millennium (Rev. 20:4, 6; Matt. 16:28); it is also the kingdom of God (Matt. 13:41, 43). The believers have been regenerated into the kingdom of God (John 3:5) and are, in the church life, living in the kingdom of God today (Rom. 14:17). Not all believers will participate in the millennium; only the overcoming ones will. The unclean, defeated ones will have no inheritance in the kingdom of Christ and of God in the coming age.

According to John 3, all those who are regenerated are in the kingdom of God. Romans 14:17 also indicates that in the church life we are in the kingdom of God today. However, the millennium will be the kingdom in a way that is more practical than what we are experiencing in the church today. Only in the millennium does the kingdom of Christ also become the kingdom of God. Therefore, the term the kingdom of Christ and of God refers not to the kingdom today in the church life, but to the manifestation of the kingdom in the coming millennium. Today all believers are in the kingdom of God, but not all of them will have an inheritance in the coming millennial kingdom. Both the defeated ones and the overcoming ones may be in the church as the kingdom of God. But only the overcoming ones will inherit the kingdom during the millennium. The fornicators, the unclean persons, and those of unbridled greedy lust will have no share in the reign of Christ in the millennium.

V. THE WRATH OF GOD
COMING UPON THE SONS OF DISOBEDIENCE

Verse 6 continues, "Let no one deceive you with vain words, for because of these things the wrath of God is coming upon the sons of disobedience." The wrath of God will come upon the sons of disobedience mainly because of the three evil things spoken of in verse 3. The sons of disobedience are the unbelievers. We, the believers, are beloved children of God. Nevertheless, some of God's children behave as if they were sons of disobedience. Therefore, the wrath of God will come upon them. For this reason, in verse 7 Paul tells us, "Do not become partakers together with them." We should be good imitators of God and not be partakers of any unclean thing.

VI. WALKING AS CHILDREN OF LIGHT

In verse 8 Paul says, "For you were once darkness, but now light in the Lord; walk as children of light." We were once not only dark, but darkness itself. Now we are not only the children of light, but light itself (Matt. 5:14). As light is God, so darkness is the Devil. We were darkness because we were one with the Devil. Now we are light because we are one with God in the Lord.

In this verse Paul exhorts us to "walk as children of light." As God is light, so we, the children of God, are also the children of light. Because we are now light in the Lord, we should walk as children of light.

In verse 2 Paul tells us to walk in love, and in verse 8 he tells us to walk as children of light. The first seven verses of this chapter cover the matter of love. If we walk in love, we shall keep ourselves from uncleanness. To walk in love is to walk in intimacy with God. An intimate relationship between a daughter and mother may illustrate what it means to walk in love. Certain young women enjoy an intimate love with their mothers. They love whatever their mothers love. Because of the love they have for their mothers, they are not willing to do anything opposed to their mothers' feeling. Rather, they walk in intimate love toward their mothers. In the same principle, we have an intimate relationship with the Father. As those who have received grace, we may come in the Son to contact the Father. In the Father's presence we not only enjoy grace, the expression of love, but we also enjoy love itself. We experience this love in a very intimate way. Because we enjoy the love of God in such an intimate way, we do not want to do anything that displeases the Father. The Father hates fornication, uncleanness, and lust. If we walk in love, we shall stay away from such things. Because we love the Father, we shall not do anything to grieve His heart. What a tender, delicate walk this is! This is not simply living by grace; it is walking in love. We should always remember that we are children of God enjoying His love. We are saints separated unto Him and saturated with Him. Therefore, in our daily walk we would always take care of the Father's feeling, for we live intimately in His tender love.

The difference between love and grace can be illustrated by the relationship between a mother and her child. Sometimes a child may want something from the mother. However, at other times the child simply wants to enjoy the mother's loving embrace. Receiving something from the mother which expresses the mother's love is grace. But resting in the loving embrace of the mother is an illustration of love. In the same principle, we have received grace, the expression of the Father's love. But as we go to the Father in fellowship, we enter into His love, which is the source of grace.

It is rather difficult to point out the difference between truth and light. In our experience we may often realize God as truth to us, as our reality. But sometimes when we get into God's presence, we sense that we are in the light. At such times, we are not only experiencing reality, but we are in the very light itself. Thus, the experience of light is deeper than the experience of truth.

We should not simply be according to truth and by grace, but in love and under light. Walking in love and in light is deeper and more tender than living according to truth and by grace.

After commanding us to walk as children of light, Paul inserts in verse 9 a parenthetical statement regarding the fruit of the light, saying that "the fruit of the light is in all goodness and righteousness and truth." Goodness is the nature of the fruit of the light; righteousness is the way or the procedure to produce the fruit of the light; and the truth is the reality, the real expression of the fruit of the light. This expression is God Himself. The fruit of the light must be good in nature, righteous in procedure, and real in expression so that God may be expressed as the reality of our daily walk.

It is significant that in speaking of the fruit of the light Paul mentions only three things: goodness, righteousness, and truth. He does not speak of holiness, kindness, or humility. The reason he mentions just three things is that the fruit of the light in goodness, righteousness, and truth is related to the Triune God. Goodness refers to the nature of the fruit of light. The Lord Jesus once indicated that the only One who is good is God Himself (Matt. 19:17). Hence, goodness here denotes God the Father. God the Father as goodness is the nature of the fruit of the light.

Notice that here Paul speaks not of the work of the light nor of the conduct of the light, but of the fruit of the light. Fruit is a matter of life with its nature. The nature of the fruit of the light is God the Father.

We have pointed out that the righteousness denotes the way or the procedure of the fruit of the light. Righteousness is the procedure by which the fruit of the light is produced. In the Godhead, the Son, Christ, is our righteousness. He came to earth to produce certain things according to God's procedure, which is always righteous. Righteousness is God's way, God's procedure. Christ came to accomplish God's purpose according to His righteous procedure. Therefore, the second aspect of the fruit of the light refers to God the Son.

The truth is the expression of the fruit of the light. This fruit must be real; that is, it must be the expression of God, the shining of the hidden light. No doubt, this truth refers to the Spirit of reality, the third of the Triune God. Therefore, the Father as the goodness, the Son as the righteousness, and the Spirit as the truth, the reality, are all related to the fruit of the light.

Verse 9 is the definition of walking as children of light. If we walk as the children of light, we shall bear the fruit described in verse 9. The fruit we bear by walking as the children of the light must be in goodness, in righteousness, and in truth. The proof that we are walking as children of light is seen in the bearing of such fruit.

VII. PROVING WHAT IS WELL-PLEASING TO THE LORD

Verse 10 says, "Proving what is well-pleasing to the Lord." This phrase is related to verse 8. We should not walk foolishly or blindly or ignorantly. Rather, we should walk as children of light, proving what is well-pleasing to the Lord.

VIII. NOT PARTICIPATING
IN THE UNFRUITFUL WORKS OF DARKNESS

In verse 11 Paul says, "And do not participate in the unfruitful works of darkness, but rather even expose them." The unfruitful works of darkness are vanity, whereas the fruit of the light is truth, reality. Just as Paul commands us to walk as children of light, he also commands us not to participate in the unfruitful works of darkness.

IX. EXPOSING THE WORKS OF DARKNESS

In verse 11 Paul commands us to expose the unfruitful works of darkness. In verse 13 he says, "But all things which are exposed are made manifest by the light; for everything that makes manifest is light." The Greek word rendered exposed may also be rendered reprove or rebuke.

It is a very difficult matter to expose or rebuke someone. Most people reject a rebuke and feel enmity toward the one who rebukes them. There is an element in the fallen human nature that rejects rebuking, reproving, or exposing. Therefore, if possible, we should not expose or rebuke anyone. However, there are times when rebuking is necessary. At such times, the one who does the rebuking must be sure that he himself is very clean. He is like a surgeon who must cleanse himself of all germs before performing surgery. If you have not been purified, you are not qualified to operate on someone by rebuking or exposing him, for the germs in you will cause the other to be contaminated. The reason most rebukes are not successful is that those who give the rebuke are not pure. Therefore, immediately after the "surgery" infection sets in. Before we can reprove or expose someone, we must be purified, or even sterilized. We must be clean in our thought, motive, feeling, and intention. We must be pure in our heart and in our spirit. This is one aspect of the matter of reproving.

Another aspect concerns the one who receives the reproof or the rebuke. If you are being rebuked by someone, you should not try to discern whether or not the one rebuking you is pure. Simply receive the rebuke, the exposure. If you do this, you will be blessed. You will be aroused from sleep, and Christ will shine on you. Every rebuke, whether pure or impure, clean or unclean, is the shining of Christ. Whenever we are rebuked, we should say, "Lord, I worship You for Your shining. This rebuke is Your shining, and I receive it." To receive a rebuke is to walk in light. This means that if we are not willing to accept a rebuke, we are walking in darkness. If we are truly walking in the light, we shall be able to profit from any kind of rebuking.

X. AWAKE AND ARISE

In verse 14 Paul says, "Wherefore He says, Awake, sleeper, and arise from among the dead, and Christ shall shine on you." The sleeping one who needs the exposing mentioned in verses 11 and 13 is also a dead one. He needs to awake from sleep and arise from death. When we expose or reprove anyone who is sleeping and in the darkness of death, Christ will shine on him. Our exposing or reproving in light is Christ's shining.

LIFE-STUDY OF EPHESIANS

MESSAGE FIFTY-ONE

LIVING BY BEING FILLED IN SPIRIT

In this message we shall consider the matter of living by being filled in spirit. This is covered by Paul in 5:15-21.

I. THE FIFTH ITEM
OF THE WALK WORTHY OF GOD'S CALLING

To live by being filled in spirit is the fifth item of a walk worthy of God's calling. The first four aspects of such a worthy walk are the keeping of the oneness, the growing up into the Head, the learning of Christ, and the living in love and light. In chapter four Paul speaks of keeping the oneness, of growing up into the Head, and of learning Christ. In chapter five he speaks of living in love and in light and of living by being filled in spirit. Thus, in chapter five there are three crucial words: love, light, and spirit. Love and light are covered in the first fourteen verses. The next section of this chapter deals with the mingled spirit.

To be filled in spirit (v. 18) is to be filled in our regenerated spirit, the human spirit indwelt by the Spirit of God. Our spirit should not be empty, but should be filled with the riches of Christ unto all the fullness of God (3:19). All the items in 5:18—6:9 are related to the one matter of being filled in spirit. Many readers of this chapter pay attention to such details as wives submitting to their own husbands or husbands loving their wives, but they fail to see the source of all these virtues, that is, being filled in spirit. When we are filled in our spirit with Christ unto all the fullness of God, then wives will be subject to their husbands, husbands will love their wives, parents will care for their children, slaves will obey their masters, and masters will treat their slaves in a proper way. All of these things are the issue of being filled in spirit.

Those from a Pentecostal or charismatic background may regard the spirit in verse 18 as the Holy Spirit. They may interpret Paul's word to mean that we should be filled with the Holy Spirit and speak in tongues. But according to the Greek text, Paul here is not saying that we should be filled with the Spirit, but that we should be filled in our spirit, that is, in our regenerated spirit. Our spirit may be empty and flat, like a flat tire. If our spirit is flat, it needs to be filled with *pneuma*. We need to go to the heavenly "filling station" and get our spirit filled with *pneuma*. In this way we shall be filled in spirit. According to chapter three, we are to be filled with the riches of Christ unto all the fullness of God. If our spirit is filled with the riches of Christ, we shall have no problems in our Christian life.

We have pointed out that living by being filled in spirit is the fifth aspect of a walk worthy of God's calling. The first aspect is the keeping of the oneness. This is for the Body life, the church life. The second aspect is the growing up into Christ the Head in all things. This is for the building. Following this, we learn Christ by being placed into the mold, the standard of a living according to the truth in Jesus. We Christians have a high standard with an uplifted principle to govern our daily walk. To learn Christ is to take Him as the standard and to take His life as the principle. Fourthly, a life worthy of God's calling is a life in love and in light. We must live not only according to truth and by grace, but also in light and in love. We need to be those who live in intimacy with God and walk in His presence. Our daily life must be altogether according to God's heart and in His presence. If we have these four aspects of a worthy walk, we shall spontaneously be filled in our spirit.

These five items are arranged in a marvelous sequence. Firstly we keep the oneness, and then we grow in Christ. After this, we learn Christ and live in love and in light. Then we are spontaneously filled in our spirit with the riches of Christ unto all the fullness of God. Out of this inner filling will come submission, love, obedience, care, and all the other attributes of a proper Christian life, church life, family life, and community life. Therefore, the fifth aspect of a walk worthy of God's calling is the issue of the first four aspects; that is, it is the issue of keeping the oneness, growing in Christ, learning Christ, and living in love and in light. What a life we have when we demonstrate these five aspects of a worthy walk! If we are filled inwardly unto the fullness of God, there will be no problems at home, in the church, or in the community. This is the crucial point in this message.

II. WALKING NOT AS UNWISE, BUT AS WISE

Verse 15 says, "Look therefore carefully how you walk, not as unwise, but as wise." The word "therefore" in this verse indicates that verse 15 is a conclusion drawn from verses 1 through 14. If we walk in love and in light, then we shall walk, not as unwise, but as wise. The unwise are the nations, the Gentiles, in chapter four, whereas the wise are the beloved children of God.

III. REDEEMING THE TIME

Verse 16 is related to the walk presented in verse 15. In verse 16 Paul says, "Redeeming the time, because the days are evil." To redeem the time is to seize every available opportunity. This is to be wise in our walk.

We must redeem the time because the days are evil. In this evil age (Gal. 1:4, Gk.), every day is an evil day, full of pernicious things which destroy, injure, and spoil our time. Therefore, we must walk wisely that we may redeem the time, seizing every available opportunity. If we do not seize every opportunity, our time will be wasted. Many evil things will come in to distract us and frustrate us. We may be distracted by telephone calls, letters, or visitors. We may be enjoying the presence of the Lord and suddenly be attacked through a negative telephone call. Because the days are evil, we must be on the alert to take advantage of every opportunity.

IV. NOT BEING FOOLISH,
BUT UNDERSTANDING THE WILL OF THE LORD

Verse 17 continues, "Therefore do not be foolish, but understand what the will of the Lord is." To understand the will of the Lord is the best way to redeem our time. Not knowing the will of the Lord is the main cause of our time being wasted.

V. NOT DRUNKEN WITH WINE,
BUT FILLED IN SPIRIT

In verse 18 Paul says, "And do not be drunk with wine, in which is dissipation, but be filled in spirit." To be drunk with wine is to be filled in the body, whereas to be filled in our regenerated spirit is to be filled with Christ (1:23) unto the fullness of God (3:19). To be drunk with wine in the body causes us to be dissipated, but to be filled with Christ unto the fullness of God causes us to overflow with Him in speaking, singing, psalming, giving thanks to God, and subjecting ourselves one to another. Day by day we need to be filled in our spirit with the riches of Christ.

A. Speaking, Singing, and Psalming

Verses 19 through 21 are related to "be filled in spirit" in verse 18. Psalms, hymns, and spiritual songs are not only for singing and psalming, but also for speaking to one another. Such speaking, singing, and psalming are not only the outflow of being filled in spirit, but also the way to be filled in spirit. Psalms are long poems, hymns are shorter ones, and spiritual songs are the shortest. All are needed in order for us to be filled with the Lord and to overflow with Him in our Christian life.

According to the New Testament, psalms, hymns, and spiritual songs are good not only for singing, but also for speaking. Sometimes we are inspired by singing. But on other occasions, speaking that is filled with *pneuma* may be more inspiring than singing. If we are flat, short of *pneuma,* then our speaking will afford no inspiration. But if we are full of *pneuma,* then our speaking will have impact and will inspire others. This is not eloquence; it is utterance with impact.

In 1967 I visited the church in Jakarta, Indonesia. In one of the meetings I suggested to the saints that we not only sing the hymns, but speak the hymns as well, according to Ephesians 5:19. Immediately we practiced this in the meeting. This speaking was marvelous, filled with the Holy Spirit.

Sometimes we need to practice this in the meetings, without making it a legality. Before we sing a hymn, we may speak it to one another. The brothers may speak the first line and the sisters may respond by speaking the second. However, in doing this we should not fall into an unwritten form. I must admit that some of our meetings are not as living as they should be. Hence, we need to experience the indwelling Spirit in a living way in our singing and speaking.

Verse 19 also speaks of psalming. Singing may be short. Psalming is always long. Sometimes just by singing we cannot express what is within us to praise the Lord; we need psalming to pour out our praise to the Lord adequately.

B. Giving Thanks

Verse 20 goes on to say, "Giving thanks at all times for all things in the name of our Lord Jesus Christ to God and the Father." We should give thanks to God the Father, not only at good times, but at all times, and not only for good things, but for all things. Even at the worst times, we should give thanks for all things to God our Father.

This verse tells us to give thanks in the name of our Lord Jesus Christ. The reality of the name of the Lord is His Person. To be in His name is to be in His Person, in the Lord Himself. This implies that we should be one with the Lord in giving thanks to God.

C. Subject to One Another
in the Fear of Christ

In verse 21 Paul speaks of being "subject to one another in the fear of Christ." Being subject to one another is also the way to be filled in spirit with the Lord and also the overflow of being filled. Our subjection should be one to another, not only the younger ones to the older ones, but also the older ones to the younger ones (1 Pet. 5:5).

According to the context of the following verses, to be in the fear of Christ is to fear offending Him as the Head. This is related to Christ's headship (v. 23) and involves our subjection one to another. Christ is the Head of the Body. If we mistreat any member of the Body, we offend the Head of the Body. We need to keep the relationship with the members of the Body in the fear of the Head.

The life of speaking, singing, psalming, and thanking is a life of subjection. When we speak, sing, psalm, and give thanks in the name of the Lord Jesus Christ, we are willing to submit ourselves to one another. We all submit to Christ the Head and also to the Body. But this submitting comes from the speaking, the singing, the psalming, and the giving of thanks, which in turn come from the infilling. When we are filled in our spirit, we sing, we psalm, we speak, and we thank. Spontaneously, we also submit. However, if we are not filled, there will be no speaking, singing, psalming, or thanking God, and consequently there will be no submitting. The proper church people are those who are submissive by speaking, singing, psalming, and giving thanks to God from their inner being. They live in the way of being filled in spirit with all the riches of Christ unto the fullness of God.

LIFE-STUDY OF EPHESIANS

MESSAGE FIFTY-TWO

LIVING IN THE RELATIONSHIP
BETWEEN WIFE AND HUSBAND

In this message we come to 5:22-33, where we see the proper living in the relationship between wife and husband.

I. AN ASPECT OF THE LIVING FILLED IN SPIRIT UNTO ALL THE FULLNESS OF GOD

In 4:1-24 Paul gives us the principle of a life worthy of God's calling. This principle is a matter of having put off the old man and of having put on the new man. From 4:25 through 6:9 Paul presents the details of a proper living. If we would fulfill all these detailed requirements, we need to live according to the truth and by grace. Furthermore, we must live in love and in light, and we must be filled in our spirit. As we have pointed out, being filled in spirit is an aspect of the life worthy of God's calling.

The relationship between wives and husbands is connected to the matter of being filled in spirit. It is an aspect of the daily living of those who are filled in spirit unto all the fullness of God. Therefore, when we speak about the relationship between wives and husbands, we should not neglect the infilling. Only by being filled in our spirit can we have a proper married life.

II. WIVES

Verse 22 says, "Wives, be subject to your own husbands as to the Lord." This is one of the kinds of subjection implied in verse 21. In the exhortations concerning married life, the apostle deals first with the wives, since the wives, like Eve in Genesis 3, more easily get out of line than the husbands.

In the same principle, Paul deals with children before parents, and slaves before masters. Regarding the relationship between children and parents, most of the problems are caused by the children, not by the parents. The children are disobedient to their parents, but, in actual practice, the parents are obedient to their children. The same is true of the relationship between wives and husbands. Husbands, in your married life, do you obey your wife more than she obeys you, or does she obey you more? Most husbands would have to answer that they obey their wives more than their wives obey them. You may think that it is not right for husbands to obey their wives or for parents to obey their children. Although this may seem backwards according to doctrine, it is true according to practice. If husbands do not know how to obey their wives, they will not have a peaceful married life. Any husband who does not obey his wife does not know how to sympathize with her and to love her. In order for a husband to love his wife, he must sympathize with her and even obey her. Only obedience can beget obedience. Only obedience can pay the price to produce obedience in others. If a husband never obeys his wife, it will be very difficult for his wife to obey him.

First Peter 3:7 says that wives are weaker vessels. This is the reason Paul speaks to wives first here in Ephesians 5. In his exhortations concerning wives and husbands, children and parents, and slaves and masters, Paul takes care firstly of the weaker side and then of the stronger side. Those on the stronger side should not place demands on those on the weaker side. If a husband realizes that his wife is the weaker vessel, he will not be demanding of her.

What we have said thus far does not deny the obvious fact in 5:22 that wives are to be subject to their husbands. Because we all are familiar with this exhortation, there is no need for us to say anything to strengthen it or to intensify it.

A. Subject to Their Own Husbands

In verse 22 Paul exhorts wives to be subject to their own husbands. Most wives appreciate and respect others' husbands. Hence, the apostle exhorts the wives to be subject to their *own* husbands, no matter what kind of husbands they are.

Paul's word about wives submitting to their own husbands indicates that there is the tendency for wives to compare their husbands with the husbands of others. Husbands may do the same thing regarding their wives. If we are short of grace and do not live in the light of God, we may make such comparisons. This is the subtlety of Satan to damage married life. During your engagement, you may have thought that the one you were planning to marry was the best. But after you married him, you may have begun to compare him with others. Therefore, Paul exhorted the wives to submit to their own husbands and not to make comparisons.

In the same principle, when Paul addresses the husbands, he exhorts them to love their own wives (vv. 28, 33). This indicates that they should not compare their wives with the wives of others. We must hate such comparisons. They originate with the enemy, Satan, and can lead to separation or even divorce. If we desire to live a life worthy of God's calling, a life according to truth, by grace, and in love and light, we must not compare our wife or husband with others. Rather, wives should submit to their own husbands, and husbands should love their own wives.

B. As to the Lord

According to Paul's word in verse 22, wives are to be subject to their own husbands "as to the Lord." The wives need to realize that in the eyes of the Lord the husband represents the Lord. The reason the wife must submit to her own husband is that in married life he is as the Lord. I doubt that many married sisters regard their husbands as the Lord. The situation regarding married life today is deplorable, filled with disobedience and rebellion. Nevertheless, as

Christ is the Head of the church and the Savior of the Body, wives must be subject to their husbands as to the Lord. Sarah, the wife of Abraham, was a good example of this. According to 1 Peter 3:6, "Sarah obeyed Abraham, calling him lord."

C. Taking the Husband as the Head

Wives must also take their husbands as the head. Verse 23 says, "For a husband is head of the wife as also Christ is head of the church, being Himself the Savior of the Body." As head of the wife, a husband typifies Christ as the Head of the church. In addition to being the Savior of the Body, Christ is also the Head of the church. The Savior is a matter of love, whereas the Head is a matter of authority. We love Christ as our Savior, but we must also be subject to Him as our Head. It ought to be the same in the relationship between wives and husbands.

D. In Everything

In verse 24 Paul goes on to say, "But as the church is subject to Christ, so also the wives to their husbands in everything." The thought here is this: although husbands are not the savior of their wives as Christ is of the church, the wives still need to be subject to their husbands as the church is to Christ. According to divine ordination, the subjection of the wives to their husbands should be absolute, without any choice. This does not mean that they should obey their husbands in everything. To obey is different from being subject. In sinful things, things against God, the wives should not obey their husbands. However, they should still be in subjection to them.

E. Fearing the Husband

In verse 33 Paul says that the wife should see that "she fear her husband." Because the wife should respect her husband as the head, the one who typifies Christ as the Head of the church, she should fear her husband in the fear of Christ (v. 21). As the head of the wife, the husband is the representative of the Lord. For this reason, the wife should fear the husband.

III. HUSBANDS

A. Loving Their Wives

Paul exhorts the husbands to love their wives. The opposite of subjection is ruling. However, the apostle does not exhort the husbands to rule over the wives, but to love them. In married life, the wife's obligation is subjection and the husband's, love. The wife's subjection plus the husband's love constitutes proper married life and typifies the normal church life, in which the church is subject to Christ and Christ loves the church.

B. As Christ Loved the Church
and Gave Himself Up for Her

Verse 25 says, "Husbands, love your wives even as Christ also loved the church and gave Himself up for her." A husband's love for his wife must be like Christ's love for the church. This means that a husband ought to give himself up for his wife.

The requirement for the husband is much heavier than that for the wife. Submitting to someone is not as difficult as giving yourself up for someone. To give yourself up is to be a martyr, to sacrifice your life. Husbands are to love their wives at such a cost to themselves. They must be willing to pay a great price, even to die for their wives.

C. As Their Own Bodies

Verse 28 says, "So the husbands ought also to love their own wives as their own bodies. He who loves his own wife loves himself." In this verse Paul twice speaks of husbands loving their own wives. As we have pointed out, this indicates that a husband is to love his wife without comparing her to others.

In this verse Paul exhorts the husbands to love their own wives as their own bodies. Everyone loves his body. A husband should regard his wife as part of his body and care for her as his own body.

1. Nourishing

Verse 29 goes on to say, "For no one ever hated his own flesh, but nourishes and cherishes it, even as Christ also the church." We show love for our body by nourishing and cherishing it. To nourish is to feed. Concerning physical nourishment, it is the wife who nourishes the husband. It is a somewhat abnormal situation for the husband to do the cooking for the wife. But spiritually speaking, husbands are to nourish their wives. Just as we eat for the sake of our body, so husbands need to take in something of the Lord for the sake of their wives. In doing this a husband regards his wife as part of his body. A husband needs to nourish his wife, to take care of her need, just as he takes care of the need of his body. This is the meaning of nourish in verse 29.

To take in something to meet the wife's need reveals a deep love. I have known some husbands who were skillful in cooking. They even cooked for their wives. Eventually I learned that they were cooking only for their own enjoyment, but they neglected the real need of their wives. To nourish your wife does not mean to serve food to her. It means that you take in something of the Lord to care for her need. In this way you nourish her just as you nourish your own body. This is real love.

2. Cherishing

Husbands should also love their wives as their own bodies by cherishing their wives. To cherish is to nurture with tender love and foster with tender care. This is the way Christ cares for the church as His Body. To cherish something is to care for it deeply and tenderly. It is to soften it through tender warmth. For example, a mother bird softens baby birds with the warmth of her body as she holds them under her wings. Under her embrace, the little birds are warmed tenderly. The heat from the loving embrace of the mother's body softens and warms the cold little birds.

Sometimes wives are like cold birds. They may not argue with their husbands or even be angry with them, but they may become cold. They may use coldness as a weapon to subdue their husbands. At such times, a husband should tenderly warm and soften his wife, just as a mother bird warms her baby birds by embracing them. This is cherishing. A brother who by grace and in love cherishes his wife in this way will surely be a good husband.

The warmth conveyed through such cherishing does not burn others; it soothes them tenderly and even melts their hearts. This is exactly what the Lord does to us in the church. Although we love the Lord, sometimes in our experience we become "cold birds." We may not rebel against the Lord, but we may become cold. At these times, the Lord embraces us, spreading His wings over us in order to warm us up. By the warmth of His embrace He softens the "cold birds" and melts our hard hearts. This is the Lord's tender love for His Body.

D. Leaving Father and Mother and Being Joined to the Wife as One Flesh

Verse 31 says, "For this cause a man shall leave his father and mother and shall be joined to his wife, and the two shall be one flesh." Christ and the church being one spirit (1 Cor. 6:17), as typified by the husband and wife being one flesh, are the great mystery.

For a proper married life, a man must leave his father and mother and be joined to his wife as one flesh. A man and a woman get married for the sake of their own married life, not for the sake of their parents' family life. Neither the parents of the wife nor those of the husband should interfere with the marriage. It is absolutely against the biblical principle for a married couple to live either with the husband's parents or with the wife's parents. Such an arrangement spoils married life. According to biblical principle, a man should leave his father and mother and be one with his wife. This principle, of course, also applies to the wife. I know of some young women who became engaged with the condition that after marriage the couple would live with the wife's parents. This is wrong. Only when the husband and the wife both leave their parents can they have a proper married life. This is the teaching of the Word of God.

E. Loving Their Own Wives as Themselves

Finally, in verse 28 Paul says that the husband ought to love his own wife as his own body. He also says, "He who loves his own wife loves himself." The same point is stressed again in verse 33. This indicates the depth of the love a husband must have for his wife.

LIFE-STUDY OF EPHESIANS

MESSAGE FIFTY-THREE

A MYSTERIOUS TYPE
OF CHRIST AND THE CHURCH

In his exhortation in chapter five, the apostle presents the church as the Bride of Christ. This aspect of the church reveals that the church comes out of Christ as Eve came out of Adam (Gen. 2:21-22), that she has the same life and nature as Christ, and that she, as His counterpart, becomes one with Him as Eve became one flesh with Adam (Gen. 2:24). The church as the new man is a matter of grace and truth, whereas the church as the Bride of Christ is a matter of love and light. The apostle's exhortation in chapter four is focused on the new man with grace and truth as its basic elements, but his exhortation in chapter five is focused on the Bride of Christ with love and light as its basic substances. In grace and truth we should live as the new man, and in love and light we should conduct ourselves as the Bride of Christ.

Many Christians know that husband and wife are a type of Christ and the church. However, most know this type only in a superficial way. Their knowledge of this mysterious type does not touch their being or affect their living. We need to get into the depths of this type in order that our being and our life may be changed by it.

A COMPLETE PICTURE OF CHRIST AND THE CHURCH

The first couple in the Bible, Adam and Eve, present a significant and complete picture of Christ and the church. According to the book of Genesis, God did not create man and woman at the same time and in the same way. Firstly, God formed man's body from the dust of the ground. Then He breathed into his nostrils the breath of life, and man became a living soul (Gen. 2:7). After God created man, He said, "It is not good that the man should be alone; I will make him a help meet for him" (Gen. 2:18). The animals and the fowl were brought to Adam, and Adam named them. But for Adam "there was not found a help meet for him" (Gen. 2:20). Within Adam there was the desire to have a counterpart, to have someone to match him. Among the cattle, the beasts, and the fowl, there was no counterpart to Adam. In order to produce such a counterpart, "the Lord God caused a deep sleep to fall upon Adam" (Gen. 2:21). While Adam slept, the Lord took one of Adam's ribs and used it for the building of a woman (Gen. 2:22, Heb.). In life, nature, and form the woman was the same as the man. Therefore, when God brought the woman to Adam, Adam exclaimed, "This time it is bone of my bones, and flesh of my flesh" (Gen. 2:23, Heb.). Adam knew that at last he had found his counterpart.

Genesis 2:24 indicates that a man and his wife are one flesh. We should regard a husband and wife not as two separate persons, but as one complete person, as two halves of a whole unit. A husband and a wife as a complete unit are a marvelous picture of Christ and the church as one entity.

Because there was no counterpart for Christ in the created universe, God caused Christ to die on the cross. As He slept there, His side was opened, and blood and water came forth (John 19:34). Because in Genesis 2 the problem of sin had not come in, that chapter mentions only the rib that was taken out of Adam; it says nothing about blood. But John 19 speaks of blood, which solves the problem of sin. The water signifies the flowing life of Christ, the eternal life, which produces the church. This life is also typified by the rib. According to John 19, not one of the Lord's bones was broken when He was on the cross. This was a fulfillment of the Scripture which said, "Not a bone of him shall be broken" (Psa. 34:20). The unbroken bone of Christ signifies Christ's unbreakable eternal life. Hence, Adam's rib typifies the unbreakable eternal life of Christ. It is with this eternal life that the church is built up as the Bride, the counterpart prepared for Christ. In this building up of the Bride, Christ gains the church as a match for Himself.

We have pointed out that Eve had the same life and nature that Adam had. This signifies that the church has the same life and nature that Christ has. Furthermore, just as Eve had virtually the same image as Adam, so the church bears the same image as Christ. Moreover, in stature Eve was very nearly the same as Adam. This indicates that the church has the same stature as Christ.

A COMPLETE UNIT

Together Adam and Eve made a complete unit. In the same principle, Christ and the church make a complete unit. The church is Christ's other half. Adam and Eve became one flesh, but Christ and the church are one spirit (1 Cor. 6:17). We can say to the Lord, "Lord Jesus, without the church, You are just a half. You are not complete. Likewise, without You, we are not complete either." Praise the Lord that when Christ and the church are joined as one, they make a complete unit!

In the church there is no place for our natural life and fallen human nature. The human life and nature are not adequate to match Christ. In order to be His counterpart, we need to be one with Christ in life and in nature. This means that Christ and the church as one unit have the same life and nature. Furthermore, Christ and the church have the same image and stature. We should not merely know this as a doctrine, but see it as a heavenly vision. We need to see why we must receive Christ as our life and partake of His divine nature and, furthermore, be transformed into His image from glory to glory. We also need to see that we must attain to the measure of the stature of the fullness of Christ because we are to be Christ's counterpart. If we see this vision, we shall be able to understand the type of Christ and the church in chapter five of Ephesians.

CHRIST NOURISHING THE CHURCH

At this point we need to go on to consider how Christ

nourishes and cherishes the church. When we are nourished, something enters into our being to meet our need. Nourishment, therefore, must come out of a supply. Without a supply, it is impossible to have nourishment.

Christ nourishes the church with all the riches of the Father. Christ is the embodiment of the fullness of the Godhead. Hence, all the riches of God are in Him, and He enjoys these riches. Then He nourishes the church with the very riches of the Godhead that He Himself has enjoyed.

This is proved by John 15. In this chapter the Lord Jesus says that He is the vine and that the Father is the husbandman. The Father is the cultivator, the planter, the farmer. We, the believers in Christ, are the branches. The vine nourishes the branches with what the vine absorbs from the soil. God the Father is the soil, the water, and everything to Christ as the vine. The vine absorbs the riches from the soil and the water, digests them, and then transmits them to the branches. This is the nourishing. Christ nourishes the church with the riches of the Father which He has absorbed and assimilated. By nourishing the church, Christ meets the inward need of the church.

It is correct to say that Christ nourishes the church with His life and with His word. But neither life nor His word is the source. The source is the Father. What Christ receives of the Father becomes the life and the life supply which are embodied in the Word. For this reason, the Word is the word of life, even the bread of life or the supply of life. If we would be nourished by Christ today, we need to abide in Him to absorb His content into our being as life and the life supply. In order to experience this in a practical way, we daily need to contact the living Word, for the Word is the embodiment of life and of the life supply. The more we abide in the Lord and contact the Word, the more we experience His nourishing. This is the way Christ nourishes the church.

All the members of the church need to practice abiding in the Lord. There should be no insulation, no separation, between us and the Lord and no detachment from Him. As soon as we are detached from Him, the supply of nourishment is cut off. Along with abiding in the Lord constantly, we must daily come to the Word and take it in as our life and life supply. Then we shall receive nourishment. Furthermore, all the meetings of the church should be meetings of nourishment. Morning watch and our fellowship with the saints should also be times of nourishment.

As we are nourished by the life and the life supply, we grow and we are purified. In the following message we shall see that the nourishing word is also the washing word, the cleansing word. The water we drink cleanses the fibers of our inner being. As we abide in the Lord to receive the riches of the Father and as we contact the Word to receive the life and the life supply, we are nourished by Christ. In this way Christ nourishes the church He loves.

CHRIST CHERISHING THE CHURCH

According to the New Testament, Christ's care of the church has two aspects. The inner aspect is the nourishing, and the outer aspect is the cherishing. To be nourished is to have something imparted into us inwardly, whereas to be cherished is to be warmed and comforted outwardly. Cherishing is related to environment. In our environment or circumstances the Lord Jesus is often real to us as a warm, tender breeze blowing upon us. As this warm breeze comes upon us, we have the sense of being soothed tenderly. Although this takes place in the environment, it is something more than the environment itself. It is even something that surpasses the Lord's presence. When the Lord's presence becomes a gentle breeze, we experience His cherishing. This cherishing includes soothing, comfort, and rest.

In the environment of the church life, we often experience the Lord's cherishing, although we may not even be conscious of it. However, if for any length of time we are in an environment where there is no church, we sense that the climate has changed and that the environment is different. Then we begin to sense that we have lost something, that the tender, warm breeze is no longer blowing upon us. We may have everything necessary for our material existence, but we know that something we formerly enjoyed is missing. When we return to the church life, we immediately and spontaneously enter into the environment and atmosphere of the Lord's cherishing. Once again we are warmed, soothed, and comforted. This is cherishing.

Just as a child is cherished by the very presence of his mother, so we are cherished by the Lord's presence. My little granddaughter often desires simply to be intimately in her mother's presence. Simply to be in the presence of her mother is a comfort to her. The presence of her mother provides a tender, warm atmosphere. In like manner, the Lord's presence produces an atmosphere of tenderness and warmth to cherish our very being.

We experience such an atmosphere in the church meetings. I am saddened whenever there are saints who do not care for the meetings, but prefer simply to have fellowship in their homes. No matter how enjoyable the fellowship may be in your home, the atmosphere there is not nearly as cherishing as the atmosphere in the meetings. How pleasant is the spiritual climate in the gathering of the saints! As soon as we enter this atmosphere, we are cherished by the Lord's presence. It is by the atmosphere produced by the Lord's brooding presence that the Lord cherishes the church. To be in this climate, this atmosphere, this environment, gives us rest, comfort, healing, cleansing, and encouragement. No atmosphere can compare to the atmosphere of the church meetings. For this reason I do not want to miss even one meeting of the church.

Nourishing and cherishing go together. Through the nourishing we enjoy the supply of life inwardly, and through the cherishing we experience the soothing, comforting atmosphere outwardly. Whenever we are in an atmosphere of cherishing, we can absorb every word of the ministry. This indicates that under the cherishing we receive nourishing. A church that is nourished and cherished in such a way will be strong and healthy.

The nourishing and the cherishing are the church's portion, and they should be found in every meeting. If there is no nourishing and cherishing in the meetings, then there is a problem. The problem, however, may be with you and not with the church. If you are proper, normal, and healthy, you will enjoy the cherishing atmosphere of the Lord's presence in the church and in this atmosphere receive the nourishing supply of life. Praise the Lord for the way He cares for the church! The church people have the privilege of enjoying the Lord in such a fine, tender, intimate, real way.

CHRIST'S INCREASE

As Eve was Adam's wife, so the church is Christ's Bride (John 3:29; Rev. 19:7; 21:2, 9). Furthermore, Eve was Adam's increase, and the church is Christ's increase (John 3:30). When John the Baptist was told of the many who were coming to Christ, John said, "He who has the bride is the bridegroom" (John 3:29). Then he went on to say, "He must increase, but I must decrease" (v. 30). The increase in verse 30 is the Bride in verse 29. For the Lord to increase means that He must have the Bride. All the following must go to Him. All those who believe in Him should follow Him to be His increase. Although John spoke a clear word regarding this, he was not willing to practice it. This was the reason that God allowed him to be imprisoned and later beheaded. Eventually, John the Baptist received nothing, and all the increase, the Bride, went to the Bridegroom to be His increase. Just as Eve was Adam's increase, so the church as the Bride of Christ is Christ's increase.

THE MARRIED LIFE AND THE CHURCH LIFE

If we are impressed with the various aspects of the mysterious type of Christ and the church unveiled in this chapter of Ephesians, we shall have not only a proper church life, but also a proper married life. The wives will know what their responsibility is, and the husbands will know their responsibility. Paul's burden here was to cover both married life and the church life at the same time. In his writing he did not separate married life from the church life. Rather, he blended the two together, for he knew that married life is actually part of the church life. Without the married life being proper, it is difficult to have a proper church life. We thank the Lord that through the proper church life our married life also can become proper. How wonderful! This is a mysterious type of Christ and the church.

LIFE-STUDY OF EPHESIANS

MESSAGE FIFTY-FOUR

CHRIST SANCTIFYING THE CHURCH
BY CLEANSING HER

In the foregoing message we pointed out that the church has the same life and nature as Christ. This is revealed in the type of Adam and Eve. If the church did not have the life and nature of Christ, the church could not be Christ's counterpart and could never be a match for Christ. If two halves of a unit did not have the same life and nature, they could not make a complete whole. Christ and the church as one entity share the same life and the same nature.

We have also pointed out that Christ nourishes and cherishes the church. He supplies the church and cares for the church in order that the church may grow. Although the church has received Christ's own life and nature, there is still need for supply and for care so that there may be growth. Growth is implied in the formation of Eve, who is a type of the church. God created Adam as a full-grown man. Hence, with Adam, there was no need for growth. However, Eve was built from a rib taken out of Adam's side. This building implies growth. Firstly, Eve received the life and nature of Adam. Then she grew into a woman by being built into a woman. The reference to nourishing and cherishing in Ephesians 5 indicates the need for growth. Nourishing and cherishing are not related to the initial impartation of life. They are related to supplying and caring for the life that has already come into existence so that this life may grow to its full measure.

Consider the vine tree as an illustration. The vine firstly receives nourishment from the soil and the water. The nourishing element is absorbed into the vine to supply life to meet the inward need of the vine. As the vine is nourished, it is simultaneously cherished by its environment, mainly by the fresh air and the sunshine. The wind and the sun regulate the atmosphere to promote the growth of the vine. If the weather is too cold, the sun warms the vine. If the temperature is too high, the wind cools the vine. This outward regulation of the environment is what we mean by cherishing, as distinguished from the inward supply of life, the nourishing. Today Christ is nourishing the church from within and also cherishing the church from without. He supplies us with life, and He regulates the atmosphere so that we may grow properly.

In this message we shall consider a third aspect concerning Christ and the church—the aspect of sanctifying by cleansing. Christ sanctifies the church by cleansing her (5:25-27). The purpose of Christ in giving Himself to the church is to sanctify her, not only separating her to Himself from anything common, but also saturating her with Himself that she may be His counterpart. This is accomplished by cleansing her with the washing of the water in the Word.

I. CHRIST LOVING THE CHURCH
AND GIVING HIMSELF UP FOR HER

Verses 25 through 27 are actually one long sentence. In these verses Paul is saying that husbands should love their wives as Christ loved the church and gave Himself up for her. He did this that He might sanctify her, cleansing her by the washing of water in the Word, in order that He might present the church to Himself glorious, without spot, wrinkle, or any such things. Christ's purpose in loving the church and in giving Himself up for the church was to sanctify her by the washing of the water in the Word. Sanctifying is by cleansing, cleansing is by washing, washing is by water, and water is in the Word.

Christ is sanctifying the church so that He might present the church to Himself. In the past, Christ gave Himself up for the church; in the present, He is sanctifying the church; and in the future, He will present the church to Himself as

His counterpart for His satisfaction. Therefore, loving is for sanctifying, and sanctifying is for presenting.

The first point in these three verses is that Christ loved the church and gave Himself up for her. The second point is the sanctifying in verse 26, and the third is the presenting in verse 27. The first point is for the second, and the second is for the third.

Christ's loving the church and giving Himself up for her was for redemption and for the impartation of life. According to John 19:34, blood and water came out of the Lord's pierced side. The blood was for redemption, and the water was for the impartation of life so that the church might come into existence. In Ephesians 5:25 we have the church coming into existence through Christ's loving her and giving Himself up for her.

After the church has come into existence, the church needs the sanctifying. The process of sanctification includes saturation, transformation, growth, and building up. Although sanctification includes separation, the main aspect of sanctification is saturation. The church needs to be saturated with all that Christ is. Saturation is accompanied by transformation, growth, and building. Through such a process of sanctification with all these aspects, the church becomes complete and perfect, the reality of what is typified by Eve in Genesis 2.

After Eve had been prepared for Adam by being built out of Adam's rib, she was presented to Adam, the source from which she came. In like manner, the church will be presented to Christ, who is her source. This presentation will be done not by God, but by Christ Himself. Verse 27 says that Christ will present the church to Himself glorious. Hence, He will be both the presenter and the receiver.

Without separation, saturation, transformation, growth, and building, the church cannot be perfected and grow into the measure of the stature of the fullness of Christ. Only through an all-inclusive process of sanctification can the church become complete and attain to the measure of the stature of Christ's fullness so that Christ can present a perfect church to Himself.

In these verses we have three stages of the production of the church. Firstly, the church is brought into existence. Secondly, the church is sanctified and thereby perfected and completed. Finally, the church is presented to Christ as a glorious church without spot, wrinkle, or any such thing. It is presented to Him holy and without blemish. We are presently in the second stage of the production of the church, the stage of sanctification. When this stage is complete, we shall be presented to Christ as a glorious church.

II. CHRIST SANCTIFYING THE CHURCH

A. Separated and Saturated

In this message we need to dwell on the matter of the all-inclusive sanctification of the church. In the church meetings we are nourished inwardly and cherished outwardly. We are also sanctified. Not many of us have been separated unto the Lord simply through our private time with the Lord. On the contrary, most of us have been separated from the world unto God through the help we have received in the church meetings. We need to be nourished and cherished in order to be separated from the world. As we are separated, we are also saturated. It is the nourishment that brings in the saturation. Furthermore, the more we are cherished by the atmosphere in the meetings, the more we are willing to give up the things of the world. By the cherishing we simply lose our taste for those things, for we realize that they are the very things which cause us to be cold toward the Lord. The cherishing also helps us to be saturated with Christ. This saturation spontaneously produces transformation. You may not be conscious of how much you have been transformed, but others are aware of it. They can see the change in your life and in your living.

Transformation does not come through teaching or correction or through chastisement. It comes through the nourishing and the cherishing. If you faithfully come to the meetings to be nourished and cherished, spontaneously you will be separated from the world and saturated with the riches of Christ. Then with you there will be growth, transformation, and building. This is the way the Bride will be prepared for Christ. Eventually, the Bride will be complete, perfect, and grown to the measure of the stature of the fullness of Christ. Then the Lord Jesus will come and present this prepared Bride to Himself.

B. The Washing of the Water in the Word

Now we must see the way the Lord sanctifies us. In verse 26 Paul says that Christ sanctifies the church by cleansing her through the washing of the water in the Word. According to the divine concept, water here refers to the flowing life of God typified by flowing water (Exo. 17:6; 1 Cor. 10:4; John 7:38-39; Rev. 21:6; 22:1, 17). The washing of such water is different from the washing of the redeeming blood of Christ. The redeeming blood washes away our sins (1 John 1:7; Rev. 7:14), whereas the water of life washes away the blemishes of the natural life of our old man, such as "spot or wrinkle or any such things" (v. 27). In sanctifying the church, the Lord firstly washes away our sins with His blood (Heb. 13:12) and then washes away our natural blemishes with His life. We are now in such a washing process in order that the church may be holy and without blemish.

With Eve in Genesis 2 there was no need of cleansing because in that chapter she had not fallen. Rather, she was pure and without mixture. But because we are fallen, contaminated, and defiled, we today need to be cleansed. Many things in us must be purged away: the flesh, the self, the old man, the natural life. Furthermore, we have many spots and wrinkles from which we need to be cleansed.

If we had the nourishing and the cherishing without the cleansing, our problems would remain with us. The Lord's nourishing and cherishing always issue in His cleansing. In the process of spiritual metabolism brought about by the cleansing, the "germs" in our being are killed and the negative things are discharged. Through the nourishing and the cherishing with the cleansing, we become healthy and strong. In the meetings the cleansing takes place within us unconsciously. The more we are nourished and cherished in the meetings of the church, the more we are cleansed metabolically.

It is the nourishment that we receive that makes the cleansing possible. If the nourishment ceases, the cleansing will cease also. But if we continually take in the spiritual supply, the elements we absorb into our being will cleanse us inwardly and carry away the old, dead, and unclean things. This metabolic process is taking place day by day in the church life.

The cleansing is the sanctifying. The cleansing by the washing of the water of life is in the Word. This indicates that in the Word there is the water of life, which is typified by the laver between the altar and the tabernacle (Exo. 38:8; 40:7). In Greek the word rendered washing in verse 26 means laver. This Greek word is used in the Septuagint to translate the Hebrew word for laver. In the Old Testament, the priests wash themselves from earthly defilement in the laver (Exo. 30:18-21). Now the washing of the water washes us from defilement. Therefore, we are cleansed by the laver of the water in the Word.

In a very real sense, the Word of God is a laver. According to the Old Testament, the priests who served God in the tabernacle had to have their sins dealt with by the blood on the altar, and they had to have their defilement dealt with by washing in the laver. I believe that Paul's concept here is that the church is cleansed by the laver of the water in the Word. Hallelujah, we have the real laver! The priests had only a type, a material laver made of brass. But we have the real laver, the laver in the Word of God.

As the priests in the Old Testament came firstly to the altar and then to the laver, so we come firstly to the cross to be saved, redeemed, and justified, and then we come to the Word to be cleansed. Day by day, morning and evening, we need to come to the Bible and be cleansed by the laver of water in the Word. By coming to the Word in this way, we are cleansed from the defilement we have accumulated in our contact with the world. Whenever you contact the world in the course of your human living, you need to come to the Word to be cleansed.

In the laver of the Word there is water. This is not the water that quenches our thirst; rather, it is the water that washes us. Here Paul is concerned not about thirst, but about the removal of negative things. These things are washed away by the water in the Word.

One day Brother Nee was speaking about Bible reading. A certain sister told him that she had a poor memory and forgot everything she read in the Word. She asked Brother Nee what was the purpose for her to go on reading the Bible. In his answer, Brother Nee spoke of the way women in China wash rice in a willow basket. They dip the basket in and out of the water a number of times. Every time they take the basket out of the water, all the water flows out of the basket. Nevertheless, although the basket retains no water, both the basket and the rice are washed. He then applied this illustration to the reading of the Word. Although we may not retain anything of what we read, we are washed by it nonetheless, and we are cleansed. Let us be encouraged to come to the Word again and again to be washed. Let us place our basket in the water of the Word and draw it out. The water may flow through the basket, but we shall be cleansed.

C. Dealing with Spots and Wrinkles

The washing in verse 26 does not deal mainly with sins, but deals with spots and wrinkles. Spots are something out of the natural life, and wrinkles are signs of oldness. Only the water of life can metabolically wash away such defects by the transformation of life. All the spots and wrinkles in the church will be washed away through the inner cleansing of the water in the Word. The more we come to the Word, the more we are nourished. The nourishment we receive brings about an inner cleansing from the defects caused by the natural life and from the wrinkles caused by oldness. We all need such an organic, metabolic washing to take away our defects and the marks of our oldness. As the church is washed organically and metabolically in this way, the church is renewed and without blemish.

Such a washing takes place entirely by life and by the nourishment of life. Let us be encouraged to abide in Christ as the source of nourishment and to contact the Word to receive the nourishing element so that we may be washed organically and metabolically from all defects and oldness. By means of such a washing, the church will be perfected and become glorious.

III. CHRIST PRESENTING THE CHURCH TO HIMSELF

A. A Glorious Church

It is such a glorious church that Christ will present to Himself at His coming back. Glory is God expressed. Hence, to be glorious is to be God's expression. Eventually, the church presented to Christ will be a God-expressing one. Such a church will also be holy and without blemish. To be holy is to be saturated and transformed with Christ, and to be without blemish is to be spotless and without wrinkle, with nothing of the natural life of our old man.

The church that comes out of Christ will go back to Christ just as Eve came out of Adam and went back to Adam. As Eve became one flesh with Adam, so the church which goes back to Christ will be one spirit with Christ.

The church presented to Christ will be glorious; it will be the expression, the manifestation, of God. For the church to become glorious means that the church becomes God's expression. Because the nourishing, the cherishing, and the sanctifying will cause the church to be saturated with the essence of God, the church will eventually become the Bride to express God. Every local church today must be God's expression. The only way for us to become His expression is to be continually saturated with the divine essence. If we would experience this saturation, we need Christ's nourishing, cherishing, and sanctifying.

B. Holy and without Blemish

We have pointed out that the glorious church, the church

that expresses God, will be holy and without blemish. To be holy is to be separated to the Lord from common things and then saturated and permeated with the divine nature, with all that God is. The church that has become holy in this way will also be without blemish. Blemish here is like a defect in a precious stone. This defect comes from mixture within the stone. If we would be pure, we must be without mixture; that is, we must not have anything other than God in our being. One day, the church will be like this. It will be not only clean and pure, but also without blemish, without mixture. The church will be the expression of God Himself mingled with a resurrected, uplifted, and transformed humanity. This is the glorious church, the church that is holy and without blemish. In the future such a glorious church will be presented by Christ to Himself. Today, however, the church is undergoing the process of Christ's nourishing, cherishing, and sanctifying.

LIFE-STUDY OF EPHESIANS

MESSAGE FIFTY-FIVE

CHRIST IN THREE STAGES

Ephesians 5:25-27 presents Christ to us in three stages. Verse 25 says that Christ loved the church and gave Himself up for her. Here we see Christ in the stage of the flesh. Verse 26 speaks of Christ sanctifying the church, cleansing her by the washing of the water in the Word. In this verse we have Christ in the stage of the life-giving Spirit. Finally, a third stage of Christ is revealed in verse 27, which speaks of Christ presenting the church to Himself in His coming back. Hence, in this stage Christ will be the Bridegroom receiving His Bride. The first of these three stages was in the past, the second is in the present, and the third will be in the future. In the first stage Christ was the Redeemer; in the second, He is the life-giving Spirit; and in the third, He will be the Bridegroom.

In this message we need to consider certain points found in these verses. However, I wish to point out that our concern is not doctrinal. In the Lord's recovery there is no need for us to pay very much attention to doctrine. The important matter is that we see what a Christ we have and come to experience and enjoy Him more and more.

THE GOD-MAN

Although Christ is God, He is not God only. If He were simply God, He could not be our Christ. To be the Christ to us, He had to be incarnated. Through incarnation, Christ became a man with flesh, blood, and bones. How wonderful that God put on human nature! Our God is not merely God. In Christ He has become a God-man.

It was in the flesh that the Lord gave Himself up for us. If He had not given Himself up as a man in the flesh, there would have been no way for us to gain Him. We are not spirits; we are flesh. Angels are spirits. God has no intention for us to become spirits like angels. God's concern is not with angels, but with men of flesh. Nothing is more pleasing to God than a man of flesh. At times we regret that we are fleshly. However, if we see ourselves from God's point of view, we shall realize that there is a positive aspect of the flesh. According to Hebrews 2, Christ did not take on the nature of angels, but He did take on blood and flesh. Furthermore, John 1 says that the Word which was God and was with God became flesh (v. 14). Great is the mystery of godliness—God was manifest in the flesh (1 Tim. 3:16). God cannot be manifest in angels; He can be manifest only in the flesh. The portion of the angels is to behold the manifestation of God in the flesh.

The Word became flesh and God was manifested in the flesh. Yes, we must condemn the sinful flesh. But there is also a positive aspect of the flesh. We are not spirits as angels are—we are flesh! Our Christ did not become an angelic spirit; He became flesh. The Christ who gave Himself up for us was God incarnate.

If Christ had not put on human nature, it would be impossible for us to receive Him into us. The very Christ we take as our person is the God-man. It is impossible for us to take in God directly. Only after God has become the God-man can we take Him into our being to be our life and our person.

A PROPER HUMAN LIFE

Some Christians think that they should behave as if they were angels. They try to live like heavenly beings. In the eyes of God, this kind of living is abnormal. He does not want His children to imitate angels; on the contrary, He wants them to be very human. All the members of the church should have a genuine humanity. For this reason, Ephesians, a book dealing with the church, covers various human relationships: the relationship between wife and husband, between children and parents, between servants and masters. In order to have a proper church life, we must have a proper human life.

The very Christ we have received and gained is not an angel or some kind of heavenly being, but a God-man. It was as a man in the flesh that He gave Himself up for us. Furthermore, it is as a man that He is able to fit into our situation and meet our need. He has put on human nature in order to be like us. Now He lives in us as our life and as our person to be manifested from within us. When a sister takes Christ as her person in submitting to her husband, her submission will be glorious, full of the reality of Christ lived out from within her. Likewise, when a brother takes Christ as his person in loving his wife, Christ will be expressed in his love for her. Such a manifestation of Christ is possible because as the God-man He gave Himself up for us.

THE SPEAKING SPIRIT

According to verse 26, Christ gave Himself up for the church so that "He might sanctify her, cleansing her by the washing of the water in the word." After the Lord Jesus gave Himself for us in the flesh, He was resurrected and in resurrection became the life-giving Spirit (1 Cor. 15:45). As the life-giving Spirit, He is the speaking Spirit. Whatever He speaks is the word that washes us. The Greek word rendered word in verse 26 is not *logos,* the constant word, but *rhema,* which denotes the instant word, the word the Lord presently speaks to us. As the life-giving Spirit, the Lord is not silent; He is constantly speaking. If you take Him as your person, you will discover how much He desires to speak within you. Idols are dumb, but the indwelling Christ is always speaking. No one who takes Christ as his life and his person can remain silent. On the contrary, he will be constrained by Christ to speak. As I minister to the Lord's children, I experience Christ speaking within me.

In John 6:63 the Lord Jesus said, "The words which I have spoken unto you are spirit and are life." The Greek word rendered words here is also *rhema,* the instant and present spoken word. This differs from *logos,* the constant word, as in John 1:1. As the speaking Spirit, the Lord is speaking the *rhema* to us. Whatever He speaks is spirit.

If day by day there is no speaking of the Lord within us, it is an indication that there is some problem within us. If there is no speaking, no *rhema,* then in our practical experience the Spirit is absent, for the Lord's speaking actually is the Spirit. As long as we have the Lord's present word, we have the Spirit, the life-giving Spirit. We cannot separate Christ as the life-giving Spirit from His speaking. His presence consists in His speaking. How can we know that Christ as our person is present with us? We know it by His speaking. If we do not have His speaking within us, we do not have His presence. But if we turn to Him, to mean business to take Christ as our life and our person. His speaking will begin again. His speaking is the living word. The living word is the Spirit, and the Spirit is our wonderful Christ Himself. How practical, subjective, intimate, and real He is as the speaking Spirit!

METABOLIC CLEANSING AND TRANSFORMATION

This Spirit is the water that washes us. The more the Spirit speaks, the more we are washed, cleansed. Every time He speaks within us we should experience cleansing.

This cleansing is a metabolic cleansing that removes what is old and replaces it with what is new. How different this is from some type of outward cleansing! It is by the inward, metabolic cleansing that we have transformation. By the metabolic cleansing that comes from the speaking of Christ as the life-giving Spirit, we are truly changed, transformed.

Because such an inward transformation is taking place within us, there is no need for outward correction in the church life. God's way in His economy is not to change us outwardly. His way is for Christ to give Himself up for us and then to come into us as the life-giving Spirit. In a very practical sense, the Lord's presence is one with His speaking. Whenever He speaks, we realize His presence within us.

This speaking of the life-giving Spirit within is the water that cleanses our inner being. This cleansing water deposits a new element into us to replace the old element in our nature and disposition. This metabolic cleansing causes a genuine change in life. This change is what we mean by transformation. Outward correction has no value. What the church needs is the inward metabolic cleansing that comes from allowing Christ as the life-giving Spirit to be our life and our person.

In verse 26 we have Christ not in the stage of the flesh, but in the stage of the life-giving Spirit. As we have pointed out, the life-giving Spirit is the speaking Spirit. Christ's speaking is the Spirit; it is the very presence of the life-giving Spirit. If we honor the speaking of the Spirit within us, the Spirit's speaking will become the water that cleanses, purifies, sanctifies, and supplies us with the element of Christ. This element replaces and discharges our old element and brings about genuine transformation. In this way we are purified and sanctified; in this way we also experience the practicality of the church life.

NOT OUTWARD CORRECTION,
BUT CHRIST AS OUR LIFE AND PERSON

Suppose two brothers who live together in a brothers' house have a problem with each other. One may contact an elder for help, and another may go to an elderly sister for fellowship. The elder may tell the one brother that in the church life we all must learn patience, whereas the elderly sister may tell the other that the Lord has put him into his situation so he could learn certain lessons. Such advice may be mere religious talk. If these brothers try to follow it, they will have even greater problems. Eventually, they may choose to move out of the brothers' house and even leave the church life.

In the church life we do not need outward correction. Instead, the church life is a life in which we all take Christ as our life and person. The elders and the elderly sisters need to help the saints to realize that their need is to take the Lord Jesus as their person. The more all the saints do this, the more they will experience the speaking of Christ as the life-giving Spirit. This speaking will be to them the cleansing, purifying water. This water will spread the element of Christ throughout their being, and it will discharge all oldness. Eventually, brothers like those in the illustration above will no longer be bothered by problems with each other, but will grow together and be built up together. This is the proper church life. Oh, how we all need the inward cleansing, the metabolic purification that transforms us!

What I am ministering to you in this message is something I have learned through years of experience in the Christian life as well as in the church life. I am familiar with various teachings concerning the inner life, holiness, and spirituality. Although I put these teachings into practice, most of them were not very effective. Many of us can testify that although we endeavored to practice what we read on holiness and spirituality, what we read did not work very well in our experience. Out of failure and disappointment many have come to believe that it simply is not possible to have the proper church life today. They claim that for this we must wait until the next age. By the Lord's mercy I can testify that it is possible to have the genuine church life. We have the church life not by trying to carry out teachings in an outward way, but by taking Christ as our life and as our person. Then we enjoy and experience Christ as the life-giving, speaking Spirit. We enjoy the speaking that cleanses us, transforms us, and causes us to grow.

As we grow in life, we are spontaneously built up with others. In such a building there is no place for division or strife concerning opinion and doctrine. We in the church in Los Angeles can testify that we do not care for opinions, suggestions, or proposals. We care only for taking Christ as our life and as our speaking person. We treasure His speaking because His presence as the life-giving Spirit is in His speaking. By His speaking He cleanses us, purifies, and sanctifies us. Eventually, all the spots and wrinkles are swallowed up by life.

A GLORIOUS CHURCH

Through the Lord's speaking within us as the life-giving Spirit, we are becoming a glorious church, a church holy and without blemish. Today we are waiting for the Lord's coming back, knowing that when He comes, He will present us to Himself a glorious church, holy and without blemish. At that time, we shall experience Christ in the third stage as the Bridegroom coming for His Bride. Until then, our need is to daily take Christ as our person and to be cleansed, purified, and sanctified through the speaking of the life-giving Spirit. In this way we shall undergo a metabolic change leading to the transformation in life which is necessary for the church life.

LIFE-STUDY OF EPHESIANS

MESSAGE FIFTY-SIX

SANCTIFYING, CLEANSING, NOURISHING, AND CHERISHING

(1)

God's economy is not a religion, but a wonderful, unlimited, immeasurable, unsearchable, and all-inclusive Person, Christ Jesus Himself. Christ is the embodiment of God and the content of the church. This Christ is to be our life and our person.

NOT RELIGION BUT A WONDERFUL PERSON

However, in today's Christianity God's economy has become a mere religion. Under the influence of this religion, Christians believe that God loved the world and gave His only begotten Son to die on the cross for our sins. After Christ's resurrection, He ascended to the heavens. Until He comes back, we are to study the Bible and follow its teachings. But teachings are not the living Person of Christ Himself. God's economy is not a matter of religion with doctrines and teachings; it is a matter of a wonderful, living Person. Now this Person must become our person. Our need today is not to be concerned with doctrine, but to be concerned with contacting the living Christ within us.

RECOVERED TO THE SUBJECTIVE CHRIST

Many Christians pay more attention to the Bible than to Christ. This indicates that even the Bible can be utilized to distract people from Christ. Surely, we believe, respect, and honor the Bible to the uttermost. But we recognize that the Bible is the revelation of the living Person of Christ. If we do not pay attention to the Christ revealed in the Bible, then we ignore the main function of the Bible, which is to reveal this very Christ to us. How we need to be recovered fully to Christ Himself!

We need to be recovered not merely to the objective Christ in the heavens, but to the subjective Christ in our spirit. This subjective One is seeking to spread Himself into our heart. Not only is Christ our Savior objectively, but He is our life and our person subjectively. We need to devote our full attention to such a subjective Christ. In Galatians 2:20 Paul could say, "Not I, but Christ who lives in me." Here Paul did not speak of the life of Christ, the work of Christ, or the power of Christ; he spoke of Christ Himself living in him. Hallelujah, the very Person of Christ is living in us!

In the foregoing message we pointed out that when Christ was in the flesh, He gave Himself up for us. Then in resurrection He became the life-giving Spirit. This life-giving Spirit is the One we are to take daily as our person. As the life-giving Spirit, Christ is washing us, sanctifying us, cleansing us, nourishing us, and cherishing us. We shall consider these matters in this message.

BECOMING HOLY DISPOSITIONALLY

Perhaps you have heard messages or read books about sanctification. In order to know the true meaning of sanctification, we need to contact the life-giving Spirit indwelling our spirit. One aspect of sanctification involves separation. To be sanctified is to be separated positionally, to undergo a change of position. However, this is not the only aspect of sanctification. In sanctification something that once was natural gradually becomes holy in nature. Hence, as we are sanctified subjectively, we become holy dispositionally.

This aspect of sanctification can be illustrated by the process of making tea. When tea is placed in a cup of water, the water is "tea-ified." As the water is "tea-ified," it becomes tea-water. We can compare ourselves to the cup of water and Christ to the tea. Just as water is "tea-ified" by the element of tea, so we are sanctified by the element of Christ. Therefore, to be sanctified is to have Christ Himself added into our being. The more Christ is added into us, the more we have the appearance, taste, and aroma of Christ. Day by day, our need is to take more of Christ as the heavenly tea into us so that more of His element may be added into our being. In this way we shall be "Christ-ified."

Suppose Christ were simply an objective Christ at the right hand of God in the heavens. Could we be sanctified dispositionally simply by trying to follow in an outward way the teachings of the Bible? Certainly not. Nothing of the element of Christ could be added into our being. We thank the Lord for showing us that subjective sanctification is a matter of having Christ added into us. The only way this can happen is by our taking Him as our life and as our person.

CHRIST'S INTENTION IN HIS SPEAKING

We have pointed out that when we take Christ as our person, we experience Him speaking in us as the life-giving Spirit. The Lord's intention in His inward speaking is not simply to tell us to do certain things or not to do other things; it is to impart Himself into us by speaking to us. The more the Lord speaks within us, the more He imparts Himself into us. Whenever we tell the Lord that we want Him to be our person, He begins to speak within us.

Even if we do not hearken to His speaking, He will still impart Himself to us by His speaking. Many times we may disobey the Lord's inner speaking, but He spreads within us a little more nevertheless. The Lord's main concern is not with how much we obey Him, but with how much opportunity He has to impart Himself to us and to spread Himself within us. As soon as you say, "Lord Jesus, I take You as my person," the Lord begins to impart Himself into you. However, should you change your mind and tell the Lord that you want to withdraw your promise, He will say, "Even if you withdraw your promise, I have already imparted Myself into you." If we tell the Lord that we are not able to obey Him, He will reply, "I am not concerned whether or not you feel you are able to obey Me. I only care to be given the opportunity to get Myself into you." Even as we are speaking to the Lord about not wanting to fulfill the promise we have made to Him or about being unable to obey Him, He is imparting Himself into us. The more we speak to Him, the more we are "Christ-ified."

Sanctification comes from our dealing with the living Person of Christ. I have the full assurance that those who have told the Lord that they are willing to take Him as their person cannot escape the Lord's speaking. As the Lord speaks, He imparts Himself into us. This impartation is sanctification.

CLEANSED BY THE SUBJECTIVE CHRIST

We come now to cleansing. In sanctification a new element is added into us, whereas in cleansing a particular element is removed from us. We all need our natural disposition to be cleansed. No matter how good or kind you may be naturally your natural disposition is a problem. Furthermore, we have the problems of our habits, customs, and self-made ordinances. All these things need to be eradicated.

Contrary to religious teachings, we are not cleansed by self-correction. This means that we are not cleansed by dealing with ourselves in an outward way. For example, it is impossible to remove wrinkles, signs of oldness, by washing the skin outwardly. During our first period of time in the church life, we may experience a church honeymoon. However, inevitably oldness sets in and wrinkles appear. In order for our wrinkles to be removed, our youthfulness in life must be restored. As the life-giving Spirit, Christ is doing such a work of restoration among us today. Christ will not come back for a bride with wrinkles. If we would be His Bride, we must be kept up to date with Him. Wrinkles are not taken away by teaching or by trying to obey the doctrines in the Bible. Wrinkles are removed as we take Christ as our person and allow Him to live in us. It is not the objective Christ in the heavens who cleanses us; on the contrary, it is the subjective Christ, the Christ so intimate and available, who cleanses us. Whenever we contact

Him, we are refreshed, renewed, and made more youthful in life.

Ephesians 5:25 and 26 say that Christ gave Himself up for the church that He might sanctify her, cleansing her by the washing of the water in the word. In the foregoing message we pointed out that the water in the word is Christ as the speaking Spirit. The more Christ speaks within us, the more He flows within us. This flowing water is not in the *logos,* the constant word, but in the *rhema,* the present, instant word. As this water washes us, it carries away our oldness. This washing is a metabolic washing. It supplies a new element to replace the old. This leads to transformation. Therefore, cleansing is not a matter of teaching, but a matter of taking Christ as our living person. When we take Him as our person, He adds Himself into us and washes us metabolically.

NOURISHED BY TAKING CHRIST AS OUR PERSON

In verse 29 there are two important words: nourish and cherish. To nourish is to feed. In the past many of us attended so-called Christian services or read the Bible without receiving any nourishment. But if we take Christ as our person, we shall experience Him nourishing us. We shall continually have the sense of His inward nourishment. To be nourished by Christ is to be supplied with His riches. I believe that we all have experienced the nourishment that comes from taking Christ as our person.

Nourishment brings about transformation. We all become what we eat. This means that if we eat Christ, we shall eventually be constituted with Christ. We shall be transformed by the element of Christ that has been dispensed into us. The more we take Christ as our person, the more He nourishes us. Through Christ's nourishment we are transformed. This means that we become a new person with a new element and substance. Hallelujah, Christ nourishes us with Himself, with the riches of all He is! What we need today is not doctrine or religion, but the enjoyment of the all-inclusive Christ.

OUR BURDEN

In these messages our burden is not to pass on more teachings to the saints. Our burden is to minister the living Christ. Today the need of the Lord's people is to take Christ as their person for nourishment. Because we are conscious of this need, we are not interested in mere objective teachings. Our desire is to help others come in touch with the living Christ, to open to Him, and to take Him as their life and person. I hope that many will say, "Lord, I have been a Christian for years, but I have not taken You as my person. Lord, by Your mercy, I want to begin now to take You as my person." If your husband or wife troubles you and you are tempted to exchange words, that is the time to take Christ as your person. Instead of arguing with others or defending ourselves, we should allow Christ to make His home in our heart.

"WRECKED" BY CHRIST

Many of us can testify that we have been "wrecked" by Christ. On the one hand, Christ rescues us; but on the other hand, He "wrecks" us and makes us useless for anything other than Himself and the church life. The more we take Christ as our person, the more He "wrecks" us. Actually, this ministry is a "wrecking" ministry. Through it, thousands have been "wrecked" for Christ and the church. Now nothing other than the living Christ and the proper church life can satisfy us.

WARMED AND SOFTENED

Along with the nourishing we have the cherishing. To be cherished is to be softened by being warmed. When we are hard and cold, we need Christ to cherish us. We need Him to warm our hearts. After some experiences of His warming, we are softened. Many can testify that through their contact with the church in the Lord's recovery, they have been warmed and softened. Before coming into the church life, they were somewhat cold and hard. But Christ, the nourishing and cherishing One, has made them warm and soft.

Many of us can give testimony of what it is to be cherished by Christ in such a tender, intimate way.

Just as a mother cherishes a child by holding the child to her breast, so the Lord cherishes us by holding us close to Him. Although I am an elderly person, I still need Christ's cherishing. Sometimes I tell Him, "Lord, You know how small I am." He replies, "Yes, I know. This is why I am here not only to sanctify, cleanse, and nourish you, but also to cherish you." How tender, sweet, and warm the Lord Jesus is! By resting on Him, we who once were hard and cold become soft and warm. Such a change takes place through the Lord's care for us from within. Inwardly the Lord warms us and softens us as we enjoy His tenderness, sweetness, and lovingness. Praise Him, He is the cherishing One! May we all take Christ as our person and experience more of His sanctifying, cleansing, nourishing, and cherishing. In this way we enjoy Him and experience Him in a living way.

LIFE-STUDY OF EPHESIANS

MESSAGE FIFTY-SEVEN

HOW CHRIST GLORIFIES THE CHURCH

We have seen that 5:25-27 presents Christ in three stages. In the first stage, the stage of the flesh, Christ gave Himself up for the church. In the second stage, He as the life-giving Spirit is sanctifying, cleansing, nourishing, and cherishing the church. Eventually, in the third stage, He will present a glorious church to Himself as His Bride.

HOW CHRIST PRESENTS THE CHURCH TO HIMSELF

We need to consider how Christ will present the church to Himself as a glorious church. When I was young, I thought that Christ was merely in the heavens and that the church was on earth. My concept was that at His coming back from the heavens to the earth, He would suddenly take up the church and present her to Himself. According to this concept, Christ is far away in the heavens, and we on earth are making ourselves ready to be presented to Him. I realized later, however, that this is a natural concept that makes Christ too objective.

God's economy is altogether different from the natural concept and from religion. In His economy, God is working Christ into us. Eventually, Christ will present the glorious church to Himself not by coming merely in an objective way, but by expanding within us and then by coming out of us.

Romans 8 indicates that God has not only called us and justified us, but that He will also glorify us. Years ago I was taught that one day the Lord would suddenly descend from the heavens and sweep us up into glory. But this concept of glorification is not according to God's economy. Christ will glorify us not by descending upon us from the heavens, but by coming forth from within us. The hope of glory is not the

Christ in the heavens, but the Christ who is in us (Col. 1:27). If we do not take Christ as our life and our person, we shall have no way to enjoy the glory that is within us. We need to say, "Lord Jesus, I take You as my life and my person. Lord, I offer my heart to You. Take my heart, Lord. Possess it, occupy it, and make Your home in it." If you practice this, spontaneously you will come to know the glory within you.

THE SHINING OF THE INNER GLORY

Many of us were taught that the light of God shines upon us from outside of us. Our experience of the Lord's shining, however, is different from this. According to our experience, the light shines not from the outside, but from within us. When you take Christ as your life and your person, do not expect the heavens to open and a great light to shine upon you in an outward way. If your experience is like that of so many, the Lord's shining will be inward, a shining from within. Such a shining is an expression of the inner glory. Our hope of glory is Christ in us. Hence, when God glorifies us, He will not need to send the glory from above; rather, He will cause Christ to shine forth from within us. This indicates that glorification is a subjective experience of the indwelling Christ.

SWALLOWED UP BY CHRIST AS GLORY

Contrary to the religious concept, our glorification will not be a sudden event. Rather, it will take place gradually as Christ expands within us and saturates us with Himself. Christ glorifies us as He "eats us up" little by little. We all need to be eaten, devoured, swallowed up, by Christ as the glory within us. Within us we have Christ not only as our life and our person, but also as the very glory of God.

We may use the metamorphosis of an ugly caterpillar into a beautiful butterfly as an illustration of glorification. A caterpillar is not instantaneously transformed into a butterfly by a beauty that suddenly descends upon it and envelops it. No, the beauty of the butterfly is contained within the life of the caterpillar. As the law of this life functions within the caterpillar, the caterpillar is gradually transformed into a butterfly. As this process takes place, the beauty of the butterfly swallows up the ugliness of the caterpillar.

In the same principle, Christ is in us to be our hope of glory. As the indwelling glory, He takes every opportunity to expand within us. The inner glory saturates us and even swallows us up. One day our entire being will be saturated with the divine glory. On that day we shall be brought into glory in a full way.

This is completely different from the religious teaching that tells us we must try to behave ourselves until some-day when we hope to be suddenly transported into a realm of glory. According to the religious concept, we must try our best to please the Lord. If we are pleasing to Him, one day He will swoop down from heaven and carry us away to glory. What a contrast between this and God's economy! God's economy is to dispense Christ into us. As believers, we have Christ in us as our glory. Our need is not to behave ourselves or to endeavor to please God; it is to take care of Christ as the hope of glory and to allow this glory to be our life and person.

CHRIST COMING FROM WITHIN US

What we have within us is not simply life or the Spirit, but Christ Himself as the very glory of God. This Christ will present the church to Himself as a glorious church. However, He will do this not in a religious way, but in the way that is according to God's economy. This means that He will expand within us and saturate us with Himself until we have been wholly swallowed up by the inner glory. Then He will come forth from within us.

Most Christians expect Christ to come from the heavens. I am very familiar with the verses which speak of this. On the one hand, Christ will come from the heavens. But on the other hand, much to the surprise of many, He will come from within us. Objectively Christ is in the heavens, but subjectively and experientially He is in us. As the One indwelling us, He will come from within us.

Since the day Christ came into us, He has been seeking a way to come out through us. It is easy for Him to get into us, but it is not easy for Him to get out of us. For example, we can easily sow a seed into the soil, but it takes time and it requires a process for this seed to grow out from the soil. Nevertheless, just as the seed eventually grows and comes out from the earth, so Christ eventually will saturate us, swallow us up, and then come out through us.

THE CONTRAST BETWEEN RELIGION AND GOD'S ECONOMY

Most Christians today miss the mark of God's economy because they are veiled by religious concepts. They simply do not know what God's economy is. The contrast between religion and God's economy can be illustrated by the Lord's human living. When the Lord Jesus was on earth, the temple with all its rituals, practices, and ordinances was still in Jerusalem. In the temple the priests presented the offerings, burned the incense, and lighted the lamps. However, God was not in the temple—He was in the Lord Jesus. Sometimes the Lord stayed in the home of Lazarus, Martha, and Mary in Bethany. He visited with them and spoke with them in a normal, human way. Nevertheless, while He was in that house in Bethany, the priests continued to perform the rituals in the temple. With the priests in the temple we see the practice of religion, but with the Lord in Bethany we see God's economy. God's economy is to work Himself into man. His economy was carried out not in the temple, but in that house in Bethany, for there Christ, the embodiment of the fullness of God, was present. Those who worshipped in the temple were practicing their religion, but Lazarus, Martha, and Mary enjoyed the presence of the Lord Jesus. The local churches today should not be like the temple in Jerusalem, but be like that home in Bethany. This means that the churches should not be places of religion, but be places where God's economy is being carried out.

Religion teaches that God will bring us into a sphere, a realm, of glory. According to the religious concept, the Lord will instantaneously transport us into this objective glory. Until then we must behave ourselves and seek to order our lives according to the Scriptures. In everything and in every way we must try our best to be scriptural. Then, according to this teaching, we shall be qualified one day to be caught up into the realm of God's glory.

Contrast this concept with the economy of God. According to God's economy, the glory has already come into us and is now dwelling within us. This glory is the very Christ who is our life and our person. Christ will present a glorious church to Himself not by suddenly coming down upon the church, but by expanding within the church until the church has been wholly permeated, saturated, and swallowed up with Himself. How different this is from trying to please God in an outward way! Glorification is altogether a matter of Christ's expanding within us and swallowing us up with Himself. This is God's economy.

Let us turn from religious teachings and give ourselves absolutely to God's economy. The Bible reveals that in His economy God is working Christ into us. On the day we repented and believed in the Lord Jesus, Christ came into us as the element of glory. Now He is in the process of presenting a glorious church to Himself by spreading Himself within us. According to Ephesians 3:17, Christ's expanding within us is actually His making His home in our heart. Christ is saturating us and even "eating us up." This will go on until He comes out of us. By this process Christ is presenting the church to Himself as a glorious church.

NOT ONLY VICTORIOUS, BUT ALSO GLORIOUS

Ephesians 5:27 does not say that Christ will present to Himself a nice church nor even a victorious church, but it says that Christ will have a glorious church. It is possible to be victorious without being glorious. Many books tell us how to be victorious, but I do not know of a book that tells us how to be glorious. Likewise, many messages have been given on the way to have victory. But have you ever heard a message about how to be glorious? Christ wants a glorious church, not merely a victorious one.

BACK TO THE INDWELLING CHRIST

Not many of us have the confidence to say that we are glorious. The reason for this is that we realize that we have not given the Lord the full opportunity to saturate us and to come out through us. After receiving the Lord Jesus into us, many of us became distracted or snared by religious teachings. Instead of concentrating on the indwelling Christ, we paid attention to other things. Therefore, in the Lord's recovery we all must be brought back to the indwelling Christ. From the depths of our being we need to tell the Lord that we want to take Him as our life and our person and give Him the full ground within our being.

If the Lord were only in the heavens, He could not be our life and our person. But Christ is both in the heavens and in us. It is this indwelling One whom we must take as our life and person. When we do this, He makes His home in our heart. He expands in us, saturates us, and gradually swallows us up. Eventually, at the time of His coming back, He will be fully expressed from within us. This is God's economy in life.

THE PROCESS OF GLORIFICATION

In God's economy, Christ is even now in the process of presenting the glorious church to Himself. As this process takes place, He is making His home in our heart by becoming our life and our person. In this way, He saturates our inner being with Himself. It is not His intention to correct us, adjust us, or to improve us. His aim is to glorify us. In order to achieve this goal, He is now carrying on the process of glorification within us.

No matter how nice, good, right, or victorious you may be, you are not yet glorious. Christ's intention is not to obtain a church that is nice, right, or good, but to obtain a church that is altogether glorious. Hence, Christ cares only to glorify us by saturating us with Himself and by swallowing us up. Day by day, He is devouring us and replacing us with the element of what He is. This process transpires in the depths of our being. Oh, how we need to experience such an intimate, personal Christ! Our Christ must not be a Christ in teaching, but be a Christ making His home in our heart, a Christ saturating our being with His element.

A MUTUAL EATING

A well-known hymn tells us to trust and obey. God's economy, however, is more than just trusting and obeying; it requires that we be "eaten up" by Christ. Christ wants us to eat Him, and He wants to eat us. Hence, in God's economy there is a mutual eating. My burden in this message is to point out that Christ's intention is to "eat us up." When we have been consumed by Christ in a full way, He will then present the church to Himself as a glorious church.

Do you know why the church today is not very glorious? The reason is that not many have allowed Christ to eat them up. If the church is to become glorious, we need to allow the indwelling Christ to consume every part of our inward being. According to verse 25, Christ gave Himself up for the church. Now He is working within us to saturate us and to come out of us. However, He does not intend to come out of us and leave us aside. On the contrary, He wants to come out of us by saturating us and devouring us. We need to pray, "Lord Jesus, eat me up!" When Christ has finished consuming us inwardly, He will be able to boast to Satan, "Satan, look at My glorious church!"

The goal of God's economy is to gain a glorious church. God has ordained us unto glory (1 Cor. 2:7). This is not an objective glory, but a glory that is subjective and experiential. Such a glory is actually the very Christ whom we eat and by whom we are being eaten up. Our desperate need today is to eat the Lord and to allow Him to consume us. Only in this way will the church become the glorious church for which Christ is longing.

LIFE-STUDY OF EPHESIANS

MESSAGE FIFTY-EIGHT

SANCTIFYING, CLEANSING, NOURISHING, AND CHERISHING

(2)

In 5:26 and 29 there are four crucial words: sanctify, cleanse, nourish, and cherish. Because the enemy has veiled these matters, not many Christians have a clear understanding of their significance. For this reason, I am very burdened of the Lord to consider them further in this message.

THE ADDITION OF THE ELEMENT OF CHRIST

God's intention in His economy is not to correct us or to improve us. Neither is it to have good people in place of bad people. In the eyes of God, it does not matter whether we are good or bad, for the only thing of value in His economy is Christ Himself. Therefore, God's desire is to work Christ into us. Whether we are good or bad, we need the element of Christ added into us. This involves Christ's work in sanctifying us. Sanctification in 5:26 does not mean merely to be separated from what is common, but it means to have the very element of Christ added to us.

Sanctification is not a matter of adjusting ourselves outwardly to fit into the situation of the church life. For example, a young brother may have been rather loose before coming into the church. Now that he is living in a brothers' house he constantly reminds himself to behave properly. This behavior is not sanctification—it is religion. In the eyes of God, such religious behavior is included in what Paul calls dung (Phil. 3:8). The Lord does not want our self-improvement or self-adjustment; He wants to saturate our whole being with Himself. Hence, sanctification is not behavior, but the addition of the element of Christ to our being.

NOT DELIBERATE BEHAVIOR, BUT A SPONTANEOUS EXPRESSION

As one who is familiar with both the Bible and the teachings of Confucius, I have come to realize that in their daily living many Christians live as if they were disciples of Confucius. Under the influence of the religious concept, they regard the Bible as a book of doctrines and ethical teachings. For example, a sister may try desperately to submit to her husband. In doing this, she is actually living like a follower of Confucius, all the while believing that she is being a good Christian. She explains her behavior by saying that, according to the Bible, her husband is the head and she is obligated to submit to him. Such a word sounds very good, but it is religious, for it is not according to God's economy to work Christ into us. We all know that in 5:22 Paul exhorts the wives to be subject to their own husbands. But do not forget that this follows his word about being filled in spirit (v. 18). This indicates that a wife's submission should come out of the infilling of the Spirit, not out of an outward, deliberate attempt to be submissive.

Often in Christian weddings a pastor will charge the bride and groom according to Paul's word in Ephesians 5 regarding husbands and wives. The wife promises to submit to her husband, and the husband vows to love his wife. However, neither the bride nor the groom realizes that submission and love are the issue of being filled in our spirit with the Triune God.

If a sister's submission is genuine, it will not require deliberate effort. On the contrary, she will submit spontaneously out of her experience of Christ and her enjoyment of Him. She may not even realize that she is submissive, for she submits without purposely trying to do so. Such submission comes out of the element of Christ that has been imparted into that sister. How different this is from submitting because she has been taught to be under the headship of her husband! Such deliberate submission is religious and is not according to God's economy.

TAKING CHRIST AS OUR LIFE AND OUR PERSON

There is a great difference between sanctification and behavior. In sanctification we do things without trying on purpose to do them. They are the spontaneous expression of our taking Christ as our life and our person. When Christ is our life and our person, He lives within us. It is He who is loving and submissive. To submit because of the indwelling Christ is one thing, but to submit because of behavior or outward correction is an altogether different matter.

The leading ones in the churches should not tell others what to do. Instead, we all must be able to testify that we live, not according to outward teachings, but according to the Christ who dwells in us to be our life and our person. Our aim is not to behave in a particular way, but simply to take Christ as our life and our person. Then what we do will be the outflow of the inner life. Spontaneously, the wives will submit to their husbands, the husbands will love their wives, and the children will be obedient to their parents. However, this kind of living will not be deliberate; it will be the issue of being filled in spirit with the Triune God.

When the young people are helped by a message, they may say that they will never be the same. But even this may be religious, for the young people may unconsciously try to improve themselves. They may try by their own effort to do what they heard in that message. Striving to make ourselves different is not sanctification.

In order to be sanctified in a genuine way, we simply need to contact the Lord and take Him as our life and our person. We need to pray, "Lord Jesus, You are my life and my person. Lord, take me, occupy me, and possess me. O Lord, come into every corner of my heart, fill my heart with Yourself, and make Your home in my heart. Lord, I don't care whether or not I'll be different, and I'm not concerned about behavior. I care only that You fill me and come out through me." If you contact the Lord in this way, He will gradually and spontaneously be added into your being. This addition of Christ will sanctify you.

A HEAVY BURDEN

Subjective sanctification does not take place by teaching, but takes place by the inward working of the living Christ. This is the reason we emphasize the fact that in the Lord's recovery we care little for doctrine in letters, but very much for the experience of Christ as our life and our person. I cannot express how heavy is the burden on my heart concerning this matter. If I can help the saints realize what sanctification is, I believe that this burden will be discharged. Please be impressed that sanctification definitely is not a matter of outward behavior or improvement. God desires to daily dispense the element of Christ into our being. It is this element alone that causes us to be sanctified.

WASHING AWAY THE NATURAL DISPOSITION

In subjective sanctification something of Christ is added to us, but in cleansing something of us, especially our natural disposition, is subtracted. As we are cleansed, our natural disposition is washed away. Disposition is the most inward aspect of our constitution; it is the very root of our being. We were born with a certain disposition. Disposition, therefore, is altogether inward. However, character, a combination of disposition, custom, and habit, is partly inward and partly outward, whereas behavior is wholly outward. The Lord Jesus cares little about our behavior, more about our character, but very much about our disposition. As Christ is adding His element into us, He is also cleansing us and subtracting our natural disposition. His cleansing washes away the natural element from the depths of our being.

We have pointed out that the Lord will wash the church from all wrinkles. Wrinkles are caused by our natural disposition. Hence, the only way these wrinkles can be removed is for the element of our natural disposition to be cleansed away.

With the young people it is easy to point out what their disposition is. However, if the Apostle Paul were with us, it would be difficult to discern his disposition, because he has been so deeply cleansed and purified. His old, natural disposition has been washed away by the element of Christ.

The washing away of our natural disposition cannot be accomplished by teaching, but can be accomplished only by the impartation of the element of Christ into our being. At the same time the element of Christ is being added, something of ourselves is being carried away. Therefore, on the one hand, we have the addition of Christ, but, on the other hand, we have the subtraction of the natural disposition. Gradually, Christ is being added into our being, and our natural disposition is being subtracted. The result of this process is transformation, a metabolic change in which the new element is constituted into us and the old element is carried away.

THE WORK OF THE LIVING CHRIST

We have pointed out that 5:25-27 presents Christ in three stages. When Christ was in the first of these stages, the stage of the flesh, He went to the cross and there gave Himself up for the church. Then in resurrection He became the life-giving Spirit (1 Cor. 15:45). In this second stage He is sanctifying and cleansing us. If we open to Him and tell Him that we are willing to take Him as our life and our person, He will work within us as the life-giving Spirit to add Himself to us and to carry away our oldness and our natural disposition. This is the work of the living Christ in sanctification and cleansing.

NOURISHMENT AND SATISFACTION

We proceed to the nourishing and the cherishing. When I was young, I spent a great deal of time studying the book of Ephesians. Nevertheless, I did not understand what it meant to be nourished and cherished. But through experience I have come to know what it is to be nourished and cherished by Christ. Whenever we open to the Lord Jesus and take Him as our life and our person, He sanctifies us and cleanses us. At the same time He gives us nourishment. We know this by the fact that we have a wonderful sense of satisfaction within. Satisfaction comes from nourishment.

CLEANSING AND NOURISHING

Only by receiving the life supply can we endure the Lord's cleansing of our disposition. Surgeons realize that for a patient to withstand surgery, he must have nourishment. For this reason, blood and glucose are transfused into the patient. The Lord's cleansing is a kind of spiritual surgery, surgery on the depths of our inner being. The Lord's cleansing is His operating. For such an operation we surely need His nourishing.

I know of a certain brother whose natural disposition was rude, mean, and even cruel. Sometimes he came to me in tears distraught over the kind of person he was. He admitted that no one could satisfy him. Regarding himself as the most loathsome person on earth, he was desperate to know what to do about his situation. I could not do anything to help him in an outward way. But I can testify that the Lord gradually cleansed and purified him thoroughly. He loved the Lord very much and was completely open to Him. Because he gave the Lord the ground within him, the Lord could come in to sanctify him and to cleanse him. The Lord operated on him and washed away the element of his natural disposition. In order to bear such extensive surgery, we need the supply of the Lord's inward nourishment. This brother could testify of the nourishment and enjoyment the Lord gave to him as He was cleansing him. Be assured, whenever the Lord sanctifies and cleanses, He also nourishes.

Any sanctification or cleansing that is not accompanied by nourishment is not genuine. It is the product of self-effort. Whenever you try to sanctify yourself or cleanse yourself, you will have the sense of spiritual starvation. But if the Lord does the sanctifying and the cleansing, He will supply the nourishment, and you will enjoy sweet satisfaction. The more the Lord purifies you, the more of His nourishment you will receive. Instead of suffering under the process of purification, you will enjoy the Lord and His abundant life-supply.

CHERISHED BY THE LORD'S TENDER WARMTH

As the Lord nourishes us, He also cherishes us. He is like a mother who cherishes her child even as she feeds him. How the little ones enjoy the warmth and comfort of their mothers! If you consider your experience, you will realize that when the Lord sanctifies, cleanses, and nourishes you, He cherishes you with His tender warmth. His cherishing comforts you, soothes you, and calms you. Hallelujah for the Lord's sanctifying, cleansing, nourishing, and cherishing!

PLACING OUR TRUST IN THE LIVING CHRIST

Only the living Christ can do all this. Doctrines cannot do it and not even the Bible can do it. If you want the sanctifying, the cleansing, the nourishing, and the cherishing, you must place all your trust in the living Christ. Tell Him, "Lord Jesus, nothing can replace You. Lord, I love You, I open my heart to You, and I give You all the ground in my being. Lord, possess me and be my life and my person. Lord, I don't care about outward things, not even about the church life in an outward way. I care only that You, Lord, will be my life and my person." If you contact the Lord in this way, you will discover how living, real, available, and present He is. He will sanctify you by adding Himself to you. He will cleanse you by washing away the old element of your natural disposition. He will also nourish you with His riches and cherish you with His warmth. As all this is taking place within you, you will have a marvelous enjoyment of the Lord. This is the way the Lord is preparing His Bride. In this way we are becoming the glorious church Christ will present to Himself at His coming back.

LIFE-STUDY OF EPHESIANS

MESSAGE FIFTY-NINE

GOD'S DESIRE FOR A GLORIOUS CHURCH

We have seen that God's intention in His economy is to obtain a glorious church. Strictly speaking, God is not seeking a spiritual church, a heavenly church, nor even a victorious church. He wants a church of glory. Glory is the expression of God and it is altogether different from human morality and behavior. When God filled the tabernacle and the temple, both of them were filled with glory, with the very manifestation of God. The church should be characterized by glory—not by anything else, not even spirituality. I am not happy to hear talk about a so-called spiritual church. The only way God can have a glorious church is through Christ's sanctifying, cleansing, nourishing, and cherishing. As we experience these things in a personal and practical way, the church becomes glorious.

The Bible does not speak of a spiritual church. But in Ephesians 5 Paul speaks of a glorious church. One of Brother Nee's books is entitled *The Glorious Church*. Many Christians have as their goal a so-called spiritual church. Instead of seeking spirituality, we should seek to be filled with glory so that Christ may have His glorious church.

GOD'S GOAL

Because of religious teachings, many have been blinded to God's desire for a glorious church. In a sense, some have been helped by those teachings, but in another sense, they have been frustrated by them. Religious teachings can keep the saints from seeing the revelation of the glorious church and can cause them instead to seek such things as spirituality, gifts, and victory. Ultimately, it is not God's intention to have a church that is merely spiritual, victorious, or heavenly. His goal is a glorious church. Do not aspire to be like the angels. They may be spiritual, heavenly, and victorious, but they are not glorious, for they do not bear the glory of God. Praise the Lord that we who believe in Christ bear God's glory! Religion actually brings people down to the level of angels. Under the influence of the religious concept, many Christians are envious of the angels. If we see God's economy, we shall reject such an influence and desire to become filled with glory in order that God may reach His goal.

NOT VICTORIOUS BUT GLORIOUS

It is possible to be victorious without being glorious. For example, a brother may be pleased at his success in overcoming his temper. He may have been defeated by his temper for years and now at last he has gained victory over it. Such a victory, however, may be completely lacking in glory. God's economy is not a matter of becoming victorious over such things as our temper. It is a matter of taking Christ as our life and our person and allowing Him to live in us. The result of this is the expression of God as glory. In ourselves we may be victorious, but in order to be glorious we need Christ to be our life and our person.

THE DECEPTIVENESS OF RELIGION

In a sense, religion is deceptive. While it is helping us, it is also deceiving us. The reason is that religion is part truth and part falsehood. This mixture of truth and falsehood is a subtle form of deception. For example, it is rather easy to preach the gospel to the heathen and to bring people to the Lord. However, it is very difficult to bring someone to the Lord who has had a background in Catholicism, for he has been cheated by the half-truths of that religious system. On the one hand, we have been helped by the religious teachings we received in the past. But on the other hand, these same teachings have veiled us in relation to God's economy. Therefore, we need to discard religious concepts and teachings and come back to the whole truth of the pure Word of God.

GOD EXPRESSED THROUGH MAN

According to the truth in the Word, God has no intention of gaining a group of spiritual beings. He already has myriads of angels. God's goal is to have a glorious people as His expression. In the midst of this dark, evil age, God desires to have on earth a people full of His glory. If the meeting hall were filled with angels, we would probably think that the situation of the church is glorious. We perhaps would marvel at all the spiritual, heavenly, victorious beings. However, such a situation would not be a true manifestation of God's glory. God expresses Himself not through angels, but through man. Although we are men in the flesh, we can take Christ as our life and our person. When we do this, even the angels will marvel at the expression of glory in us. The angels may say, "Look at these people. They are full of God's glory!"

Do you still desire to have a spiritual church, a heavenly church, a victorious church? If you know God's economy, your desire will be for a glorious church. We should be able to say to the angels, "Angels, we don't envy your spirituality, victory, or heavenliness. We have Christ within us as our life and our person, and we are being filled with glory. Angels, do you have Christ as your life and your person? Gabriel could announce the birth of Christ, but he does not have the privilege of taking Christ as his life and person. Angels, we would like to tell you that Christ dwells within us. You may be spiritual, heavenly, and victorious, but we are glorious."

Verse 27 of Ephesians 5 has been in the New Testament for centuries, but it has been lost as far as the experience of believers is concerned. Therefore, today the Lord is in the process of recovering the glorious church. Let us read this verse again: "That He might present the church to Himself glorious, not having spot or wrinkle or any such things, but that she should be holy and without blemish." Christ is sanctifying, cleansing, nourishing, and cherishing us so that we may be a glorious church. He is not doing these things simply to make us spiritual, heavenly, or victorious.

A CORPORATE MAN

The glorious church is a corporate man. This means that every part of this corporate man is glorious. Are you a part of this glorious man in a practical way? In other words, are you being filled with glory? Even after reading all these messages, we still may be occupied with the thought of victory and may seek to be victorious over our temper or a difficult situation. We may be very appreciative of those whose teaching can lead us into the way of victory. Oh, may the Lord impress us with His desire to have a glorious, shining people! The goal of His economy is to gain a church that shines with His glory.

CHRIST COMING FROM WITHIN US

The concept of glorification common among believers today is that Christ will suddenly descend from the heavens and sweep us away into a realm of glory. Until then, we are simply to wait until the Lord Jesus comes to glorify us. But as we pointed out in message fifty-seven, Christ will come from within us. I fully realize that certain verses in the New Testament indicate that Christ will come objectively from the heavens. Nevertheless, other verses indicate that He will come forth from within us and will glorify us in a very subjective way.

THE GOSPEL OF THE GLORY OF CHRIST

A number of verses in the New Testament show that the experience of glory is subjective. Second Corinthians 4:4 says, "In whom the god of this age hath blinded the thoughts of them that believe not, lest the light of the gospel of the glory of Christ, who is the image of God, should shine unto them" (Gk.). In this verse Paul does not speak of the gospel of forgiveness or of justification by faith. He speaks instead of the gospel of the glory of Christ. Our gospel is not simply a gospel of redemption, forgiveness, and regeneration. It is also the gospel of the glory of Christ.

Only this gospel has the ability to shine into us. Firstly it shines into us and then it shines out from within us. The more the glory shines within us, the more it penetrates into our being and saturates it. Eventually, the inner glory will consume, swallow up, our entire inward being. Then the light of the gospel of the glory of Christ will shine out through us. Such a shining cannot come by way of teaching, but only through the experience of Christ who is Himself the glory of God and the manifestation of God. Hallelujah, Christ has shone into the depths of our being and now He is shining within us! The time is coming when He will shine throughout our inward being. Hence, the light of God's glory will shine not in an outward way, but will shine from within us. The more Christ shines, the more we are filled with glory.

CONCENTRATING ON THE LORD'S INWARD SHINING

When we are in a difficult situation, we do not need to strive to be victorious. Forget about trying to be victorious and pay attention to the inner shining of Christ as the glory within. Learn to say, "Hallelujah, Christ is shining in me and through me! He is my life and my person. How sweet and pleasant is His inward shining!" As we concentrate on the Lord's shining within, we shall spontaneously be victorious without any conscious effort on our part.

The goal of God's economy is that we all shine forth His glory. As we are under such a shining, we enjoy the sweetness of Christ living in us to be our life and our person. This comes not by teaching, but by Christ's saturating us with Himself according to God's economy. The saints taking the way of God's economy are those built up with the glory of God.

THE FACE OF JESUS

In 2 Corinthians 4:6 Paul also speaks of glory: "For God, who commanded the light to shine out of darkness, hath shined in our hearts, to give the light of the knowledge of the glory of God in the face of Jesus Christ." The word face here refers to the Lord's countenance, to His presence. How we need to have the presence of the Lord Jesus within us! His presence is the very glory of God, for the glory of God is in the face of Christ. If our Christ is only a Christ objectively in the heavens, we shall not have the shining of His face within us. Neither shall we have the experience of His indwelling glory. We have pointed out that glory is the manifestation of God. Now, according to this verse, we see furthermore that glory is simply the face of Jesus. When we have His face, we have the glory. When we are in the presence of Christ and before His countenance, we are in glory.

TRANSFORMED FROM GLORY TO GLORY

In 2 Corinthians 3:18 Paul says, "But we all, with unveiled face beholding and reflecting as a mirror the glory of the Lord, are being transformed into the same image from glory to glory, even as from the Lord Spirit" (Gk.). Our need today is to behold and reflect the glory of the Lord. As we behold His glory, we are transformed. Notice that Paul does not say that we are corrected, adjusted, or even changed. He points out that we are being transformed into Christ's image. We are not being transformed from behavior to behavior, from spirituality to spirituality, nor from victory to victory. Hallelujah, we are being transformed from glory to glory! The source of this transformation is not doctrine in letters; it is the Lord Spirit. The more we behold the Lord's glory and are transformed by the Lord Spirit from glory to glory, the more the Lord will gain the glorious church He desires.

LIFE-STUDY OF EPHESIANS

EXPERIENCING CHRIST
IN GOD'S ECONOMY

Christ is sanctifying, cleansing, nourishing, and cherishing us in order to present to Himself a glorious church. Contrary to the religious concept, this presentation will not take place suddenly, without any preparation, when the Lord Jesus appears in His coming back. Rather, Christ's presentation of the glorious church involves a process which began at the time of the Apostles and which has been going on throughout the centuries. Today we also are participating in the process through which Christ is presenting the glorious church to Himself. This presentation is the goal of His sanctifying, cleansing, nourishing, and cherishing.

Since the day we first called upon the Lord Jesus and received Him into us, He has been seeking opportunities to work Himself into our being. The more His element is worked into us, the more we are saturated with Himself and the more we are sanctified, cleansed, nourished, and cherished. The ultimate consummation of this process will be the presentation of the church to Himself in glory.

SATURATED WITH CHRIST

Christ's working Himself into us is not a matter of behavior or self-improvement. It is a matter of our being inwardly saturated with the Shekinah glory of God. Suppose a steel rod, hard, cold, and black, is thrust into fire and held there. Eventually, the fire will saturate the steel and cause it to glow. In this way the steel loses its natural color and becomes white hot. In a sense, the color of the steel is swallowed up by the fire. Now the steel is shining, glowing. However, it would be useless, even ridiculous, for someone to teach steel to shine. What can cause the steel to shine is not teaching, but burning. It must be burned until fire has saturated its very substance. This will cause the steel rod to become a bearer of light. If this steel is to keep on glowing, however, it must remain in the fire. If it is kept out of the fire for any length of time, its natural color and darkness will return. In a similar way, what we need today is not doctrine in letters; we need to be burned by Christ and saturated with Him as the indwelling glory of God.

COMING TO CHRIST IN THE WORD

I can testify that most of the teachings I received in Christianity did not afford me very much help. They actually hindered me and frustrated me from going on with the Lord. Today to me the Bible is not mainly a book of teachings, but a book that reveals the Person of the living Christ. As I read the Word, I open to the Lord, and immediately I experience His burning within me. Since I have His burning, what need do I have for mere teachings?

In John 5:39 and 40 the Lord Jesus said to the religionists, "You search the Scriptures, because you think that in them you have eternal life, and it is these that testify concerning Me; and you are not willing to come to Me that you may have life." These verses indicate that religion may even help people to honor and respect the Bible, but that very respect for the holy Word may be used to keep them away from the presence of the living Christ. If we read the Word properly, it should always bring us to the Lord. Whenever we come to the Bible, we must also come to Him so that we may have life.

AN UNVEILED FACE

We have seen that God's desire is to obtain a glorious church. Only Christ who is the expression of God's glory can make the church glorious, for only He Himself is the fire of glory that burns His glory into us. Moses had an experience along this line. After Moses had spent forty days in the Lord's presence on the mountain, the skin of his face shone with God's glory (Exo. 34:29-35). The glory of God had been burned into him. This was not the result of religious teaching; it came from directly beholding the glory of God.

In 2 Corinthians 3:18 Paul tells us that we all, with an unveiled face, need to behold and reflect as mirrors the glory of the Lord (Gk.). Pay attention to the term "unveiled face." This term indicates a face that used to be veiled and from which the veil has been removed. I am deeply concerned that many of us are still veiled by religious concepts and teachings. Oh, how we need a face unveiled to behold the Lord! Hence, we all should pray, "Lord, remove the veils from me."

How pitiful it is to be veiled. Nevertheless, many believers are covered by layers of veils they do not even realize are there. For this reason, Paul was burdened that the saints would be unveiled. Then with unveiled faces we can behold and reflect the glory of the Lord. In this way we are genuinely transformed from one degree of glory to another. Such a transformation takes place through the Lord Spirit. Therefore, we do not behold doctrines and teachings; we behold the glory of the Lord. Moreover, we are not taught or corrected, but we are transformed into the image of Christ from glory to glory.

In the Lord's ministry we are fighting to remove the veils from the saints. How subtle is the influence of religion! Its subtlety is seen in the fact that it causes the Lord's people to become veiled. Although many are sincerely seeking the Lord, they have been completely veiled by religion with its teachings and concepts. Therefore, I say once again that we are here not for doctrine in letters, but for the genuine recovery of the experience of Christ. We all need an unveiled face to behold the Lord.

Various things can be veils to us today, just as they were veils to the Jews. The Jews were veiled by the Scriptures, by the law, by the ordinances, and by Judaism as a religious system. Today Christians are veiled especially by teachings and ordinances. I am burdened that all the veils would be removed so that the saints may have an unveiled face to behold the glory of the Lord.

VEILED BY ORDINANCES

Let us consider in more detail the matter of ordinances as veils. Sometimes in our meetings we shout praises to the Lord. Visitors may be troubled by our shouting. They may even think that our enthusiasm in the meetings matches that of a crowd at a sporting event. Such a criticism of shouting comes from an ordinance regarding meetings. Others may criticize the meetings because they see no exercise of such gifts as speaking in tongues. This indicates that they have an ordinance concerning gifts. Still others may react to the way certain of the saints dress. This indicates that they have an ordinance concerning the proper way to dress for a church meeting. Let us drop all the ordinances and come back to the living Person of Christ.

In message after message we desire to do just one thing: to point out your need for the living Christ. You need to be sanctified, cleansed, nourished, and cherished by Him. Nevertheless, no matter how much we emphasize the need to experience Christ as our life and our person, many are still preoccupied with secondary matters related to our meetings or our practice of the church life, because they are still veiled by their ordinances. Therefore, we wish to declare that we are not here for any particular practice. We are here for the wonderful Person of the Lord Jesus Christ.

Over the years Christians have been divided by various ordinances and are still being divided by ordinances today. For example, to insist upon the practice of pray-reading is wrong. We are not a church of pray-reading. However, to reject pray-reading is also wrong. In either case, there would be an ordinance regarding pray-reading. We need to turn from all ordinances to the Christ who sanctifies, cleanses, nourishes, and cherishes us.

It is a mistake to come to Los Angeles with the intention of learning how we practice the church life. Because we are constantly changing, not even we ourselves know the way to have the church life. Prior to 1966 we did not have pray-reading, and before 1968 we did not have the practice of calling on the name of the Lord. Perhaps after another period of time, the Lord will show us something further that we should practice. To insist that we know the way to have the church life is to cause trouble.

Christians are easily divided over practices. Some like to shout praises to the Lord, but others oppose shouting. The same is true regarding quiet meetings or speaking in tongues. If we have truly seen the church, then we shall realize that all ordinances regarding practices must be set aside, for all such ordinances are divisive. Many dear saints love the Lord and seek Him, but they do not realize the divisiveness of their ordinances.

GOD'S ECONOMY

God's economy is so simple: it is just to work Christ into us so that He may live in us and we may live by Him. If we take the way of God's economy, the church will eventually become glorious, for Christ, the glory of God, will continually burn His glory into us. We are not here for a particular practice or way of having the church life. We are here only for Christ. The church is the issue of the enjoyment of Christ. The proper church life is a matter of us all enjoying Christ and then coming together to express Him, without insisting upon any particular way of expressing Christ. What we need in the Lord's recovery today is not a particular practice—it is only the living Christ.

Concerning the living Christ, we have pointed out that in His coming back Christ will come out from within us. He will spread within us, saturate us with Himself, and swallow up every part of our inward being. Then He will come out through us. When some hear of this, they may argue that the New Testament teaches that Christ will descend from the heavens. Yes, a number of verses tell us that the Lord is in the heavens and that in His coming He will descend from the heavens. However, for many, the teaching of the Lord's coming from heaven has become a religious preoccupation. Therefore we must also pay attention to the verses which emphasize the fact that Christ is in us. For example, Colossians 3:4 says that when Christ appears we shall appear with Him in glory, but Colossians 1:27 says that Christ in us is the hope of glory.

NO SYSTEMATIZING

Certain religious teachers attempt to systematize the revelation in the New Testament. Under the influence of such systematic teachings, some suppose that since Christ is in the third heaven He cannot be elsewhere, particularly not in us. Nevertheless, the Bible says that Christ is both in the third heaven and in us as well (Rom. 8:34, 10). Furthermore, although Christ is in us already, He is coming. This means that He is both here now and He is coming. I cannot reconcile this. I simply believe both aspects because the New Testament reveals both.

Recently a young man approached me and asked if I believed that the Lord Jesus was at the right hand of God in the heavens. I assured him that I did. Then he asked me if I believed that the Lord had been resurrected with a body. I told him that I definitely believed this also. Then I encouraged him not to systematize the truth of God's revelation in the New Testament. On the day of His resurrection, the Lord Jesus entered the room where the disciples were gathered. Although the doors were closed, He suddenly appeared in their midst. According to Luke 24:37, "They were terrified and affrighted, and supposed that they had seen a spirit." The Lord said to them, "Behold my hands and my feet, that it is I myself: handle me, and see; for a spirit hath not flesh and bones, as ye see me have" (v. 39). Certainly the Lord in resurrection still had a physical body. How then was He able to enter that closed room? Instead of trying to explain this or to systematize it, we should simply believe the plain word of the Bible. The New Testament says that Christ is the life-giving Spirit indwelling our spirit. As such an indwelling One, He is spreading within us and saturating us with Himself, seeking the opportunity to come out through us. But the Bible also reveals that Christ is on the throne in the third heaven and that in His coming back He will descend to the earth. Instead of trying to reconcile the subjective aspect and the objective aspect of the Lord's coming, let us simply believe both because both are revealed in the New Testament.

EXPERIENCING THE INDWELLING CHRIST

The problem many believers have is that they have been religiously indoctrinated regarding the objective aspect of the Lord's coming, to the neglect of the subjective aspect. They pay their full attention to the Christ in heaven and firmly believe in His coming back. However, they neglect the fact of the indwelling Christ, perhaps not even realizing that Christ is now within them. As we are awaiting Christ's coming back from the heavens, we need to enjoy Him inwardly. The Lord Jesus said, "Behold, I stand at the door and knock; if anyone hears My voice and opens the door, I will come in to him and dine with him and he with Me" (Rev. 3:20). The Lord's word here indicates that He is here already. How we need to experience the living, subjective, indwelling Christ!

My burden is to minister such a Christ to the Lord's people. It is not to teach the saints how to interpret the Bible. What is the use of knowing how to rightly interpret the Bible if we do not have a direct, precious, and intimate enjoyment of the living Christ? How we must fight the battle so that all the children of God may have such an enjoyment of the Lord! This is our need in the Lord's recovery today.

Let us forget the ordinances and practices, and let us say, "O Lord Jesus, I have not realized how much I need to take You as my life and as my person. Lord, I open my being to You, and I take You as my life and as my person. I don't care about my concepts concerning the way to practice the church life. I care only to have the living, intimate, and personal enjoyment of You."

GOD'S CONCERN IN HIS ECONOMY

Regarding the church, we should have no intention of either imitating or of opposing. Our only aim should be to enjoy the living Person of Christ and to inwardly experience Him more and more. We should not be concerned about practices, methods, or ways. Consider as an illustration the various kinds of eating utensils. The Chinese use chopsticks, the Americans use a knife and fork, and the Indonesians may use their fingers. We should not be concerned about what we eat with, but only about what we eat. As long as people take the proper food into them, we should not be concerned whether they use chopsticks, a knife and fork, or their fingers. However, some may boast that the best way is to use a knife and fork. Spiritually speaking, we may do the same thing regarding the practice of the church life. We may be proud of our way, but we may not have any food on our plate. Let us not care for spiritual table manners; let us care only for spiritual eating. Many of us were starving for years because we cared only for manners, not for food. In so many religious groups everything is well-mannered and in excellent order, but there is no food for the Lord's people to eat. Therefore, in His recovery today the Lord is recovering the food on the table, not the manner of eating the food.

In His economy God is not concerned about utensils. His concern is that we experience Christ's sanctifying, cleansing, nourishing, and cherishing. Only as we experience Christ in such a way will He be able to present a glorious church to Himself. Praise Him that the process of this presentation is inwardly taking place day by day. May we all see that in His economy God cares not for forms or practices, but only for His dear Son, the Lord Jesus Christ. May we all receive mercy to experience and enjoy Him.

LIFE-STUDY OF EPHESIANS

A SUMMARY OF THE EXHORTATION
IN CHAPTER FIVE

In this message we shall present a summary of Paul's exhortation in chapter five, concentrating on love and light. We have seen that firstly we receive God in Christ as grace and realize God in Christ as truth. Then we come to enjoy God as love and light. Love and light are inward elements, whereas grace and truth are outward elements. For this reason, the exhortation in 5:1-33 is deeper than that in 4:17-32. Love is the inner substance of God that can be sensed, and light is the expressed element of God that can be seen. According to the revelation of Ephesians 5, both love and light are to be the inner source of our walk.

BASIC ELEMENTS AND BASIC FACTORS

Paul's writing in Ephesians is both profound and deep. As he was writing this Epistle, he drew upon the deep concepts that were within him. These deeper concepts are the basic elements and basic factors in each chapter. In our reading of Ephesians, we must endeavor to determine what these basic elements and basic factors are, for they are the very components of the book. We have pointed out that the basic elements in chapter four are grace and truth and that the basic elements in chapter five are love and light. Along with these basic elements, there are the basic factors. In chapters four and five Paul's intention is not simply to give a number of exhortations regarding stealing, putting off falsehood, submission, and love. Nevertheless, many pay attention to such details, but not to the basic elements and basic factors.

We have seen that in chapter four the basic factors, on the positive side, are the life of God and the Spirit of God and, on the negative side, the Devil. Now we must go on to see that the most important basic factor in this chapter is the church as the new man. This means that the exhortation here is related to this aspect of the church. The main factor in chapter five is the church as the Bride. Therefore, just as Paul's exhortation in chapter four is related to the new man, so his exhortation in chapter five is related to the Bride.

THE KEY TO CHAPTER FOUR

Remember, the subject of the book of Ephesians is not behavior or virtue; it is the church. In giving us the long exhortation recorded in chapter four, Paul never loses sight of his main point—the church. As he presents the principle and the details, he is fully conscious of the church as the new man. Hence, the living described in chapter four must be for the church as the new man; that is, the church as the new man must be according to truth and by grace. As the new man, the church should live a life according to God's standard, according to the truth as it is in Jesus. The only way the church as the new man can have such a life is by God's all-sufficient grace. This grace supplies us so that we may live according to the mold, the model, the pattern, of the life of Jesus. This is the key to chapter four.

If we apply this key in our reading of this chapter, the entire chapter will be open to us. Keep in mind that Ephesians 4 deals with the church as the new man. If we would be the church in this aspect, we must live a life according to the standard of the truth as it is in Jesus and by God's all-sufficient grace.

LOVE AND LIGHT IN CHAPTER FIVE

In the same principle, the main point in chapter five is the church as the Bride. The main point is not Paul's exhortation regarding wives submitting to their own husbands or husbands loving their own wives. As the Bride, the church needs something finer and deeper than truth and grace. There is the need for love and light. Truth is not as fine as light, and grace is not as deep or intimate as love. With respect to the church as the Bride, in chapter five Paul speaks of love and light.

The fact that the church as the Bride requires a living in love and in light can be proved by our own experience in married life. If a husband and wife live together merely by grace and according to truth, their married life will be very poor. If my wife were to deal with me according to grace but offer me no love, I would be extremely dissatisfied. She would feel the same if I dealt with her according to grace without love. Married life is based not upon grace, but upon love. In like manner, married life is based not upon truth, but upon light. How pitiful it would be if a husband and wife were always considering the right way to behave toward each other. For the intimate relationship between husband and wife, mere truth is not adequate. There must be light. Therefore, a proper marriage is not merely according to truth and by grace, but is in love and in light.

Is your married life according to truth and by grace, or is it in love and in light? Suppose a wife says to her husband, "Everything I do for you is according to truth and by grace. Nothing I do is wrong or false. Furthermore, everything is by the Lord's sufficient grace." This does not sound like the intimacy of a marriage, but sounds like the coldness of a law court. In married life the relationship between wife and husband should be fine, bright, and intimate.

LIVING IN THE REALM OF LIGHT

Although it is rather easy to understand the difference between love and grace, it is more difficult to understand the distinction between light and truth. Perhaps it will help if I illustrate from my own experience in married life. My wife and I have been married for a good many years. During this time, I cannot recall ever dealing with her according to what I thought was right. On the contrary, by the Lord's enabling, I have behaved toward her always in light. When we are in the light, we are outside the realm of right and wrong. There is no need to discern what is right and what is wrong, what we should do and what we should not do. If we are in the light, we simply act and behave spontaneously in a certain way. However, when we are in darkness, we need to discern, to guess, and to grope for a way to do things. But when we are in the light, there is no need for groping, guessing, or discerning.

Suppose I am about to lose my temper with my wife. There is no need for me at such a time to ask if this is according to truth. I do not need to wonder what my children or the elders of the church will think about it. To ask such questions with respect to husband or wife is to descend from the realm of light to the realm of truth. It is to consider what is according to the standard of the pattern of the life of Jesus. If we remain on the mountaintop in the realm of light, there will be no need for such considerations. As those in the light, we shall not try to discern whether or not it is right to lose our temper at that particular time.

TWO CASES

In a foregoing message I referred to the cases of the immoral women in John 4 and 8. In both cases the word truth is used. In John 4:24 the Lord Jesus speaks of worshipping God in spirit and in truth. In John 8:32 He says that we shall know the truth and that the truth will set us free. The women in these two chapters were not yet saved. When the Lord was dealing with them, they were candidates for salvation. As such, they were in darkness and in falsehood. However, they were about to be delivered out of darkness and falsehood into the realm of truth and righteousness. I believe that both these women were saved and brought into the realm of truth. However, having entered into this realm, they were to go on to contact the Father and enter into the presence of God where all is light. Here in the realm of light we no longer consider what is right and what is wrong, what is false and what is real. Instead of such considerations, there is simply the shining of light.

A SPONTANEOUS LIVING

If our married life is proper, we shall not consider whether our behavior with our spouse is according to truth or up to the standard. If we think in this way in relation to our husband or wife, we are quite far from the realm of light. In fact we are not even fully according to truth. If our married life is in the sphere of light, we shall not consider how to behave. Rather, we shall simply and spontaneously live in light. We shall do certain things and behave in certain ways simply because we are in the light, not because we regard such things or such behavior as according to the truth as it is in Jesus.

In the early years of my Christian life, I lived in the sphere of truth. I tried to be right in everything I did. I was afraid to do certain things because of what others might say. Therefore, I behaved in a way that others would regard as praiseworthy. This means that my behavior was according to truth. Later, by the Lord's mercy, I was brought more into His presence. I learned how to abide in His presence and to live in intimacy with Him in a relationship full of love and light. As a result, I was kept from doing things not because I had reasoned they were wrong, but simply because I was in the light. As one in the light, I acted, behaved, and spoke in certain ways without considering what was according to truth or what was right. No longer was I concerned about what others might say. I no longer thought about what kind of behavior would be appreciated or what would be criticized. I was in the light, and I no longer reasoned about what actions were according to truth.

To be the church as the new man it is necessary and appropriate to live according to truth and by grace. But this is not adequate for the aspect of the church as the Bride. As the Bride, the church must have an intimate relationship with the Lord Jesus in love and in light. In everything and in every way the church as the Bride must be bright. Therefore, in chapter five love and light are the basic elements.

THE WARRIOR

In every chapter of Ephesians different aspects of the church are revealed. Each of these aspects is related to various basic elements. For example, in chapter six we see the church as the warrior. What a warrior requires is neither grace and truth nor love and light, but strength and armor for fighting. As the warrior, the church must be strong to stand and must have the armor with which to fight.

THE BODY OF CHRIST

Let us now trace the basic factors and the basic elements in chapters one, two, and three. The major factor in chapter one is the church as the Body of Christ, the fullness of the One who fills all in all. The infinite, unlimited, eternal power that raised Christ from among the dead, uplifted Him to the third heaven, and made Him the Head over all things, is to the church which is His Body. In order for the church to be the Body, the church must have the well-speaking of the Triune God. Hence, the major factor in chapter one is the church as the Body of Christ, and the basic element is the well-speaking of the Father, Son, and Spirit.

GOD'S DWELLING PLACE

In chapter two we see various aspects of the church: the masterpiece, the new man created by Christ on the cross, the commonwealth of God, the kingdom where the citizens have civil rights and responsibilities, the household of God, and finally the dwelling place of God, God's habitation. Although all these aspects are covered, the major factor in chapter two is the church as the dwelling place of God. To be God's habitation, the church must have both resurrection and the Spirit. These are the basic elements in this chapter. In the first part of the chapter the main concept is that of resurrection life, and in the second part the main thought is the Spirit. Both are necessary for the church to be the habitation of God.

THE FULLNESS OF GOD

In chapter three, the deepest chapter in Ephesians, the major factor is the church as the fullness of God. For the church to be the fullness of God, we need the unsearchable riches of Christ. Thus, the unsearchable riches of Christ are the basic element in this chapter.

THE CHURCH LIFE ACCORDING TO GOD'S DESIRE

Let us review the major factors and the basic elements in the six chapters of Ephesians. In chapter one the major factor is the church as the Body of Christ, and the basic element is the well-speaking of the Triune God. In chapter two the major factor is the church as the habitation of God, and the basic elements are resurrection and the Spirit. In chapter three the major factor is the church as the fullness of God, and the basic element is the unsearchable riches of Christ. In chapter four the major factor is the church as the new man, and the basic elements are grace and truth. In chapter five the major factor is the church as the Bride, and the basic elements are love and light. Finally, in chapter six the major factor is the church as the warrior, and the basic elements are might and the armor.

Because the church life as the Bride in love and light requires something fine and intimate, Paul uses married life as an illustration. In married life there is no place for might or for armor. Neither are such things characteristic of the church as the Bride. With the church as the Bride there is no emphasis on grace, truth, nor even the riches of Christ. Furthermore, there is no mention of resurrection, the Spirit, nor the well-speaking of the Triune God. Specifically what is required here is God Himself as love and light. As we have pointed out, love is the inner essence of God, and light is the element of God expressed visibly. When we get into God to touch His inner substance, we experience Him as love and light. The proper church life should be in this realm.

Why then does Paul include chapter six? This chapter is necessary because God's enemy remains to be dealt with. If there were no enemy, we could stop with the church as the Bride in chapter five.

According to Revelation 19, the warrior who fights with Christ in the battle against the enemy is firstly the Bride of Christ. This means that firstly we must be the Bride in love and in light, and then we can go forth as the warrior with Christ to war against the enemy. Thus, a couple, Christ and His Bride, will defeat the enemy.

May we all be impressed that the church life according to God's desire must be in love and in light, both of which are the very elements of God Himself. In the inner substance of God we have love and light. Here we have the top church life, the church as the Bride. The goal of the book of Ephesians is to bring us into God's inner substance to know Him as love and light. Here we are to live in intimate fellowship as we enjoy the shining light and love in its sweetness.

LIFE-STUDY OF EPHESIANS

MESSAGE SIXTY-TWO

THE BELIEVERS' LIVING IN THE RELATIONSHIP
BETWEEN CHILDREN AND FATHERS
AND BETWEEN SLAVES AND MASTERS

Through the sanctifying, cleansing, nourishing, and cherishing Christ will gain a glorious church as His Bride. Just as Eve came out of Adam and went back to Adam to be one flesh with him, so the church comes out of Christ and will go back to Christ to be one spirit with Him. God's desire is that the church which comes out of Christ and returns to Christ will be a glorious church, a church that expresses God and manifests Him. By the sanctifying, cleansing, nourishing, and cherishing the church is being saturated with the essence of God. In this way the church is becoming the Bride to express Christ. Every local church today must be such an expression of God.

The glorious church, the church that expresses God, must also be holy and without blemish. As such a holy church, she must be first separated from everything common and then permeated and saturated with the element of God.

In order to be without blemish, the church must be without mixture. To be unclean is one thing, and to have some mixture within us is another. We need to be both pure and without mixture. To be without mixture means that in our being we have nothing other than God. For example, we are like precious stone that has no foreign element or substance within it. One day the church will not only be clean and pure, but also without blemish, without mixture. She will be altogether the mingling of the Triune God with a resurrected, uplifted, and transformed humanity. In order that Christ may gain such a church, we are presently undergoing His sanctifying, cleansing, nourishing, and cherishing.

The first four chapters of Ephesians cover the fulfillment of God's eternal purpose. For the fulfillment of His purpose, God needs the universal new man, the church as the full-grown man in chapter four. In this respect, the new man is the highest aspect of the church. From the church as the assembly we proceed to the church as the household of God, then to the church as the Body, and finally to the church as the full-grown man.

Along with the need for God's purpose to be fulfilled, there is also the need for Christ to be satisfied. Within Christ there is the longing, the deep desire, for satisfaction. Only the church as the Bride can satisfy the longing in Christ's heart.

Even in the relationship between husband and wife, the wife should care for her husband's satisfaction and not merely do certain things for her husband. Before the creation of Eve, the Bible says, "It is not good that the man should be alone" (Gen. 2:18). Therefore, the woman was created to fulfill the man's need for satisfaction. According to the Bible, the satisfaction of a man depends upon the woman. In Ephesians 5 Paul presents the church as the Bride for Christ's satisfaction. As we have seen, what is required for the church to be the Bride is not just truth and grace, but light and love.

The church, who is the new man for the fulfillment of God's purpose and the Bride for the satisfaction of the longing in Christ's heart, is also the warrior for the defeat of God's enemy. Through the spiritual warfare of the church as the warrior, God's problem with the enemy is solved. If the church is to be the warrior to defeat the enemy, she must have both might and the whole armor of God. Therefore, the church is the new man for the fulfillment of God's purpose, the Bride for Christ's satisfaction, and the warrior for the defeat of God's enemy.

Between the section on the church as the Bride (5:22-33) and the church as the warrior (6:10-20), we have 6:1-9, which deals with the relationship between children and fathers and between slaves and masters. If we neglect this portion of the Word, we cannot be a proper Bride or a proper warrior.

I. THE RELATIONSHIP
BETWEEN CHILDREN AND FATHERS

A. Children

Verse 1 says, "The children, obey your parents in the Lord, for this is right." In exhorting the children and the parents, the apostle deals with the children first, since trouble comes mostly from them.

In this verse Paul does not simply speak of children, but of *the* children. By using the definite article before children Paul indicates that the children of believers are not common. They are different from the children of people in the world. Therefore, the particular children, those in the families of believers, are exhorted to obey their parents in the Lord.

The phrase "in the Lord" indicates obedience to the parents by being one with the Lord. It also indicates that this should be done not by self-effort, but by the Lord, and not according to the natural concept, but according to the Lord's word. The children of believers should realize that they are to obey their parents by being one with the Lord. Moreover, they are to obey their parents not by their own strength, but by the Lord Himself. Their obedience is to be according to the Lord's word, according to the Scriptures.

In this verse Paul says that for the children to obey their parents in the Lord is right. The Greek word may also be rendered just. To obey the parents is both right and just.

In verses 2 and 3 Paul goes on to say, "Honor your father and mother, which is the first commandment with a promise, that it may be well with you, and that you may live long on the earth." This is not only the first commandment with a promise, but also the first commandment concerning man's relationship with man (Exo. 20:12). The promise, mentioned in verse 3, is that it may be well with the children and that they may live long on the earth. The first part of the promise is related to prosperity in material blessing; it also refers to living in a peaceful situation. The second part is to have lon-gevity. According to this commandment, prosperity and longevity are God's blessings in this life to those who honor their parents.

Honoring is different from obeying. Obedience refers to an action, whereas honor denotes an attitude. It is possible for the children to obey their parents without honoring them. In order to honor their parents, the children need a certain attitude, a certain spirit. All the children need to learn to obey their parents with honor.

If we would live long on the earth, we need to honor our parents. Those who fail to honor their parents commit sui-cide in a gradual way. They actually shorten their life on earth. If you wish to prolong your days, learn to obey your parents with honor. In the Bible this is the unique condition for having a long life. Anyone who desires a long life needs to fulfill this condition.

B. Fathers

In verse 4 Paul turns to the fathers: "And the fathers, do not provoke your children to anger, but nurture them in the discipline and admonition of the Lord." Provoking to anger damages the children by stirring up their flesh. It is always destructive for parents to be angry with their children. For this reason, I counsel the parents not to lose their temper when dealing with their children. Not provoking the chil-dren's anger requires the fathers' anger to be dealt with by remaining under the cross. The only way we can keep from losing our temper is to stay on the cross. In dealing with your children's wrongdoings or misbehavior, you must firstly go to the cross and stay there. Otherwise, you will lose your temper, and this loss of temper will provoke your children's anger.

Instead of provoking the children to anger, the fathers are to nurture them in the discipline and admonition of the Lord. To nurture children means to bring them up, to raise them, by nourishing them. Raising children requires that the parents give them the needed instruction related to human life, family life, and social life. The word admonition here includes instruction. Paul was probably referring to the Old Testament requirement that parents instruct their children with the word of God (Deut. 6:7). This means that we are to teach our children with the Bible. Along with this instruction, we sometimes must discipline them, chastise them. It is crucial that parents learn to nurture the children in the discipline and admonition of the Lord.

As parents, we must do our duty with respect to our children. This means that we should not only teach them, but also set up an example for them to follow. Just as the Lord Jesus sanctified Himself for the sake of His disciples (John 17:19), so parents should sanctify themselves for the sake of their children. Those who do not have children may be free to do certain things, such as sleep late in the morning. But those with children do not have the liberty to do these things. For the sake of their children, they must be restricted. Children always imitate their parents. Therefore, it is the parents' responsibility to set up a high standard and a proper pattern and example for their children to follow.

However, no matter how good an example is set by the parents, how the children develop depends on God's mercy. On the one hand, the parents must keep a high standard, but on the other hand, they need to trust in the Lord. Day by day we should tell Him, "Lord, these children are not mine; they are Your possession placed in my custody for a period of time. Lord, what I am doing with them is simply fulfilling my responsibility. How they will turn out, Lord, depends absolutely on Your mercy."

It is possible for parents to be selfish concerning the spiritual welfare of their children. If their children get saved and become spiritual, they are very happy. However, these parents may not be happy to see the children of other families becoming more spiritual than their children. Most parents in the church hope that their children will become the future apostles, elders, and deacons. Thus, even in this matter, we are selfish.

I once read of a certain woman who prayed desperately for her child to be saved. Although she prayed daily for years, still her child was not saved. One day she inquired of the Lord why He did not answer her prayers and keep His promise. The Lord told her that He would surely keep His promise and answer her prayers. However, she was too selfish. If she would stop praying so much for her child and begin to pray for the children of others, she would see His faithfulness. From that time onward, she began to pray for other children to be saved. After a short while, her child was saved.

This story illustrates the fact that we may be selfish even in praying for the salvation of our children. Not to pray for our children is wrong, but to be fully occupied with prayer for them in a selfish way is also wrong. Hence, the matter of the salvation of our children and their spiritual welfare is also a test to us.

II. BETWEEN SLAVES AND MASTERS

A. Slaves

In 6:5-9 Paul deals with the relationship between slaves and masters. Concerning this relationship, he exhorts the slaves first because the source of trouble is mostly with them. Verse 5 says, "The slaves, obey your masters according to flesh with fear and trembling, in singleness of your heart, as to Christ." In the apostle's time, slaves were purchased by their masters, and the masters had the right over their lives. Some slaves and some masters became brothers in the church. As brothers in the church, they were equal. But in their homes those who were slaves still had to obey the brothers who were their masters according to flesh.

Paul exhorts the slaves to obey with fear and trembling, in singleness of heart, as to Christ. Fear is the inward motive, and trembling is the outward attitude. Singleness means to be pure in motive, with only a single purpose. The slaves are to be single; they are not to have a double purpose. That is, they are not to serve their masters with the intention of receiving some gain for themselves.

The slaves are to be in obedience to their masters as to Christ. This means that the slaves are to regard their masters as if they were the Lord. The relationship between slaves and masters is a type of our relationship with Christ, our Master. We should obey Him as a slave, in singleness of heart.

In verse 6 Paul goes on to say, "Not with eye-service as men-pleasers, but as slaves of Christ, doing the will of God from the soul." If a brother in slavery stands in his position and obeys his master, he is in the eyes of the Lord a slave of Christ, doing the will of God, and his service is as to the Lord and not to men (v. 7). Such a slave is to do the will of God from the soul. The words "from the soul" here equal from the heart, from the inner being. This means to serve not only with the physical body, but with the heart. The slaves were to serve "as to the Lord and not to men." This indicates that Paul's intention was to direct the slaves to the Lord. His desire was that they would learn to serve their masters as the Lord.

Concerning the slaves, Paul concludes in verse 8, "Knowing that whatever good thing each one does, this he shall receive from the Lord, whether a slave or a freeman." The word this refers to the good thing. Whatever good thing we do, we shall receive the same from the Lord. If the slaves do something good, the Lord will return to them that same good thing. This means that the good thing they do will become a reward to them.

B. Masters

In verse 9 Paul says, "And the masters, do the same things toward them, giving up threatening, knowing that both their Master and yours is in the heavens, and there is no respect of persons with Him." The masters who had the right over the lives of their purchased slaves should give up threatening, because the Lord in the heavens is the real Master of both them and the slaves. In the flesh, some may be slaves, and others may be masters. But in the eyes of the Lord, there is no difference between slaves and masters.

According to Colossians 3:11, in the new man there is no slave or freeman. In the church, we all are brothers. However, in the flesh there still is the distinction between slaves and masters.

Regarding all these exhortations, Paul is making one key point: For the sake of the church life, we need to have a proper human living in this present age. This is an extremely important lesson for us all to learn.

LIFE-STUDY OF EPHESIANS

MESSAGE SIXTY-THREE

WARFARE TO DEAL WITH THE SPIRITUAL ENEMY

In this message we come to 6:10-20, a strategic section of this book dealing with spiritual warfare. As we have seen, in Ephesians Paul covers various aspects of the church. The Greek word for church, *ekklesia,* denotes a gathering, an assembly, of called ones. For example, when city officials in ancient times called the people of the city together for a meeting, that meeting was known as an *ekklesia.* The church is such an assembly of God's called people. In Ephesians 1 Paul reveals that the church is the Body of Christ. Just as a person's body is his stature and expression, so the church as the Body of Christ is the stature and expression of Christ. As Christ's Body, the church is the fullness of the One who fills all in all.

In 2:10 Paul indicates that the church is God's poem, His masterpiece, a poetic writing that expresses the desire of the writer's heart. In this chapter Paul goes on to point out that the church is the corporate new man created in Christ Jesus, the commonwealth of God, and the household of God. Furthermore, in this chapter the church is also the dwelling place of God (v. 22).

In 3:4 Paul speaks of the mystery of Christ. The mystery of God is Christ, and the mystery of Christ is the church. As the mystery of God, Christ is the definition of God. In the same principle, as the mystery of Christ, the church is the definition of Christ.

In 3:19 Paul uses the term the fullness of God. This term is similar to the expression "the fullness of the One Who fills all in all" (1:23). The fullness of God refers mainly to the source, and the fullness of the One who fills all in all refers mainly to the outcome. For example, the fullness of God is like a fountain, and the fullness of the One who fills all in all is like the stream that flows forth from the fountain. The church is both the fullness of God and the fullness of Christ as the One who fills all in all.

In chapter four Paul again speaks of the new man (v. 24). Chapter two covers the creation of the new man, but not the living of the new man. The new man is composed of two peoples, the believing Jews and the believing Gentiles. Concerning the living of the new man, chapter four covers both the principle and the details. The principle is related to the truth as it is in Jesus, the mold established by the living of Jesus on earth. The details are related to God's grace. By grace the new man carries out God's eternal purpose.

In chapters five and six we see two further aspects of the church: the Bride to satisfy the desire of Christ and the warrior to defeat God's enemy. As the Bride, the church needs love and light. As the warrior, the church needs might and the whole armor of God.

I. THE NEGATIVE SIDE
OF THE CHURCH'S RESPONSIBILITY

Of the twelve aspects of the church covered in Ephesians, the main aspects are the new man, the Bride, and the warrior. The new man includes the aspect of the Body, and the Body includes the fullness and the dwelling place. Therefore, the first ten aspects of the church are all included in the new man who fulfills God's eternal purpose and carries out His economy. This new man is used by the Triune God to accomplish what He planned in eternity past for eternity future. Nevertheless, although God's plan is fulfilled with the new man, Christ's desire still needs to be satisfied, and God's enemy still must be defeated. Hence, there is the need for the church to be both the Bride and the warrior.

The passage from 1:1 to 6:9 completes the revelation on the positive side concerning the church for the fulfilling of God's eternal purpose. Yet on the negative side, that is, for dealing with God's enemy, something still remains to be covered. In the first five chapters the church is portrayed in many ways, on the positive side, to fulfill God's eternal purpose. On the negative side, the church is seen in chapter six as a warrior to defeat God's enemy, the Devil. To do this, the church must put on the whole armor of God.

In 1928 brother Nee held his first overcomer conference on spiritual warfare. In that conference Satan, the evil one, was exposed to the uttermost. Brother Nee pointed out that in the universe there are three wills: the divine will, the satanic will, and the human will. If we would know how the church can be God's warrior to engage in spiritual warfare, we must know these three wills, these three intentions. God's will, being self-existing, is eternal, uncreated. As created beings, the angels also have a will. One of these angels, an archangel, was appointed by God to rule the universe that existed before the creation of Adam. Because of his high position and his beauty, this archangel became proud. This pride gave rise to an evil intention, which became the satanic will. Therefore, in addition to God's intention, God's will, there is a second intention, a second will, for now the satanic will is set against God's will.

All warfare has its source in this conflict of wills. Before the satanic will rose up to contradict the divine will, there was no war in the universe. The controversy in the universe began with the rebellion of the archangel against God. That rebellion was the beginning of all the fighting that is now taking place among nations, in society, in the family, and in individuals. Throughout history there have been wars between nations, groups, persons, and even within individuals. For example, you may experience an inner warfare between your reason and your lust. All the different kinds of warfare have their source in the controversy between the divine will and the satanic will.

We do not know how much time elapsed between the rebellion of Satan and the creation of Adam. We simply know that at a particular time, God created man and endowed him with a human will that was free. It is because of God's greatness that He gave man a free will. A great person will never compel anyone to follow him. By giving man a free will, God was indicating that He would not force man to obey Him. When I was young, I thought that God was not wise in creating man with a free will. If I had been God, I would have made it impossible for man to have had a choice. I would have created man in such a way that all he could do was follow God. But in His greatness God gave man freedom of choice.

In Genesis 2 we see that man was free to exercise his will to eat either of the tree of life or of the tree of the knowledge of good and evil. These two trees represent the divine will and the satanic will, respectively. Hence, in the garden there was a triangular situation, with the tree of life representing the divine will, the tree of knowledge representing the satanic will, and Adam representing the human will. Actually, the tree of life denotes God Himself, and the tree of knowledge denotes Satan. Therefore, there were three persons—God, Satan, and man—each one with a will.

Although there were three wills, the controversy involved just two parties—God and Satan. The crucial issue was whether man would choose the divine will or the satanic will. If the human will stood with the divine will, then God's will would be accomplished. But if the human will took sides with the satanic will, Satan's will would be carried out, at least temporarily. As we all know, the human will took sides with the satanic will. This means that man chose to follow Satan and sided with the satanic will. Therefore, Satan was victorious temporarily.

However, through repentance man can turn from the satanic will to the divine will, from Satan's side to God's side. The first commandment in the gospel is to repent. The next two commandments are to believe and to be baptized. Any sinner who desires to be saved must obey these three commandments. He must repent to God, believe in the Lord Jesus, and be baptized in water. To repent is to have a turn from the satanic will to the divine will. Since birth our will has stood on the side of the satanic will. The reason for this is that we were in Adam when he chose Satan's will above God's will.

Many Christians do not know the true significance of the preaching of the gospel. The Bible says that we must repent for the kingdom (Matt. 4:17). The kingdom of God is actually the exercise of the divine will. When sinners repent for the kingdom of God, they turn from the side of Satan to the side of God, which is the kingdom of God, the will of God. After a person turns from the satanic will to the divine will, he must believe in the Lord Jesus and be baptized. Through baptism he is brought out of the authority of darkness, the satanic will, and is transferred into the kingdom of the Son of God's love (Col. 1:13).

From the day we were saved, our Christian life has been a life of warfare. The same was true of the children of Israel after they made their exodus from Egypt. After eating the Passover, they marched like an army out of the land of Egypt. This indicates that their eating of the Passover lamb was a preparation for war. They were saved in an atmosphere of warfare. As soon as they came out of Egypt, the fighting began. Pharaoh and his chariots pursued the children of Israel, but God came in to fight for them. After the children of Israel had passed through the Red Sea and Pharaoh's army had been overthrown, God's people triumphantly praised Him for His victory over the enemy. The Israelites proceeded to fight their way through the wilderness, and they continued fighting in the good land. Their history thus reveals that the life of a saved one is a life of warfare.

We have seen that as the new man the church should walk according to truth and by grace and that as the Bride the church should live in love and in light. However, not only must God's eternal purpose be fulfilled and the desire of Christ's heart be satisfied, but God's enemy must be defeated. For this, the church must be a warrior. Even in the Song of Songs we see that as the seeking one enjoys the Lord's presence, the fighting is going on. Therefore, we walk according to truth and by grace, we live in love and light, and we fight to subdue the satanic will. Our walk is for the fulfillment of God's purpose, our living is for the satisfaction of Christ, and our fighting is for the defeat of God's enemy. Hence, for these three things the church must be the new man, the Bride, and the warrior.

II. EMPOWERED

Ephesians 6:10 says, "For the rest, be empowered in the Lord and in the might of His strength." The Greek word here rendered empowered has the same root as the word power in 1:19. To deal with God's enemy, to fight against the evil force of darkness, we need to be empowered with the greatness of the power that raised up Christ from the dead and seated Him in the heavens, far above all the evil spirits in the air. The fact that we are to be empowered in the Lord indicates that in the spiritual warfare against Satan and his evil kingdom, we can fight only in the Lord, not in ourselves. Whenever we are in ourselves, we are defeated.

The charge to be empowered implies the need to exercise our will. If we would be empowered for spiritual warfare, our will must be strong and exercised. We should not be like jellyfish, those who are weak-willed and vacillating. Actually, it is those with a strong will who are most able to repent. Consider Saul of Tarsus as an example. As he was traveling to Damascus with the intention of arresting all those who called on the name of the Lord Jesus, he was apprehended by the Lord. Because Saul had such a strong will, he could have a strong repentance.

In addition to preserving our conscience, God has sovereignly preserved our will. If He had not done so, the preaching of the gospel could have no effect on people. We may mistakenly think that it is difficult to preach the gospel to one with a strong will. According to my experience, most of those who were saved through my gospel preaching were those with a strong will and a definite intention. Such a will is able to function positively in repentance. Repentance requires the exercise of the will. In like manner, to be empowered also involves our will.

On the day of Pentecost Peter told the people to be saved from that crooked generation (Acts 2:40, Gk.). This command seems to be both active and passive, with the word be implying something active and the word saved, something passive. The same is true of Paul's command in 6:10 to be empowered. An active element—be—is combined with a passive element—empowered. We need to exercise our will to be empowered in the Lord.

In chapter four we see that we must be renewed (v. 23) and in chapter five, that we must be submissive (5:21). For the new man, we need to be renewed; for the Bride, we need to be submissive; and for the warrior, we need to be empowered. As the warrior, we must go into battle not as a gentleman or as a lovely Bride, but as a lion. Therefore, for the new man, the Bride, and the warrior, let us be renewed, submissive, and empowered.

The fact that we need to be empowered in the Lord indicates that we cannot fight the spiritual warfare in ourselves; we can fight only in the Lord and in the might of His strength. In 6:10 Paul refers to power, might, and strength. Firstly, we are empowered by the power that raised Christ from among the dead and made Him to be the Head over all things. Then we know God's might and strength.

III. PUTTING ON THE WHOLE ARMOR OF GOD

Verse 11 opens with the words, "Put on the whole armor of God." To fight the spiritual warfare, we need not only the power of the Lord, but also the armor of God. Our weapons do not avail, but God's armor, even the whole armor of God, does.

The whole armor of God is for the entire Body, not for any individual member of the Body. The church is a corporate warrior, and the believers together make up this unique warrior. Only the corporate warrior can wear the whole armor of God; no individual believer can. We must fight the spiritual warfare in the Body, not individually.

The charge to put on the whole armor of God is an imperative, a command. God has provided the armor for us, but He does not put it on for us. Rather, we ourselves must put on the armor God has provided. For this, we need to be empowered. Although God can empower us, we still must exercise our will to cooperate with Him. In the same principle, we must cooperate with God's command to put on the armor.

IV. ABLE TO STAND AGAINST
THE STRATAGEMS OF THE DEVIL

We need to put on the whole armor of God so that we "may be able to stand" (v. 11). In chapter six the word stand is crucial. In chapter two we sit with Christ in the heavenlies (v. 6), and in chapters four and five we walk in His Body on the earth (4:1, 17; 5:2, 8, 15). Then in chapter six we stand in His power in the heavenlies. To sit with Christ is to participate in all His accomplishments; to walk in His Body is to fulfill God's eternal purpose; and to stand in His power is to fight against God's enemy.

By putting on the whole armor of God, we are able to stand against the stratagems of the Devil. These stratagems are the Devil's evil plans. Not only does the Devil have an evil will, but he also has subtle stratagems to work out his will. Even now Satan is busily working and plotting to carry out his evil, subtle stratagems.

V. OUR WRESTLING

A. Not against Blood and Flesh

In verse 12 Paul goes on to say, "For our wrestling is not against blood and flesh, but against the rulers, against the authorities, against the world-rulers of this darkness, against the spiritual forces of evil in the heavenlies." "Blood and flesh" refers to men. Behind men of blood and flesh are the evil forces of the Devil, fighting against God's purpose. Hence, our wrestling, our fighting, must not be against men, but against the evil spiritual forces in the heavenlies.

We in the Lord's recovery should realize that spiritual

warfare is not a matter of fighting against men. Even if men cause damage to the recovery, we should not fight against them. Behind them and over them is the evil power. For example, when Saul of Tarsus was desolating the church, he was under the influence of the power of darkness. The reason certain people and religious organizations oppose the Lord's recovery is that they also are being utilized by the evil power that is over them and behind them.

B. Against the Rulers, the Authorities, the World-rulers, and Spiritual Forces of Evil

The principalities, the authorities, and the world-rulers of this darkness are the rebellious angels who followed Satan in his rebellion against God and who now rule in the heavenlies over the nations of the world, such as the prince of Persia and the prince of Grecia in Daniel 10:20. This indicates that the Devil, Satan, has his kingdom of darkness (Matt. 12:26; Col. 1:13). In this kingdom, Satan is at the top, and under him are the rebellious angels.

"This darkness" refers to today's world, which is fully under the dark ruling of the Devil through his evil angels. The world-rulers of this darkness are the princes Satan has set up to rule the various nations. According to the book of Daniel, the Jewish nation was the only nation that was not under Satan's power. This nation was ruled over by Michael, the archangel who fought on behalf of Israel. All the Gentile nations, however, are ruled by devilish, rebellious angels under the administration of Satan. Therefore, in the eyes of God, darkness covers the earth and fills the atmosphere around the earth. Only God Himself remains in the light. Because of the working of Satan, who is the authority of darkness, the earth and its atmosphere have become "this darkness."

In verse 12 Paul also speaks of "the spiritual forces of evil in the heavenlies." The heavenlies here refer to the air (2:2). Satan and his spiritual forces of evil are in the air. But we are seated in the third heaven above them (2:6). In fighting a battle, the position above the enemy is strategic.

Satan and his evil forces are under us, and it is their fate to be defeated by us.

We need to be reminded again and again that our warfare is not against human beings, but against the evil spirits, the spiritual powers in the heavenlies. The rebellious angels are the evil spirits in Satan's kingdom. Thus, the warfare between the church and Satan is a battle between us who love the Lord and who are in His church and the evil powers in the heavenlies. Apparently it is people of flesh and blood who damage the church. Actually it is Satan and his evil angels working behind them who cause the damage. Therefore, we must fight against these spiritual forces.

VI. ABLE TO STAND IN THE EVIL DAY

Verse 13 says, "Therefore, take up the whole armor of God, that you may be able to withstand in the evil day." In verse 11 we are told to put on the armor of God, and in verse 13 we are charged to take it up. We have seen that the armor of God is prepared and provided by God for us. But we need to take it up and put it on; we need to use and apply God's provision. Some items of the armor, such as the sword and the shield, we take up. But other items, such as the breastplate, the helmet, and the shoes, we put on. Whether we put on the whole armor of God or take it up, we must exercise our will in a strong way.

Paul specifically mentions "the whole armor of God," not just a part or some parts of it. In order to wage the spiritual warfare, we need the whole armor. This requires the Body of Christ, not only individual believers, to take it up.

By taking up the whole armor of God, we shall be able to withstand in the evil day. To withstand is to stand against. In fighting the most important thing is to stand. In 5:16 Paul says that the days are evil. In this evil age (Gal. 1:14), every day is an evil day because Satan is at work every day.

VII. HAVING DONE ALL, TO STAND

Paul concludes verse 13 with the words, "Having done

all, to stand." In fighting we need to stand to the end. Having done all, we still must stand. As we shall see in the next two messages, verses 14 through 16 are a modifier describing how to stand.

ABOUT THE AUTHOR

Witness Lee was born in 1905 in northern China and raised in a Christian family. At age 19 he was fully captured for Christ and immediately consecrated himself to preach the gospel for the rest of his life. Early in his service, he met Watchman Nee, a renowned preacher, teacher, and writer. Witness Lee labored together with Watchman Nee under his direction. In 1934 Watchman Nee entrusted Witness Lee with the responsibility for his publication operation, called the Shanghai Gospel Bookroom.

Prior to the Communist takeover in 1949, Witness Lee was sent by Watchman Nee and his other co-workers to Taiwan to ensure that the things delivered to them by the Lord would not be lost. Watchman Nee instructed Witness Lee to continue the former's publishing operation abroad as the Taiwan Gospel Bookroom, which has been publicly recognized as the publisher of Watchman Nee's works outside China. Witness Lee's work in Taiwan manifested the Lord's abundant blessing. From a mere 350 believers, newly fled from the mainland, the churches in Taiwan grew to 20,000 in five years.

In 1962 Witness Lee felt led of the Lord to come to the United States, settling in California. During his 35 years of service in the U.S., he ministered in weekly meetings and weekend conferences, delivering several thousand spoken messages. Much of his speaking has since been published as over 400 titles. Many of these have been translated into over fourteen languages. He gave his last public conference in February 1997 at the age of 91.

He leaves behind a prolific presentation of the truth in the Bible. His major work, *Life-study of the Bible,* comprises over 25,000 pages of commentary on every book of the Bible from the perspective of the believers' enjoyment and experience of God's divine life in Christ through the Holy Spirit. Witness Lee was the chief editor of a new translation of the New Testament into Chinese called the Recovery Version and directed the translation of the same into English. The Recovery Version also appears in a number of other languages. He provided an extensive body of footnotes, outlines, and spiritual cross references. A radio broadcast of his messages can be heard on Christian radio stations in the United States. In 1965 Witness Lee founded Living Stream Ministry, a non-profit corporation, located in Anaheim, California, which officially presents his and Watchman Nee's ministry.

Witness Lee's ministry emphasizes the experience of Christ as life and the practical oneness of the believers as the Body of Christ. Stressing the importance of attending to both these matters, he led the churches under his care to grow in Christian life and function. He was unbending in his conviction that God's goal is not narrow sectarianism but the Body of Christ. In time, believers began to meet simply as the church in their localities in response to this conviction. In recent years a number of new churches have been raised up in Russia and in many eastern European countries.

10-034-001
ISBN 978-0-87083-148-5